THE STATES AND THE NATION SERIES, of which this volume is a part, is designed to assist the American people in a serious look at the ideals they have espoused and the experiences they have undergone in the history of the nation. The content of every volume represents the scholarship, experience, and opinions of its author. The costs of writing and editing were met mainly by grants from the National Endowment for the Humanities, a federal agency. The project was administered by the American Association for State and Local History, a nonprofit learned society, working with an Editorial Board of distinguished editors, authors, and historians, whose names are listed below.

District of Columbia

A Bicentennial History

David L. Lewis

W. W. Norton & Company, Inc.
New York

American Association for State and Local History
Nashville

Library of Congress Cataloging in Publication Data

Lewis, David L
    District of Columbia: a bicentennial history.

    (The States and the Nation series)
    Bibliography: p.
    Includes index.
    1. Washington, D.C.—History. I. Series.
F194.L48   975.3   76–28397
ISBN 0–393–05601–5

Published and distributed by W. W. Norton & Company, Inc.
500 Fifth Avenue
New York, New York 10036

Printed in the United States of America

2 3 4 5 6 7 8 9 0

To Jason Bradwell, born under Home Rule

Contents

Illustrations

Harold Faye

HISTORIC BUILDINGS
OF DISTRICT OF COLUMBIA

■ Existing structure □ Structure no longer existing

Date of construction shown thus: 1799

0   ¼   ½ mile

N
W ← → E
S

16th STREET
IRVING STREET

COLUMBIA HEIGHTS

Spanish Embassy

COLUMBIA ROAD NW

(BOUNDARY ROAD)

FLORIDA

LE DROIT PARK

AVENUE

Henderson Castle □

British Embassy, 1931

MASSACHUSETTS

CONN. AVE.

■ Lothrop Mansion, 1901

AVENUE

FLORIDA

S STREET

S STREET

RHODE ISLAND AVE.

Rock Creek

Dumbarton House, 1747 ■

■ Townsend House, 1900

Lars Anderson House, 1905

■ Walsh-McLean House, 1901

■ Patterson Mansion, 1902

LOGAN CIRCLE

P ST.

P ST.

DUPONT CIRCLE

Stewart's Castle, 1875

Heurich Mansion, 1894

SCOTT CIRCLE

6th STREET

NEW HAMPSHIRE AVE.

□ National Presbyterian Church, 1889

THOMAS CIRCLE

MASSACHUSETTS

M ST.

M ST.

■ Old Stone House, 1766

CONNECTICUT

16th STREET

AVE.

PENNSYLVANIA

□ Hay-Adams House

NEW YORK AVENUE

LAFAYETTE SQUARE

VIRGINIA AVE.

State, War and Navy Building, 1871-1888 ■

Octagon House, 1799-1800 ●

White House

Willard Hotel, 1901 ■

■ □ National Theater, 1835

AVENUE

POTOMAC RIVER

Van Ness Mansion, 1817 □

THE ELLIPSE

Old Post Office, 1839-1869 ■

National Bank of Washington, 1889

CONSTITUTION

AVENUE

THE   MALL

Reflecting Pool

INDEPENDENCE AVE.

Tidal Basin

ACKNOWLEDGMENTS

Among the persons and institutions contributing to this book, the following are owed a special debt of appreciation:

Dr. Hardy F. Franklin, Director, District of Columbia Public Library; Betty Culpepper, Chief, Washingtoniana Division, Martin Luther King, Jr., Memorial Library, who placed her patience and her staff at my disposal; Alexander Geiger, Readers' Advisor, Washingtoniana; and the staff of the Martin Luther King, Jr., Memorial Library.

Perry Fisher, Executive Director, Columbia Historical Society, who took time to read portions of the manuscript and who alerted me to a number of deficiencies; Francis C. Rosenberger, Editor, *Records* of the Columbia Historical Society, who provided an important unpublished monograph on Capitol Hill.

Louise D. Hutchinson, Director, Anacostia Studies Project, Center for Anacostia Studies of the Smithsonian Institution, who has done much to fill in the past of this neglected community.

Albert Gollin, Research Associate, Bureau of Social Science Research, Inc., who, once again, generously shared his time and considerable knowledge.

The library and research staffs of the National Capital Planning Commission; the Redevelopment Land Agency; and the Pennsylvania Avenue Development Corporation; the staffs of the Moorland-Spingarn Foundation (Howard University); the Washington Center for Metropolitan Studies; and those of Council Members Sterling Tucker and Julius Hobson, Sr.

Letitia Brown, Professor of History, George Washington University, who carefully read and helpfully worried about chapter two.

Maceo Dailey, presently a faculty member at Smith College, who helped with research and suggestions.

Charles Cooney, formerly of the Manuscript Division, Library of Congress, whose archival advice, general knowledge, and reading of several chapters are deeply appreciated; and the staff of the Library of Congress.

Joseph L. Brent III, Professor of History, Federal City College, who passed along notes and thoughts about Washington's nineteenth-century scientific community; Steven Diner, also of Federal City College, whose seminar students unknowingly rendered a service.

Hon. Walter Fauntroy, Delegate, U.S. House of Representatives, who made the regulation fifteen-minute interview profitable; Hon. Sterling Tucker, Chairperson, City Council of the District of Columbia, who gave more than the regulation fifteen minutes and filled them with uncommon candor; and the Rev. Douglas Moore, Council Member, whose willingness to talk almost matched mine to learn.

Mrs. Julia Barbour, Mrs. Mary Hundley, and Mrs. Helen Webb Harris; Professor Charles H. Wesley and Professor Rayford W. Logan, Washingtonians by birth or adoption, whose example or assistance meant much to the author.

Marcie and Jill and, once again, Charles for Haiti.

My wife, Sharon, who continues editing me for the better.

David L. Lewis

May 1, 1976

Invitation to the Reader

IN 1807, former President John Adams argued that a complete history of the American Revolution could not be written until the history of change in each state was known, because the principles of the Revolution were as various as the states that went through it. Two hundred years after the Declaration of Independence, the American nation has spread over a continent and beyond. The states have grown in number from thirteen to fifty. And democratic principles have been interpreted differently in every one of them.

We therefore invite you to consider that the history of your state may have more to do with the bicentennial review of the American Revolution than does the story of Bunker Hill or Valley Forge. The Revolution has continued as Americans extended liberty and democracy over a vast territory. John Adams was right: the states are part of that story, and the story is incomplete without an account of their diversity.

The Declaration of Independence stressed life, liberty, and the pursuit of happiness; accordingly, it shattered the notion of holding new territories in the subordinate status of colonies. The Northwest Ordinance of 1787 set forth a procedure for new states to enter the Union on an equal footing with the old. The Federal Constitution shortly confirmed this novel means of building a nation out of equal states. The step-by-step process through which territories have achieved self-government and national representation is among the most important of the Founding Fathers' legacies.

The method of state-making reconciled the ancient conflict between liberty and empire, resulting in what Thomas Jefferson called an empire for liberty. The system has worked and remains unaltered, despite enormous changes that have taken place in the nation. The country's extent and variety now surpass anything the patriots of '76 could likely have imagined. The United States has changed from an agrarian republic into a highly industrial and urban democracy, from a fledgling nation into a major world power. As Oliver Wendell Holmes remarked in 1920, the creators of the nation could not have seen completely how it and its constitution and its states would develop. Any meaningful review in the bicentennial era must consider what the country has become, as well as what it was.

The new nation of equal states took as its motto *E Pluribus Unum*—"out of many, one." But just as many peoples have become Americans without complete loss of ethnic and cultural identities, so have the states retained differences of character. Some have been superficial, expressed in stereotyped images— big, boastful Texas, "sophisticated" New York, "hillbilly" Arkansas. Other differences have been more real, sometimes instructively, sometimes amusingly; democracy has embraced Huey Long's Louisiana, bilingual New Mexico, unicameral Nebraska, and a Texas that once taxed fortunetellers and spawned politicians called "Woodpecker Republicans" and "Skunk Democrats." Some differences have been profound, as when South Carolina secessionists led other states out of the Union in opposition to abolitionists in Massachusetts and Ohio. The result was a bitter Civil War.

The Revolution's first shots may have sounded in Lexington and Concord; but fights over what democracy should mean and who should have independence have erupted from Pennsylvania's Gettysburg to the "Bleeding Kansas" of John Brown, from the Alamo in Texas to the Indian battles at Montana's Little Bighorn. Utah Mormons have known the strain of isolation; Hawaiians at Pearl Harbor, the terror of attack; Georgians during Sherman's march, the sadness of defeat and devastation. Each state's experience differs instructively; each adds understanding to the whole.

The purpose of this series of books is to make that kind of understanding accessible, in a way that will last in value far beyond the bicentennial fireworks. The series offers a volume on every state, plus the District of Columbia—fifty-one, in all.

Each book contains, besides the text, a view of the state through eyes other than the author's—a "photographer's essay," in which a skilled photographer presents his own personal perceptions of the state's contemporary flavor.

We have asked authors not for comprehensive chronicles, nor for research monographs or new data for scholars. Bibliographies and footnotes are minimal. We have asked each author for a summing up—interpretive, sensitive, thoughtful, individual, even personal—of what seems significant about his or her state's history. What distinguishes it? What has mattered about it, to its own people and to the rest of the nation? What has it come to now?

To interpret the states in all their variety, we have sought a variety of backgrounds in authors themselves and have encouraged variety in the approaches they take. They have in common only these things: historical knowledge, writing skill, and strong personal feelings about a particular state. Each has wide latitude for the use of the short space. And if each succeeds, it will be by offering you, in your capacity as a *citizen* of a state *and* of a nation, stimulating insights to test against your own.

James Morton Smith
General Editor

The
District of Columbia

1

The City of Magnificent
(and Some Not So) Intentions

ROM his weed-covered perch atop Capitol Hill, Benjamin Henry Latrobe, the Capitol's fifth architect, peered down the one-mile swath of rutted, dirt thoroughfare and espied the tragic figure shambling through the poplars President Thomas Jefferson had ordered planted along Pennsylvania Avenue. "Daily through the city," Latrobe's *Journal* noted, "stalks the picture of famine, L'Enfant and his dog." More than a decade had passed since Maj. Pierre Charles L'Enfant, planner of Washington City in the District of Columbia, had been reluctantly dismissed by Gen. George Washington. For two decades more, until his death in 1825, he would continue "haunting the lobbies of the Capitol . . . pacing the newly marked avenues," as Ambassador Jules Jusserand wrote later, everlastingly fixed upon his dream of the city made marble and stone from his great plan.[1] Periodically, there were attempts to heal past wounds and to bestow upon L'Enfant some reward or position worthy of his unique services. Congress voted the sum of $2,500 as compensation for his twelve-month employ by the Commissioners of the District of Columbia. In

---

1. Jules J. Jusserand, *With Americans of Past and Present Days, A History* (New York: Scribner's, 1916), p. 182.

1812, Secretary of State James Monroe urged him to accept a professorship at West Point. The major summarily rejected such offers.

Sinecures and money meant little to Pierre L'Enfant. By the time he was thirty-five he had already the esteem and income in America that would eventually have placed him among the ranks of the new Republic's notables. Since following Lafayette to the colonies, L'Enfant's career had been constantly upbeat. As a captain leading a gallant charge, he had been wounded at Charleston. Captured shortly thereafter, he was exchanged for a Hessian officer. Decorated and compensated by King Louis XVI he declined service in the armies of France, preferring idealistically to return to the United States. L'Enfant had earned the respect of his adopted countrymen. The respect was abundantly shown. There had been the charge from the Order of the Cincinnati to supervise the creation in Paris of its emblems. There had been the prestigious commission from New York City to design the meeting hall for the itinerant Continental Congress. And even after his unfortunate relations with George Washington and the territorial commissioners, distinguished opportunities had come. Alexander Hamilton's Society for the Establishing of Useful Manufactures retained him to lay out the city of Patterson in New Jersey, a project which finally aborted for lack of funds. Robert Morris of Philadelphia contracted to have L'Enfant design his palace—the grandest in America—but later unjustly blamed the architect for his bankruptcy. Occasionally, the War Department called upon him to supervise repairs to the fortresses ringing the federal capital. That bedraggled figure with the mangey dog seen by Latrobe was far from being an expended talent. He may have been the victim of ingratitude, but he was much more the victim of a vision.

It was the inspired idea of an otherwise cautious George Washington that had altered L'Enfant's life forever. The location of the federal capital had been a much contested issue, with a number of generous offers presented to the Congress seated at Philadelphia in the early summer of 1783. The citizenry of Kingston, New York, successfully petitioned the state legislature for permission to offer two square miles for a site. Annapolis sought and received authority to set aside three hundred choice Maryland acres. New Jersey proposed the town of Nottingham. And Virginia voted to award Williamsburg—a generous proposal including the palace, the capitol, and all the public buildings, and three hundred acres of land adjoining the said city, together with a sum of money not exceeding 100,000 pounds. Quick decisions, even in matters so crucial, were not characteristic of the jealous, contentious lawmakers of that period. Philadelphia was an elegant, comfortable place and there were powerful commercial and sectional interests which championed its superiority. The squirearchy of Virginia and the rest of the South were determined to place the national capital within the orbit of their agrarian, low tariff universe, the better to influence the people's representatives in a milieu free of the commercial and manufacturing bias of Philadelphia and New York.

Stolidly, George Washington and his allies awaited the propitious moment. After being intimidated from Philadelphia in the summer of 1783 by an angry, unpaid soldiery, after wandering like a medieval court from New Jersey (Princeton) to Maryland (Annapolis), then back to New Jersey (Trenton) before settling in New York, the government eventually decided. Southern money to fund the national debt was astutely traded by Alexander Hamilton and his supporters for eastern votes to place the capital a day's ride from Mount Vernon. By the Residence Act of 1790 and its 1791 amendment, the new capital was to be ready for occupancy at the end of the decade. Meanwhile, the nation's business would be transacted in Philadelphia.

The proposed site lay in a bowl-like depression at the base of the Cumberland Mountains, heavily forested, barely populated, and forked by the junction of two rivers—the Potomac, which the Powhatan Indians had called Cohongoronta ("River of the Swans"), and the Anacostia. It is said that the first English visitor to what was to become the heart of the city arrived in 1631, some twenty-three years after Capt. John Smith had explored the Potomac as far as its falls, and exactly thirty years before Francis Pope was granted a tract of land known as Room, or Rome, by tradition inaccurately recorded as the land on which the Capitol was built. It was in this region, now populated by the sociable, hardriding gentry descended from Addisons, Bealls, and Brents, Carrolls, Diggeses, and Roziers, that General Washington set about appointing three commissioners to superintend the building of the Federal City. The legislature of Maryland had willingly ceded sixty-nine square miles to form the new 100-square-mile territory; Virginia, for its part, gave the balance. Aside from monies to compensate landowners for property taken to build the President's Palace, the Capitol, a navy yard, and three or four other buildings, the fourteen states were not prepared to fund additional construction. The local gentry's patriotism was sound, but so was its business sense. It was expected that Congress would pay handsomely for its property.

As commissioners, the president had appointed three able, trusted men, Thomas Johnson and Daniel Carroll of Maryland, and David Stuart of Virginia, notables of the region on hunting terms with the landowners and tied to many by blood or marriage. But no agreement as to an acceptable price for the lands had been reached by April 1791. Washington's forbearance was being sorely tested. "It is of the greatest moment," he somewhat sharply advised the commissioners, "to close this business with the proprietors of the land on which the Federal City is to be that consequent arrangements may be made without more delay than can be avoided." [2] Already, a month before, Washington had met with the landowners at the Fountain Inn (commonly known as Suter's Tavern) in the old city of Georgetown, formerly located in Maryland but now one of the two townships (Alexandria being the other) encompassed by the federal territory of the District of Columbia. After a respectable number of tankards of ale, madeira, and porter, the deal had appeared to be struck: twenty-five pounds ($66.66) per acre, and for land required for streets and thoroughfares, no charge at all. No sooner returned to Mount Vernon, however, than Washington's

2. Quoted in William Tindall, *Standard History of the City of Washington* (Knoxville, Tenn.: H. W. Crew, 1914), pp. 86–87.

commissioners were reporting a plethora of ambiguities, mis-
conceptions, and plain cussed contrariness by the proprietors.
On June twenty-eighth, he was back at Suter's Tavern. (George
Washington's diary does not record whether that "churl of a
Scots landholder," David Burnes, attended; he would be the last
to come to terms.) At Suter's, George Washington, on the
twenty-ninth, addressed the gentry in his gravest voice, fixing
the recalcitrants with that famously arresting stare that one genial politician, having slapped the presidential back in effusive
greeting, said he would remember for the rest of his life. Still,
neither gravity nor frosty glances alone would have produced a
settlement.

Since mid-March the French engineer whom Washington persisted in calling "Langfang" had been observed with measuring
instruments in the woods around Tiber or Goose Creek and on
the salient known as Jenkins Hill. Rumors abounded that plans
for the new city were grandiose, that the squirearchy would be
cleared from the Potomac Basin as surely as had been the tribes
of the Algonquin Confederacy. At their insistence, Washington
unrolled the city plan. The landholders were flabbergasted. Of
the total 6,111 acres to be included within the boundaries of the
Federal City, only 541 were allocated as sites for government
offices—acreage for which the $66.66 would be paid. Some
3,606 acres were to be devoured by avenues 160 feet wide and a
vast mall extending more than two miles from the base of Jenkins Hill, future location of the Capitol building. This land, by
the terms of the tentative March understanding, must be deeded
free. The 3,606 acres were a blow to them, but the landholders
were finally seduced, doubtless as Washington and his commissioners anticipated, by the disposition to be made of the remaining 1,964 acres. Commercial plots were to be carved from this
property, the proceeds from their sales going equally to the national treasury and the proprietors. The potential value of this
land was estimated to have been enhanced tenfold. On June thirtieth, George Washington departed for Mount Vernon, leaving
his commissioners in possession of the titles to the 6,611 acres.

The plan that had staggered the Potomac gentry was L'Enfant's. Building a national capital in the American wilderness fascinated him. "Ser," he had written in shaky English to George Washington as early as September 1789,

> The late determination of Congress to lay the foundation of a Federal City which is to become the Capital of this vast Empire, offers so great an occasion for acquiring reputation . . . that Your Excellency will not be surprised that my ambition and the desire I have of becoming a useful citizen should lead me to wish to share in the undertaking. No nation had ever before the opportunity offered them of deliberately deciding on the spot where their Capital City should be fixed.[3]

The job was his. Secretary of State Thomas Jefferson finally informed him in March 1791, "You are desired to proceed to Georgetown where you will find Mr. Ellicott employed in making a survey and maps of the Federal Territory. The special object of asking your aid is to have drawings of the particular grounds most likely to be approved for the site of the Federal town and buildings." [4] The *Georgetown Weekly Ledger* reported L'Enfant's speedy arrival on March twelfth. It also related the previous arrival of two other men engaged by the commissioners:

> Some time last month arrived in this town Major Andrew Ellicott, a gentleman of superior astronomical abilities. . . . He is attended by Benjamin Banneker, an Ethiopian, whose abilities as a surveyor and astronomer clearly prove that Mr. Jefferson's concluding that race of men were void of mental endowments was without foundation.

Although Thomas Jefferson would soon proclaim his enthusiasm for Banneker to Baron Condorcet and had urged his appointment upon the commissioners, apparently he did not demand a retraction from the *Weekly Ledger*.

From Suter's Tavern L'Enfant set forth daily to discharge his mission. Fortunately for the grand scope of his plan, neither

---

3. L'Enfant to Washington, September 11, 1789, in Elizabeth Kite, *L'Enfant and Washington, 1791–1792, Published and Unpublished Documents* (Baltimore: Johns Hopkins University Press, 1919), p. 34.
4. Kite, *L'Enfant,* Jefferson to L'Enfant, March 1791, p. 35.

President Washington nor the commissioners had spelled out his precise responsibilities. It would appear that the president left it to the commissioners to instruct the major that he was their subordinate, and apparently the commissioners assumed that George Washington had explained the relationship to L'Enfant. Even had this been done, it is probable that the engineer would have stretched his commission to the limit. His prickly, nervous temperament stimulated by the unique opportunity to accomplish a task whose magnitude no engineer had been vouchsafed since the creation of Constantinople and Saint Petersburg, L'Enfant was scarcely willing to bother with matters of protocol and bureaucratic authorization. Three weeks after his arrival, Washington forwarded to him Thomas Jefferson's rough sketch for the new city, explaining that its reduced scale was done under an idea that no offer, worthy of consideration, would come from the landholders in the vicinity of Carrollsburg (to wit, from David Burnes). L'Enfant accepted the general boundaries of Jefferson's plan, a sort of wavering, bottom-heavy trapezium wedged into the fork of the Potomac and the Anacostia.

Pierre L'Enfant was to last as architect of the Federal City about a year. Whatever inspiration he may have drawn from Saint Petersburg, Christopher Wren's London, or Le Notre's Versailles (a matter still debated by architects and historians), the final plan L'Enfant forwarded to George Washington on August nineteenth was almost entirely his own and represented a quantum leap in city planning. To be sure, there were decisive contributions made by Jefferson and the commissioners. The "public walk" or mall was incorporated from Jefferson's sketch, although the major steadfastly denied the fact. And both Jefferson and the commissioners devised the nomenclature of the streets. "We have also agreed," the commissioners instructed L'Enfant in early September, "the streets be named alphabetically one way, and numerically the other; the former divided into North and South letters, the latter into East and West numbers from the Capitol." [5] L'Enfant borrowed and obeyed, but the rest was inspired innovation. Of the several

5. Quoted in Tindall, *Standard History,* p. 121.

designs drawn solely in L'Enfant's hand, only one survives. In all likelihood this is the second which, for problematical reasons, the major labelled as number one, and which deviated in several important details from the lost first plan that Washington had shown the landholders at Suter's Tavern on June twenty-ninth. The August nineteenth plan, "altered agreeably to your direction," L'Enfant wrote Washington, eliminated several major thoroughfares and irreparably distorted the function of Maryland Avenue by halving its length and of Massachusetts by bending it inward at midpoint from its destined path to one of the city's monumental (but never built) entrances. These concessions to Mount Vernon notwithstanding, L'Enfant's design emerged as a perfect balance of geography and topography.

L'Enfant's rational plan was deeply anchored in real not ideal soil. He had crisscrossed the territory ceaselessly, familiarizing himself with it like an experienced planter on new acreage. "The distinguishing and most important fact about the creation of the plan of Washington [D.C.]," William T. Partridge's still unexcelled 1930 essay on the subject tells us, "is that L'Enfant began his work not by laying out streets or by running survey lines but by the selection of dominating sites. It was from and around these sites that the plan was later developed." [6] Surely the Capitol *belongs* on its promontory as naturally and inevitably as the president's house (The White House) on the flat, low ground near Tiber Creek. The heart of the design—the Capitol-Mall-president's house composition—completed, L'Enfant proceeded to draw up the city's circulatory system with a unity of common sense and audacity which (again, whatever the arguable antecedents) achieved his conception of a city unlike any other. He slashed his radial avenues through the basic scheme of rectangular streets for several reasons that he compellingly explained to the final referee at Mount Vernon. But foremost was his intention to utilize the existing primitive arteries—Bladens-

6. William T. Partridge, "L'Enfant's Methods and Features of His Plan for the Federal City," National Capital Planning Commission (Washington, D.C.: Government Printing Office, 1930), p. 9.

burg, Ferry, Georgetown, and Rock Creek roads—that meandered above and below the city's east-west axis.

The National Capital Park and Planning Commission's "Annual Report" of 1930 points out that by "a remarkable coinci-
dence [Georgetown and Ferry roads] meet at the east-west axis
of the Capitol at the same angle and may have suggested to L'Enfant the radial pair system of avenues which makes the Washington plan unique." The major's other reasons for his radial roads
he conveyed to Mount Vernon along with the amended plan of
August nineteenth. "I opened others [avenues]," he explained,

> from every principal places, wishing by this not mearly to contrast
> with the general regularity nor to afford greater variety of pleasant
> seats and prospect as will be obtained from the advantageous ground
> over the which avenues are mostly directed but principally to
> connect each part of the city with more efficacy by, if I may so
> express, making the real distance less from place to place in
> menaging on them a resiprocity of sight.[7]

What George Washington was to understand by this garbled
elucidation was that the radial thoroughfares were intended to
break the monotony of the grid, to create monumental plazas, to
utilize the old roads (Bladensburg, Ferry, Georgetown, and
Rock Creek), to order vistas so as to guide the eye to distant
complementary ones and, finally, to afford a means of reaching
the central parts of the city by the shortest routes.

Then came L'Enfant's refinements, most of which, because
of niggardly economies or the city's growth southwesterly from
Capitol Hill, were never implemented. At the terminus of four
"outroads," he prescribed monumental gates. At the southern
extremity of the axis running south to north through the Capitol,
L'Enfant proposed an entrance of suitable magnitude to awe all
who filed through. Had L'Enfant possessed a feel for politics,
an assuaging bonhommie instead of that bristling secretiveness
in his work, the commissioners and their landholding friends

---

7. Partridge, "L'Enfant's Methods," p. 11.

might have suffered him grudgingly. Despite their dickerings at Suter's with George Washington, none of the notables had missed the potential advantages of the rapidly appreciating city plots and the commercial opportunities of a wilderness-become-metropolis; but they were not to be ridden over roughshod by an unknown arrogant Frenchman. Those receipts from the sales of the 1,964 acres were months if not years away from payment; meanwhile, the new Washingtonians were at the mercy of the major's engulfing plazas and colossal avenues. So long as the major inspired the confidence of Mount Vernon, however, the outrages of his radial and monumental extravagances had to be borne.

In September 1791, the major's behavior was sufficiently controversial to startle George Washington. Engraving delays had denied the commissioners copies of L'Enfant's plan in time for the first public auction of the 1,964 lots. "There has been something very unaccountable in the conduct of the engraver," the incredulous president confided to the commissioners, "yet I cannot be of the opinion that the delays were occasioned by L'Enfant." [8] The major blamed the Philadelphia engraver while

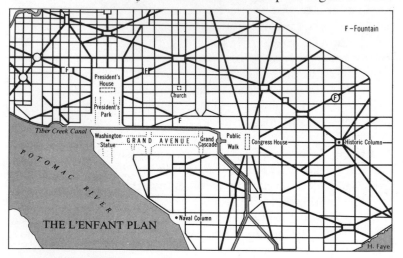

8. Quoted in Wilhelmus Bogart Bryan, *A History of the National Capital*, 2 vols. (New York: Macmillan Co., 1914), 1:156.

the apoplectic commissioners sent messengers begging him to release his working map so that it might be displayed in Suter's Tavern during the auction. L'Enfant, busy hacking Pennsylvania Avenue through the Potomac forest, refused. "Such perverseness" was unexpected, Washington admitted. He knew of L'Enfant's opposition to the auction, his repugnance at having swarms of speculators throwing up buildings of every manner and design, having shanties and saloons along his avenues, and his grand plazas desecrated by uncontrolled commercial construction. The September thirtieth auction, attended by Washington, Jefferson, and Madison, was far from a success. "I did not suppose," Washington's letter to the commissioners concluded peevishly, "[L'Enfant] would interfere further in the mode of selling lots than by giving his opinion with his reasons in support of it." [9] Surprisingly, Washington decided to say nothing to L'Enfant about the matter, weighing, in all probability, the urgency of the major's work against the risk of a time-consuming tantrum.

But L'Enfant's mandate, although he remained serenely unaware of the fact, was reaching its term. Tension between the ideal city of his imagination and the real people for whom it was conceived began to be intolerable after one of those cherished avenues, New Jersey, began its unwavering thrust from the naval yard on the Anacostia to Capitol Hill. In its path was the manor house of Daniel Carroll of Duddington, uncle of Commissioner Carroll, the largest property owner in the District of Columbia, and a member of the prolific clan descended from the lordly Roman Catholic Carrolls of Maryland. Foundations for the manor had been laid before L'Enfant's arrival. Recently, Carroll had begun to press its completion but was informed that a portion of his manor lay seven feet within the survey lines of New Jersey Avenue and that he must demolish the offending section. The record is somewhat confused at this point. Major Ellicott later testified that L'Enfant had agreed to narrow the avenue by ten feet which, if true, was certainly out of character. In any event, while the commissioners temporized and George

9. Bryan, *National Capital*, 1:157.

Washington played Solomon (suggesting either a seven-year moratorium on Duddington Manor's removal without compensation or immediate demolition with compensation), the major took matters into his own hands. In late November, despite the strict instructions of the commissioners and an injunction issued by Carroll's friend, the chancellor of Maryland, L'Enfant departed for the sandstone quarry at Aquia Creek, Virginia, leaving orders for his assistant, Isaac Roberdeau, to raze the obstruction. "It would have afforded a dangerous precedent to others to contest every step of the people employed in laying off the city," L'Enfant wrote Mount Vernon. Furthermore, "progress has already been materially slackened in consequence of that strict attention which has been paid in preserving as much as was admissible all convenience to the individual proprietors," he lectured Washington.[10] A furious Thomas Jefferson, whose feelings for the Frenchman had soured rapidly, told the president, "[L'Enfant] must know there is a line beyond which he will not be suffered to go." The secretary of state forwarded to Mount Vernon a subtly distorted account of the Duddington affair whose unmistakable thrust was that the major ought to be given his walking papers.

Equable above all else, Washington preferred to arrange for the outraged Daniel Carroll to be compensated and to bury the issue. Genius had its price, and, as he confessed to the commissioners, "I know not where another is to be found who could supply his place." [11] There was one issue, however, on which the president would not compromise further—the sale of the commercial plots. A second auction had been scheduled for the fall of 1792, but the French engraver in Philadelphia still protested that L'Enfant's drawings were too imperfect to be copied. At the end of February, Mount Vernon roared: "Every mode has been tried to accommodate your wishes on this principle, except changing the Commissioners (for commissioners there must be and under their direction the public buildings must be carried or the law will be violated)." [12] Whatever his per-

---

10. Kite, *L'Enfant,* L'Enfant to Washington, December 7, 1791, p. 90.
11. Bryan, *National Capital,* 1:167.
12. Kite, *L'Enfant,* Washington to L'Enfant, February 28, 1792, p. 154.

sonal feelings toward L'Enfant (and they seem to have been paternal), George Washington was too astute a politician to sever relations brutally. The president mistakenly feared that the Frenchman might compromise the city's prospects by making common cause with its Philadelphia and New York enemies. Behind the scenes Washington successfully urged the gentry (with the exception of Daniel Carroll of Duddington) to present L'Enfant with a testimonial of regret at his departure.

In the years that followed, L'Enfant deplored in private the alterations to the plan by his successor, Ellicott, and those who bothered to notice him wandering the city, pausing censoriously before some square intended to frame a commemorative column or monument or looking sadly upward from the Mall at unlandscaped Capitol Hill (Frederick Law Olmsted, Sr., would improve the layout in later years)—those who witnessed his wistful peregrinations knew that L'Enfant loved his creation, however flawed its growth.

Planning for Permanence

In spite of L'Enfant's vigil, the federal capital soon became a disaster area, an eastern city with the rawness of a frontier settlement, one that might never, in the words of the visiting Duc de La Rochefoucauld-Liancourt be "capable of growing to a point that could make it a bearable resting place for those fated to live in it." [13] In *Domestic Manners of the Americans*, Anthony Trollope's mother took pains to strike an upbeat note when visiting in the early 1830s: "I confess I see nothing in the least degree ridiculous about it. The original design, which was as beautiful as it was extensive, has been in no way departed from." Thirty years later, it was harder for her son to excuse the place, "as melancholy and miserable a town," Anthony grumbled, "as the mind of man can conceive." [14] A Portuguese minister dismissed it as the city of "magnificent distances," a diplomatically succinct variant of the mean-spirited doggerel by the visiting Irish poet, Tom Moore:

13. *Voyages dans les Etats-Unis fait en 1795, 1796, et en 1797* (Paris: Dupont, L'an VII de la République), p. 149. Author's translation.
14. Anthony Trollope, *North America* (New York: Alfred A. Knopf, 1951), p. 322.

This embryo capital where fancy sees
Squares in morasses, obelisks in trees,
Which second-sighted seers ev'n now adorn
With shrines unbuilt and heroes yet unborn.[15]

Mr. and Mrs. Charles Dickens paid call in 1842. *American Notes* was not unkind to Washington. Dickens was charmed by the casual good manners displayed by the company—"whatever their station"—attending President John Tyler's levee. "When I saw them turning with one mind from noisy orators and officers of state" to surround the new minister to Spain, Washington Irving, "I have seldom respected a public assembly more than I did this eager throng," Dickens ecstatically wrote. Washingtonians' admiration of Irving notwithstanding, the prevalence of chewing tobacco ("Washington may be called the headquarters of tobacco tinctured saliva") appalled Dickens, even provoking doubts about American marksmanship when "several gentlemen called upon me who, in the course of conversation, frequently missed the spitoon at five paces." The slavepens along the Mall were far more appalling. But finally, although he shared Mrs. Trollope's admiration for the magnificence of the Capitol and the classic grace of the President's Palace, Dickens joined the chorus of doubters:

> Spacious avenues that begin in nothing and lead nowhere; streets, mile long, that only want houses, roads, and inhabitants; public buildings that need but a public to be complete; and ornaments of great thoroughfares, which only lack great thoroughfares to ornament—are its leading features.

"It is sometimes called the City of Magnificent Distances," the novelist concluded, "but it might be termed with greater propriety the City of Magnificent Intentions."

Sadly, the city's magnificent intentions had been all too short-lived and much outnumbered by intentions that were neither noble nor intelligent. What happened to Washington City during the early years is a history of disappointment and lethargy. "In

15. Quoted in Mary Cable, *The Avenue of the Presidents* (Boston: Houghton Mifflin, 1969), p. 35.

passing down the Avenue from Georgetown to the President's House," Christian Hines wrote, "I recollect having seen but one house on Pennsylvania Avenue (except the Six and Seven Buildings). . . ." [16] When Abigail Adams hung the presidential wash in the unfinished East Room of the White House there were no more than five or six buildings along the avenue. The avenue, of course, was still only an absence of grass and trees (and the regular presence of dust or mud) between the White House and the Capitol guiding diplomats and lawgivers to and fro. "One might take a ride of several hours within the precincts without meeting with a single individual to disturb one's meditation," an early resident recalled. "There was a stillness and vacuity over the whole place," another remembered. James Sterling Young's *Washington Community, 1800–1828* relates the not uncommon plight of several congressmen returning from a dinner party, losing their way and spending "until daybreak in their carriage weaving through bogs and gullies in search of Capitol Hill, only a mile away." Dinners at the White House or presentation of diplomatic credentials were downright dangerous. After the horrors of his White House visit, one diplomat recorded that his vehicle had become embedded "to the axel-tree. . . . It was necessary to leave the carriage, which had to be dragged out and scraped to remove the mud and slush which stuck to it like glue." If it was mandatory to risk life and limb for the president's affairs, socializing with friends was another matter. "The house Mr. Gallatin has taken is next door to the Madisons' and three miles distant from us," a longtime acquaintance lamented. "I regret this circumstance, as it will prevent that intimate intercourse which I wished to enjoy." [17]

Washington was such a miserable aberration that Congress came within nine votes of abandoning the place after the British put the torch to its public buildings in 1814. But the legislators stuck it out, complainingly yet too parsimoniously to appropri-

16. Christian Hines, *Early Recollections of Washington City* (Washington, D.C.: 1866), p. 6.

17. Quotes from James Sterling Young, *The Washington Community, 1800–1828* (New York: Columbia University Press, 1966), pp. 42, 43, 44.

ate funds to civilize what one recent chronicler has called the "low budget Constantinople." The inconveniences were truly quite awful. If the Capitol impressed even the most fastidious visitors from Europe by its gleaming beauty, congressmen knew that it was not only jerrybuilt and poorly engineered, but practically uninhabitable. The stone from George Gibson's Aquia Creek quarry was of poor quality. Columns split under the weight of spectators' balconies in the House and Senate. The forced-air heating system, conceived as the last word in modern domestic engineering, was so thermal that the legislators had to turn it off. The glass-domed ceiling in the House chamber leaked water on the tobacco-chewing solons below. Oratory, the constant passion of those loquacious and posturing times, was nearly impossible in the House due to its poor acoustics. The justices of the Supreme Court found their chambers in the Capitol's basement so claustrophobic that they often preferred to deliberate in a nearby tavern. Had Congress decamped for Philadelphia after the War of 1812, it would have been entirely understandable.

The damage done to Washington by the invading British may have been greater than that wrought by presidents and Congresses, but it was less enduring. The recurring story of an irate Andrew Jackson, tired of experts' dickerings, storming from his office to plant his cane in a nearby field and thunderously declaring it to be the site of the new Treasury Building, is apocryphal. But Jackson's capriciousness would have been no more disastrous than the real reason for his administration's decision to erect one of the capital's finest examples of Greek Revival architecture in the worst possible place—in the middle of Pennsylvania Avenue—because, as government property, it was cheaper to do so. For more than a century, Pennsylvania Avenue, flowing wide and straight from the Capitol, has stopped abruptly a few feet from the Treasury Building and turned sharply north for a brief distance and then sharply west in order to reach the President's Palace.

That L'Enfant's mammoth artery survived largely in its original form was primarily an accident of indifference. Its neglect, save for a rare attempt at gravel seeding (the gravel immediately sank from sight), was total. Descriptions of Pennsylvania Avenue during the early years, with its innumerable furrows and pox of cavities (deep enough to conceal robbers, it was said) read like accounts of some World War One no man's land. Society folk, few of whom suffered residency elsewhere than along the square facing the President's Palace or in the shadow of the Capitol, rarely ventured the avenue's full length and never risked a nocturnal voyage, unless extraordinary business compelled it. In summer and winter inclement weather caused Tiber Creek, now widened to become Washington Canal, to overflow and swamp the artery. It had become the municipal sewer, its regular inundations turning Pennsylvania Avenue into a malodorous, pestilential quagmire. Nor had the ordinances of 1815 and 1816, authorizing a twenty-five cent reward for stray geese and half the proceeds from sales of ownerless pigs, done much to alleviate the problem of the avenue's four-footed pedestrians before the 1830s. Horace Greeley, the journalist-politician, fulminated about the wretchedness of the roads after the Civil War.

> Plagues of Egypt! Oh! Moses and Aaron, you must
> Knock under to Washington's plague of the dust.
> What whirlwinds of dust! Heads up! and mouths shut.
>   And now, facing the gust,
> Let us try this old Avenue's cyclones of dust . . . .

A poem somewhat more wretched and longer than the avenue itself.

Washington was such a ghastly embarrassment that at an 1869 convention in Saint Louis, Horace Greeley spoke eloquently for removal of the capital to the Missouri city. During this time, there was strong support for Cincinnati, Chicago, and even Kansas City as alternatives to Washington, cities better able to tie the national government to the developing West and to enhance control of trade and commerce. When some of Washington's loyalists ambitiously proposed it for the site of the 1871 World's Fair, one long-suffering senator objected, "Let us have a city before we invite anybody to see it." [18] With its embryonic police force, its fire department incapable of responding to

18. Quoted in Cable, *Avenue,* p. 139.

two simultaneous alarms, its two good hotels (Wormley's and Willard's), and its one major theatre (The National), Washington, after the Civil War, was still a backwater rather than the urban centerpiece of a proud and rich young nation. Two bright spots there were: Lafayette Square with General Jackson on his rearing mount, Saint John's Church with its gold cupola, and some of America's most history-filled mansions; and Thomas U. Walter's newly extended Capitol Building with its imposing cast iron dome, completed during the Civil War as a symbol of the federal government's determination to impose itself upon the nearby South. The Capitol's generous proportions and symmetry were challenges to the city below to measure up to its lapsed dignity.

At the end of L'Enfant's Mall, densely populated by corralled livestock, defaced by slaughterhouses, and elsewhere overrun by free-roaming sheep, pigs, and geese, there stood the ignored monument to George Washington, a truncated obelisk ringed by rotting sheds, housing blocks of marble long ago assembled for a purpose as forgotten to much of the citizenry as it was unknown to the legion of foraging animals. The cornerstone had been laid on July 4, 1848. Not even for George Washington's memory was Congress to be expected to vote tax dollars for the monument's erection; this was the responsibility of the private citizens belonging to the Washington Monument Society. Private and state subscriptions were seriously lagging when Alabama's saving idea of contributing a memorial stone instead of money was offered. The society gratefully expanded the Alabama proposal, requesting that donors contribute granite blocks four feet in length and two in height. All went well until the arrival of foreign donations excited the xenophobia of the negative American party—the Know-Nothings. In early 1854 they purloined and either pulverized or sank in the Potomac the stone from Rome's Temple of Concord, a gift of Pope Pius IX. Despite this embarrassment, Congress was sufficiently impressed by the mounting response that it voted $200,000 the next year to assist the Washington Monument Society. But the resolution was tabled when Congress learned that seven hundred fifty Know-Nothings, the night before its vote, had seized control of the society's offices and taken physical possession of monument property. Twenty-one years would pass before resumption of work on Washington's obelisk.

"Boss" Shepherd to the Rescue

Alexander Robey Shepherd was an unlikely spiritual heir of Pierre L'Enfant. William M. Maury's indispensable article in *Records* (1972), a local history journal, describes Shepherd as "an archetypal man of the Gilded Age, neither far-seeing nor short-sighted but, instead, wrapped up entirely in the problem of his own place and time." He was born in Washington, D.C., in 1836, eleven years after the major's unremarked death on the Digges family property just beyond the city limits. Alexander Shepherd rose from straitened circumstances (his prosperous father died when the son was ten) to become the most valued apprentice in the plumbing firm of J. W. Thompson. Along the way, he obtained a degree from Columbian College (later, George Washington University). Soon, he was taken into partnership and, by his late twenties, he owned the Thompson business, one of the most successful in the city. He supported the cause of the Union, shouldered a musket for three months as a private in the federal army, became president of the common council in 1862 and a member of the levy court in 1867. It was during this period on the levy court that Shepherd became one of Gen. Ulysses S. Grant's closest and most honorable intimates—all of which was remarkable, even for those free-swinging times. But what was truly extraordinary was that Alexander Shepherd, who had no formal knowledge of civil engineering, transformed Washington in a way that L'Enfant had only dreamed was possible.

Alexander Shepherd alarmed the District's gentry. Much of it had been seccessionist in sympathy during the Civil War, especially the Georgetown Brahmins. Shepherd's vigorous pro-Union politics made him unwelcome in circles where the princely Corcorans moved. The Oldest Inhabitants Society, formed in 1865 against the onslaught of parvenu ambition, excluded Shepherd and must have feared him greatly, since his

Washington roots and demonstrated intelligence and ambition made him a formidable opponent of their pretensions to civic leadership. But Shepherd's trump card was his friendship with the newly elected president, Ulysses S. Grant. A private corner in the dining room at Willard's Hotel at Fourteenth Street and Pennsylvania Avenue was reserved for the president and the youngest member of the levy court, where they were often seen in genial conference over much-replenished whiskeys.

More was at play than presidential patronage, however. Since the act of Congress of May 15, 1820, Washington City had popularly elected (but, of course, no blacks or women voted) its mayors biennially, as well as its eight-member board of aldermen and twelve-member board of common council (the latter annually renewed). Congressional liberality in granting the city local government had nothing to do with principles of democracy; the federal government wanted as little as possible to do with Washington's finances. Police, fire, and streets, sewage, poverty, and education were deemed matters for the permanent inhabitants to handle. All that changed in 1871. In February of that year Congress scrapped the city's sixty-nine-year-old charter. Georgetown, Washington City, and Washington County were merged (Alexandria had been retroceded to Virginia in 1846) into a territorial form of government. Henceforth, Washington was to be administered by a governor, presidentially appointed (and senatorially ratified) for four years, an upper chamber or governor's council of eleven members (similarly impanelled), and a twenty-two member House of Delegates, popularly elected. The board of public works, whose members served quadrennially, was also appointed and confirmed by the president and Senate. For the first time, a board of education, popularly elected, was created. Finally, a nonvoting delegate to the House of Representatives, popularly elected for a two-year term, was authorized.

President Grant had originally intended to nominate Alexander Shepherd to the governorship but relented in the face of strident opposition from the city's bluebloods and from the suspicious black leadership. Instead, Henry D. Cooke, brother of the banker, Jay Cooke, and a Shepherd ally, was appointed.

Shepherd was made vice-president of the board of public works. It made little real difference; it was the vice-president of the board of public works who made the governor's decisions. "Why is the new Governor like a sheep?" ran an opposition doggerel. "Because he is led by A. Shepherd." [19] A portrait of Shepherd in his prime shows a ruggedly handsome, uncomplicated man, the face striking by its absence of sideburns, moustache, and beard; the eyes are intrepid and intelligent. He was by all accounts a first-rate orator. During his three-year hegemony, the city was literally occupied by an army of laborers under his generalship. His audacity was boundless and his methods routinely swashbuckling.

As one of its first acts, the governor's council had approved a four-million-dollar bond issue (July 1871). Straightaway, the conservative citizenry, led by the Corcorans and the Riggses, threw up obstacles to the renovation plans, but the vice-president of the board of public works was more than a match for them. The opposition obtained an injunction. Shepherd's people riposted by authorizing the questionable disbursement of five hundred thousand dollars in anticipated revenues. The half million dollars was quickly exhausted, whereupon Shepherd stopped the laying of sidewalks and sewers and grading of roads, leaving piles of bricks, sand, and rubble throughout the city where they would do the most political good. After a chastening interval, during which construction disorders were blamed on the injunction, Governor Cooke called for a special referendum to vote the renovation plan up or down. The opposition never had a chance. The voters, who found ballots "Against Special Improvements" in scarce supply, overwhelmingly approved the plans of the board.

Resistance to Shepherd—"Boss" Shepherd, as he was beginning to be called—was not only doomed to failure but occasioned extra-legal highjinks. At what is now Mount Vernon Square, the proposed site of L'Enfant's Naval Column, a jumble of sheds and stalls comprised the Northern Liberties Market.

19. William Maury, "Alexander R. Shepherd and the Board of Public Works," *Records of the Columbia Historical Society*, 1971–1972 (394–410), 404.

Its merchants were well-organized, defiant. A local justice stood ready to issue an injunction the moment Shepherd's labor gangs approached. The merchants had been warned and temporary housing had been erected for them at Seventh and O streets, N.W., before issuance of a two-week eviction notice. On the day the period of grace expired, the merchants' judge was lured to dinner out of the city; that evening, the labor gangs invaded Mount Vernon Square; next morning it was cleared. A few weeks later, the board of public works asked the Alexandria & Washington Railroad Company to rebuild its track bed to conform to the new grade level of Maryland Avenue. The company refused. One morning soon thereafter, Washington awoke to learn that Maryland Avenue had been stripped of its railroad tracks as utterly as a deboned flounder. All that remained of the railroad's right of way was a single engine resting on a few feet of track. Shepherd's minions were known to descend by the hundreds upon a neighborhood in the morning and depart at the end of the day leaving astonished householders looking up from their front steps to a newly graded street one story higher or down from their stoops upon the exposed foundations.

More than a thousand private houses and commercial buildings followed in the wake of Shepherd's black and Irish labor gangs—Washington had finally succeeded in attracting that speculative capital opposed by L'Enfant and unresponsive to the best efforts of George Washington's commissioners. The fetid and malarial Washington Canal was largely filled in; Pennsylvania Avenue (disastrously paved with wooden blocks in 1871) was given an asphalt surface (Shepherd's enemies inaccurately blamed him for the wooden avenue); 118 miles of city and thirty-nine miles of county roads were graded and many of them surfaced; hundreds of miles of sidewalks laid; fifty thousand trees planted; nearly twenty miles of sewage and nearly thirty of gas mains connected; and several miles of water lines extended.

Shepherd's achievements made him the most hated administrator in Washington's history—and the most admired. To the majority belonging to the Oldest Inhabitants Society and to many on the *Elite List,* "Boss" Shepherd was a greater destroyer than Gen. Robert Ross, commander of the British invasion force in the War of 1812. Ross had correctly sacked and burned an enemy's public buildings; native son Shepherd, on the other hand, had not merely wantonly demolished and tyrannically rebuilt private property, he had imperilled the city's social and economic order. Fourteen years after the governor's departure from office, the *Washington Sentinel* editorialized with unabated animus (December 22, 1888),

> The outrage perpetuated [*sic*] on this community during the reign of the crew headed by Boss Shepherd exceed those committed by Tweed in New York. There was a population then of 130,000 people, of whom one-third were negroes [*sic*] paying no taxes. The burden of maintenance therefore fell on some eighty-thousand whites of whom probably one third were taxpayers, the others being women and children.

Before the end of his first year as its vice-president, the board of public works had spent itself into a $9,450,000 debt, an astronomical sum for the times, nearly thrice the total indebtedness accumulated by Washington City, Georgetown, and Washington County during the previous twenty years. Twelve hundred taxpayers petitioned Congress to stop the board and in January 1872, the House District Committee conducted a four-month investigation whose majority report fully exonerated the board of improprieties, commended its "high minded" members, and urged the Republican Congress to make "generous appropriations" in order to speed its undertakings. To placate the distraught petitioners, however, Congress imposed what it believed was a reasonable debt ceiling of ten million dollars on District spending. That left Boss Shepherd with about a half million to spend.

Three congressional enquiries failed to uncover evidence of corruption by Shepherd's regime. Waste and wretched bookkeeping, incompetence and extralegality there had been aplenty, but of enrichment at the public till there has never been proof. True enough, many years later the *Washington Post* stated matter-of-factly that Shepherd and his associates used their inside knowledge to buy property along the lines of new streets, "which lots they of course sold at an immense profit." It was also a fact that Gov. Henry Cooke's First National Bank handled the District's depreciated bonds for 60 percent of face value and further enriched his institution by collecting full value on them from the board of public works. At worst, these were venial sins for their time, shady but, withal, hardly deplorable deeds. Examples of probity such as that set by a William W. Corcoran (twenty-four years later fully reimbursing with accrued interest the depositors of a bank that had failed in 1823) were then as now, regretfully uncommon. Such standards explained much about Corcoran's animosity to Shepherd, but they no longer reflected the real world of business. As Shepherd's mouthpiece, the *Washington Star,* rhetorically observed,

> Mr. Corcoran, with all his merits as a citizen, has not been able to appreciate that Washington has needed something beside [*sic*] an art gallery and an asylum for first family widows. . . . Did Mr. Corcoran or Mr. Riggs or Mr. Davis ever move a hand to abate any of the great nuisances? . . . . Would they or would ten generations of Corcorans, Riggs or Davises ever have lifted a finger to pave or grade a street; abate the canal nuisance . . . ? [20]

What the Corcorans and Riggses deplored about the Shepherd clique—far more indeed than its pushy and arguably seamy ethics—were its fiscal improvisations. As Messrs. Corcoran and Riggs and their allies had prophesied, many homeowners were forced to surrender their properties because of greatly increased taxes and the overnight burdens of huge improvement costs assessed against them—assessments not infrequently compounded by multiple tearing up and regrading of streets and sidewalks necessitated by an absence of engineering expertise. Indisputably, Shepherd's Washington was a disconcerting metropolis. Yet the "Boss" was admired by the working classes and the Republican party's money men; his regime guaranteed profits and jobs. The almost reverential loyalty which the District's blacks rapidly developed for Shepherd was equally understandable. To Frederick Douglass, Washington's most respected black leader, Grant's presidency and Shepherd's rule were his-

---

20. Cited in Cable, *Avenue,* pp. 152–153.

toric felicities. Even the collapse, in early 1873, of Henry Cooke's bank (a consequence of the Crédit Mobilier railroad scandal) and his immediate resignation as governor failed to shake popular confidence. After all, the de facto governor, Boss Shepherd, now became governor de jure in September.

But conservative tax payers were now roiling in outrage, and the pressure for a second congressional investigation proved irresistible. This time, Shepherd's enemies struck a vein. The governor was compelled to disclose that the city's indebtedness was in excess of eighteen million dollars and that twelve million more would be required to pay for work already under contract. He had cavalierly ignored the ten-million-dollar debt ceiling. Finally, the effects of the panic of 1873 fatally compromised Shepherd's mandate. He retained President Grant's confidence until the end, but Congress had had enough of the board of public works. After nine months as governor, the District's territorial government was abolished and replaced by a three-man board of commissioners. Grant nominated his friend to the board, but the Senate refused confirmation. Two years later, 1876, Shepherd declared bankruptcy and left for Mexico.

The McMillan Commission and Beyond

Pennsylvania Avenue, in the quarter-century after Shepherd's departure, ceased being a grand causeway in search of monumental habiliments. One by one they materialized: the National Bank of Washington Building (1889) at Seventh Street, N.W.; the other Richardsonian Romanesque curiosity, the hulking yet towering Old Post Office a decade later between Eleventh and Twelfth streets, N.W.; two blocks farther along the avenue, the new Willard Hotel rising on its original site, its beaux arts ebullience to be completed in the first years of this century; and, colossal and controversial, the French Renaissance State, War and Navy Building (1871–1888, designed by Shepherd's friend Alfred B. Mullett) at the Seventeenth Street intersection, but a few paces beyond the graceful simplicity of the White House. The Grand Avenue had begun to mature to L'Enfant's conception.

Governor Shepherd's approach had been that of the shotgun. Although the board of public works established a distinguished advisory panel (Montgomery C. Meigs, the army engineer, and Frederick Law Olmsted, the landscape architect, served), "Shepherd listened to the words of the advisory panel," William Maury says, "took what he wanted, and discarded the rest." The result was that the board of public works left the cityscape ineradicably but unevenly altered. It accomplished a great deal, but there was much it had not done, and some things it had done were destructive of the L'Enfant plan. Capitol Hill languished, despite Olmsted's landscaping of the Capitol grounds and the completion, in 1897, of the Library of Congress Building. L'Enfant's Mall was as shoddily treated by Shepherd as it had been by successive Congresses. Mary Cable's delightful *Avenue of the Presidents* quotes an 1840s guidebook reminding visitors that "everyone who has gazed upon the landscape to be seen from the west front of the Capitol must have observed the large tract of waste ground. . . . It is not generally known, even to members of Congress, that this is the national mall." It was even fortunate that it had survived as wasteland, for the Mall had very nearly been auctioned for building lots by the Congress sitting in 1832. During the Civil War, Walt Whitman estimated that some ten thousand cattle were penned on the Mall. Shepherd did not offer it for sale; he did the next worst thing by granting the Baltimore & Potomac Railroad access rights across the Mall and by leasing a section at Sixth Street, N.W., for construction of a railroad depot. Shepherd's achievement had been to make Washington a place where Congress was satisfied to transact business. What remained to be done was to make the city a place congenial to L'Enfant. As the District of Columbia approached its one-hundredth birthday, a new flurry of proposals for municipal planning emerged.

Michigan's Sen. James McMillan came to Washington after a successful career as a railroad mogul. But he was not simply another rich Republican satisfying an urge to help govern what members of his class owned. McMillan had acquired passable architectural and engineering skills; he studied L'Enfant's plan with an intelligent, sympathetic eye. His politics were wilier and much less affronting than Alexander Shepherd's. What he shared with his two predecessors was tenacious commitment to make the nation's capital conform to its monumental destiny almost in spite of itself and whatever the cost or nature of the opposition. With his wry smile, astigmatic gaze, and carrot-stick goatee, McMillan became known to his senatorial colleagues as a tireless lobbyist for government-sponsored municipal reconstruction. It was fitting, then, that he became chairman of the Senate's committee responsible for the city's centennial preparations.

In May 1900, Senator McMillan recommended that Congress acquire the services of an architect, landscape architect, and sculptor to guide its renovation plans, a proposal which the House, under the hostile leadership of Speaker "Uncle Joe" Cannon, peremptorily rejected. In March of the following year, McMillan offered a revised proposal to have the Senate's District committee empower the Office of Public Buildings and Grounds of the Army Corps of Engineers to study the problem of improving the Mall, extending the White House, and designing an expanded park system, a resolution approved by the Senate. At the beginning of 1902, the senator presented his report on the work thus far accomplished, a document of surpassing importance and rather confusingly referred to as the report of the McMillan Commission, the Park Commission of 1901, or the Burnham Commission. McMillan died in August 1902, but by then the conception and pace of his plan were well established.

Four of the nation's most distinguished experts, Daniel Burnham and Charles McKim, architects, Frederick Olmsted, Jr., landscapist, and Augustus Saint-Gaudens, sculptor, had been hired by the army engineers. All four spent seven weeks in Europe during the summer of 1901 at McMillan's personal expense studying buildings and parks in London, Paris, Vienna, Rome, Venice, and Budapest. McKim, the designer of the Boston Public Library, Rhode Island's capitol, and several buildings at Harvard, was McMillan's preferred architect, but it was the more renowned and aggressive Daniel Burnham, the director of the 1893 Chicago World's Columbian Exposition, who became the commission's piston. "The damage done by the World's Fair," one of the country's more discerning architects, Louis Sullivan, decreed as beaux arts uniformity swept the land, "will last for a half century from its date, if not longer." Perhaps. But there was something to be said for an architect who knew what he wanted and, like L'Enfant, was willing to oppose the troglodytes obedient to the mediocre arrogance of Speaker Cannon. "Make no little plans," Burnham may have enjoined.

> They have no magic to stir men's blood, and probably themselves will not be realized. Make big plans, aim high in hope and work, remembering that a noble and logical diagram once recorded will never die, but long after we are gone will be a living thing, asserting itself with ever growing insistency.[21]

Here, surely, was L'Enfant *redux,* better funded and politically more astute.

Starting with Capitol Hill, the Burnham Commission successfully proposed the shifting of the Botanic Gardens at the bottom of the hill as well as the transfer of Bartoldi's graceful fountain (as well as the Chinese community) so as to "form an organic connection between the Capitol and the Mall." With equal success, the commission recommended the placement of a commemorative cluster of statuary in honor of General Grant and his valorous troops. Mount Vernon Square, dramatically levelled by Shepherd, was remembered, and with the munificence of Andrew Carnegie, Washington's Public Library à la beaux arts opened on the spot in 1903. The commission's design for the Lincoln Memorial was completed two decades after McMillan's report. McKim's bridge to Arlington was also finally completed in 1932. One of the commission's most felicitous legacies was the rococo gem, the District Building, completed in 1908, and guarded by the statue of the once vilified and now nearly forgotten "Boss" Shepherd.

Attentive to the rolling topography of the city, the commis-

---

21. Quoted in Federal Writer's Project, Works Progress Administration, *Washington: City and Capital.* American Guide Series (Washington, D.C.: Government Printing Office, 1937), p. 117. Quote recently attributed to one of Burnham's associates.

sion suggested a number of parks situated along ridges over-
looking Washington, another idea somewhat skimpily and belatedly implemented by Congress. Finally, and patently evocative
of the commissioners' Versailles visit, a reflecting pool ter-
minating at the steps of the Lincoln Memorial was included in
the Burnham Plan, an aesthetic dividend made possible by filling in the marshy area beyond the Washington Monument. The
prolongation of the Mall to the Lincoln Memorial and the plant-
ing of trees along parallel roads, aligned so as to compensate for
the two-hundred-foot southwesterly shift of the obelisk, had the
effect of visually remedying the Washington Monument's displacement (the original site having been too marshy).

As impressive as were the commission's achievements, they
were not easily won and not a few were delayed or lost to the
opposition of Speaker Cannon. Plans for fancy parks and beaux
arts facades outraged his aesthetic insensibilities, nibbled at his
power to control federal real estate, and violated his conviction
that taxpayers' money ought never be lavished upon such unre-
publican adornments. The secretary of the treasury, Leslie
Shaw, whose co-operation was crucial to the commission's
plans, blew hot and cold, usually in response to the temperature
of "Uncle Joe." The location of the Hall of Records was successfully opposed as was the site of the Department of Interior.
Congress, not the Burnham Commission, ought to determine
where the government's buildings should go, Secretary Shaw
maintained. But Burnham was stubbornly unwilling to see politics eliminate architectural reason. Writing to Shaw as didac-
tically as L'Enfant might have done, Burnham warned of the ir-
reparable harm Cannon and his men were doing:

> If the Executive yields now [August 11, 1902], it will be much
> more difficult to refuse in the future, because it will then have not
> alone the urgency of personal interest, but precedent as well to
> contend with. On all future occasions the claim will be set up that
> the Plan was abandoned by the Administration and was dropped
> definitively.[22]

22. Cited in Charles Moore, *Daniel H. Burnham, Architect, Planner of Cities* (Boston: Houghton Mifflin, 1921), p. 133.

After much caucusing, Congress acted on the commission's proposals for the Department of Agriculture Building along the Mall, for a National Museum site, and for the enlargement of the White House. Among Burnham's most significant and enduring achievements was the removal of the tracks and railroad station from the Mall. While in Europe, he had met Senator McMillan's friend, Alexander Cassatt, president of the Pennsylvania Railroad, who agreed to move to the edge of Capitol Hill if Congress would appropriate $1.5 million for a tunnel beneath the hill. Before Speaker Cannon's men could authorize the purchase of the abandoned depot for government offices, President Theodore Roosevelt hurriedly ordered its demolition. Burnham's persuasiveness, the power of the railroad lobby, and guarded presidential support extracted money from Congress for the new Union Station, the first of the commission's projects (1903–1907), and designed by Burnham himself. With its barrel-vaulted, coffered ceiling rising to ninety-six feet (Burnham was inspired by the Baths of Diocletian), its gigantic space intended to accommodate inaugural crowds of a hundred thousand, Union Station became for a time, as the McMillan Commission had ordained, "the vestibule of the capital." Today, after calls for its demolition and a science fiction design for its renovation, Union Station is once again gleaming white; its new role as the National Visitor Center began just as the capital celebrated the bicentenary.

Speaker Cannon had vowed he would "never let a memorial to Abraham Lincoln be erected in that goddamned swamp," referring to West Potomac Park.[23] But, despite his vow, the splenetic old Illinois congressman died four years after the dedication of Henry Bacon's memorial on the original site. He may have felt somewhat compensated, nevertheless, by his triumph over another commission project—Union Square. Having shifted the Botanic Gardens and the Bartoldi fountain at the foot of Capitol Hill, the planners unveiled the design for a broad sweep of parterres with L'Enfant's grand cascade of water descending from the Capitol's west front. Construction of the

23. Cable, *Avenue*, p. 192.

reflecting pool where Burnham's parterres were proposed and the controversial plan for extending the Capitol's west front would seem to preclude forever the commission's plan for Union Square. It is not much more likely, and rather fortunate, that the commission's sunken, formal monument garden around the obelisk may find favor with the National Capital Planning Commission.

In the decades since the McMillan Commission, much of Washington has become a city of marble with more statuary in its parks than any other city in North America. It has been endowed with a central advisory body, the Fine Arts Commission (1910), and, in 1926, Congress created the National Capital Park and Planning Commission to continue planning the overall development of the District of Columbia. In 1937, the justices of the Supreme Court were able to leave their hand-me-down accommodations in the old Senate chamber for Cass Gilbert's Corinthian-columned masterpiece adjacent to the Library of Congress. That same year John Russell Pope's National Archives Building on Constitution Avenue between Seventh and Ninth streets, N.W., was dedicated. The neoclassical National Archives was one of fifteen structures approved by Congress in May 1926 as part of the new four-hundred-million-dollar Federal Triangle (a McMillan proposal perfected by Andrew Mellon), whose construction was pressed forward during Franklin Roosevelt's administration. Between Sixth and Fifteenth streets, N.W., and within the wedge formed by Constitution and Pennsylvania avenues, the city's federal countenance received its major surgery to date. The face-lifting is somewhat austere, however, for although each building was designed by a different architect from the board established by Secretary of the Treasury Andrew Mellon (1921–1932), all have the appearance of a single inspiration—as though each design, more subtle than the master's, were the work of students of Germany's Albert Speer.

Among the buildings completed by 1938 were the Federal Trade Commission, the National Archives, the Department of Justice, the U.S. Post Office, the Interstate Commerce Commission, the Internal Revenue Service, and the Department of Commerce. The Federal Triangle plan called for the destruction of two of Washington's most distinctive buildings, the Richard-sonian Romanesque Old Post Office Building and the beaux arts District Building. The latter has been granted a reprieve. The controversy over the Old Post Office now appears to have been sanely resolved: the building is to stand and one of its likely occupants is the National Endowment for the Arts. Another McMillan recommendation, a national theatre building, has been belatedly realized with the erection of the John F. Kennedy Center for the Performing Arts. Architect Edward Durrell Stone's heavy marble rectangle would not please Charles McKim (it displeases many present-day Washingtonians), but it does house two fine theatres, a concert hall, restaurant facilities, and the American Film Institute; in the future, an experimental theatre will be added. What it does for the city is another matter. The McMillan plan theatre would have been located in the heart of Washington. The Kennedy Center on the banks of the Potomac literally overhangs Rock Creek Parkway and is two minutes from Whitehurst Freeway. Its location is perfect for nearby Watergate condominium owners and commuters from "west of the park" and the Maryland and Virginia suburbs who can attend the center, park their cars underground, and never come into contact with the city itself.

Since the creation by executive decree of the Pennsylvania Avenue Commission in 1965, L'Enfant's principal thoroughfare has undergone several major redesign proposals, each one somewhat improved. The first plan called for unrelieved, monumental office slabs along the avenue's undeveloped north side and a Mussolini-cold National Square the size of Paris's Place de la Concorde between Fourteenth and Fifteenth streets, on the site shared, among others, by the historic old Willard Hotel. Both the conception and the site of the proposed National Square were unfortunate, and, as Mrs. James Rowe, Jr., formerly of the National Capital Planning Commission, rightly feared would be "a place to flee from," just as the Chirico-like L'Enfant Plaza on Independence Avenue disconcerts and chills by its bloodless perfection of form and symmetry, and lies deserted after 5 P.M. The Pennsylvania Avenue Commission has mercifully reconsidered the original office slabs, of which the new J. Edgar Hoover Building would have been the mega-lithic archetype. The present design prescribes an imaginative mix of federal and commercial structures, luxury apartment buildings, and the building for the Woodrow Wilson Center for Advanced Studies, a sprawling complex for scholars proposed for the Market Square area. But the bicentenary will have long since passed before the north side of the avenue is renovated, and, until then, it will remain only half what L'Enfant en-visaged—monumental on one side and ragged on the other.

L'Enfant's cherished Mall is alive and improving. Cleared of the World War One "tempos," its perimeters are buffered not by the embassies called for by the major but by marvellously endowed museums, the latest being, in order of construction, history and technology, the bunker-shaped Joseph H. Hirsh-horn, and the colossal but unponderous Air and Space Building. The most interesting of the Mall's museums may be the Mellon family's lavish gift of an emergent structure of marble-encased pie slices to house the National Gallery's massive print collec-tion as well as temporary and loan exhibitions. The new mu-seum is being connected to the old by a sunken sculpture garden in which mostly modern pieces will be displayed. Mellon was secretary of treasury eleven years, under Harding, Coolidge, and Hoover, long enough to encourage even the most fastidious banker to confuse the accounts of the federal government with those of Wall Street. During his tenure the secretary remitted, rebated, and reduced more than six billion dollars in taxes, including a remission of $404,000 to himself. Under Franklin Roosevelt, the Internal Revenue Service mustered a query about $1.3 million in Mellon back taxes. The former secretary glibly explained that he had failed to list his art collection, donated to the A. W. Mellon Education and Charitable Trust, as a de-duction, and, even more absent-mindedly, that he had never mentioned that the foundation's paintings were to be donated to the nation. The political pressures of the New Deal constrained the former cabinet officer to fulfill his promise of a national mu-seum for his treasures. Once entrapped, Andrew Mellon spared nothing to make his gallery as splendid as the Uffizi or the Louvre. And he succeeded. With the bequests of Joseph Wi-

dener, Samuel Kress, Lessing Rosenwald, and the modern masterpieces of Chester Dale in the late sixties, the National Gallery
has become one of the world's finest museums.

The muted Freer Gallery across the Mall with its rooms filled
with oriental masterpieces, its permanent staff of Japanese
craftsmen, and its eerily beautiful Whistler room (it houses the
world's largest Whistler collection) is one of the most rewarding
aesthetic museum moments to be found anywhere. But the Mall
itself, mown and vacant, still awaits the implementation of the
Skidmore, Owings & Merrill master plan, approved a decade
ago by the National Capital Planning Commission. A beginning
has been made with the recent completion of the reflecting pool
at the foot of the Capitol. The inner roads of the Mall have been
closed to automobile traffic and the National Park Service is in
the process of turning these arteries into footpaths and of doubling the four rows of trees. Moreover, the initiative of the
Smithsonian's S. Dillion Ripley has filled the Mall every summer, since the late sixties, with the ebullience of the Folk Life
Festival, a dizzy potpourri of ethnic music, crafts, food, and
youth happenings. Director J. Carter Brown of the National
Gallery has helped make the Mall a more lively place in winter
with the recent opening of an outdoor ice-skating rink. Of
greater humanizing potential are the echoes of landscapist Andrew Jackson Downing's rejected "pleasure gardens" design
(1851), audible in the Japanese garden project, Constitution
Gardens, just completed down the Mall at Seventeenth Street.

Planning the city has become perpetual. In February 1967,
the National Capital Planning Commission released its "Green
Book" containing the twenty-year "Proposed Comprehensive
Plan for the National Capital." The comprehensive plan incor-
porates the features of the Pennsylvania Avenue Commission,
the National Capital Transportation Agency (established in
1960), Metro construction, and much more. Two major new
community settlements, at Fort Reno and Fort Lincoln, are
planned; an international center west of New Hampshire Avenue
to house foreign chanceries and international agencies is projec-
ted; a plaza (Market Square) behind the National Archives and
an "Uptown Center" for Anacostia are to be developed; several

schools and parks are called for; Buzzard Point is to be re-
claimed for parkland; and two new colleges will be established.
The new colleges—Federal City College and Washington Technical Institute—now exist and will soon merge with District of
Columbia Teachers College to become the University of the
District of Columbia. The nearly seven billion dollars of the
comprehensive plan in private and public costs is, of course, no
longer a realistic figure.

Moreover, there is a major new factor in local planning—the
elected government of the District of Columbia. No longer are
zoning, freeway, and mass transit matters exclusively determined by House District Committee members and the Army
Corps of Engineers, with encouraging nods from highway and
Washington Board of Trade lobbyists. Almost a decade before
home rule finally became a quasi-reality in January 1975, local
citizens had shown growing resentment of their colonial status
in these three areas, slowly nudging the local press and the bureaucracy of the old appointed regime onto the path of environmental restraint. Their efforts have been arduous; the engrained
belief that bigger means better and the old habits of congressional acquiescence run deep. But the orgy of freeway construction, of six-lane concrete swaths through the city, has abated—
for the moment. The damage done by the Southwest Freeway (a
dangerous roadway to Virginia severing Southwest Washington
from the rest of the city) is permanent, but Georgetown residents have probably succeeded in killing the Three Sisters
Bridge that would have created another channel for Virginia
commuters through their distinctive community. The citizens of
Brookland have also diverted construction of the North Central
Freeway, another commuter marvel designed to run parallel to
the Baltimore & Ohio Railroad tracks and through the heart of
this quiet, middle-class black neighborhood for the benefit of
Marylanders and trucking companies.

Until the long dormant citizenry roused itself, Washington
planning was imprisoned in a paradox: the more the monumental city grew to the measure of L'Enfant's ideal, the greater the
insensitivity to the needs of the residential city became. In little
more than a decade after the completing of the Federal Triangle

and the swelling of Washington's population to a 1950 high of 802,000, those who ran the city engineered a massive evacuation as if their handiwork could best be appreciated from the windows of commuting automobiles. The influx of blacks accelerated the exodus, aggravated the insensitivity, and made of Washington two cities: one for living among monuments; the other for driving through, indifferently, on ever more freeways to the suburbs. It is hardly surprising that even showcase Washington suffered at the hands of once compliant local officials, senior southern congressmen, and assorted lobbyists. There was once a plan, only recently abandoned, to ring the Lincoln Memorial with an eight-lane highway (altered, in 1967, to six lanes tunnelled under the Tidal Basin) running along the Mall (also altered to a combination tunnel and trench), and finally connecting with the Southwest Freeway.

Mass transit has been one of Washington's most bitter and complicated undertakings. Seven years ago construction began for a 98-mile subway ("Metro") system, estimated to cost $3 billion by its 1975 completion date. Now that freeway construction was clearly approaching its saturation point while the metropolitan area experienced runaway growth, an underground transit system became, so it seemed, a matter of urban survival. The fact that the privately owned bus service was becoming one of the nation's most expensive and certainly among the least efficient, hastened the decision to build. Not everyone applauded, however. Some liberal whites and many black civic leaders believed the prognosis of Edward Banfield's *Unheavenly City* that subways would fail to "make any contribution to the solution of the serious problems of the city." Suspicions have grown among Washington's poor that Metro's hidden purpose was to make the center city easier and safer to reach from the white suburbs. There is also the legitimate alarm over Metro's wholesale condemnation of residential and business property and the District's rezoning of it for intense commercial development. "Metro," one joyful Maryland congressman foretold, "will create the biggest real estate boom we have ever seen," a prospect almost as unsettling to some working-class homeowners and small businessmen as Boss Shepherd's redevelopment had been.[24]

Five billion dollars later, Washington has an embryo mass transit system that may be too expensive for the poor to ride and which fails to take them where they need to go even when they can manage the fare. Proposals that Metro and the bus service be run without fares have, unfortunately, never received the serious attention they deserve. But if Metro is about to take the city for a ride, most Washingtonians, in the few months of the first section's operation, have been euphoric about the good it will do. Architecturally, its stations are superb; it works; it is being ridden; people are proud of it; and it is appreciated as the fitting bicentennial symbol of Washington's coming of age as a vibrant world capital.

24. Lawrence Hogan, in Sam Smith, *Captive Capital, Colonial Life in Modern Washington* (Bloomington, Ind.: Indiana University Press, 1974), p. 224.

2

The Tale of the Second City

N *The Secret City,* Constance McLaughlin Green retells what is to many blacks the well-known story of Benjamin Banneker's brief role in the founding of the Federal City. Born in November 1731 of free parents near what became Ellicott, Maryland, young Benjamin received the equivalent of an eighth-grade education (a rare attainment even for whites then) and in 1753 he demonstrated remarkable intelligence by constructing a wooden clock, one of the earliest time pieces in the Maryland colony. By the time the mill-owning Ellicott clan moved into the Patapsco Valley during the mid-1770s, Banneker was a successful small farmer supporting his widowed mother and whiling away the lonely hours with the flute and violin. A friend describes him "as of a brown complexion, medium stature, of uncommonly soft, gentle manners, and of pleasing colloquial powers." [1] Friendship with the Ellicotts introduced the amateur clockmaker to a higher order of scientific challenge. George Ellicott, an accomplished astronomer, gave his friend books and a pedestal telescope, and Banneker soon astounded the American scientific community by publishing through the Baltimore firm of Goddard & Angell his *Almanack and Ephemeris for the Year of Our Lord 1792.*

1. Daniel Murray, *Banneker, the Afro-American Astronomer* (Washington, D.C.: 1921), p. 18.

Banneker had written his almanac in August 1791 and the product had so pleased him that, overcoming his customary humility, he dispatched news of the achievement together with a proud autobiographical note to the Sage of Monticello, who was known to entertain profound doubts about African intelligence. "Sir," the self-taught astronomer wrote Thomas Jefferson,

> I freely and cheerfully acknowledge that I am of the African race; and, in that color which is natural to them, of the deepest dye; and it is under a sense of the most profound gratitude of the Supreme Ruler of the Universe that I now confess to you that I am not under that state of tyrannical thraldom and inhuman captivity to which too many of my brethren are doomed, but that I have abundantly tasted of the fruition of those blessings which proceed from the free and unequalled liberty of which you are favored. . . .[2]

Jefferson had already learned of Banneker's unusual abilities from the Ellicott brothers; he was delighted to proclaim "the very respectable mathematician" and to take credit for procuring his employment as "one of our chief directors in laying out the new Federal City on the Potomac." [3] He forwarded Banneker's almanac to the Baron Condorcet. From that time on, misinformation and myth were to envelop the contribution to the District of Columbia of the Maryland mathematician, making it exceedingly difficult to know the truth.

The story goes that when L'Enfant was dismissed in February 1792, rolling up his master plan and taking it with him, the commissioners turned to his assistant, Banneker, who was able to reconstruct from memory a faithful duplicate. Banneker was never L'Enfant's assistant, however; his instructions were relayed by Major Ellicott. Furthermore, the infirmities of the sixty-year-old freedman usually compelled him to confine his activities to sedentary computations and inventories of materiel. Some knowledge of L'Enfant's plan Banneker must have gleaned from the dinners in common with the two majors and

2. Murray, *Banneker,* p. 23.

3. Silvio Bedini, *The Life of Benjamin Banneker* (New York: Charles Scribner's Sons, 1972), p. 109.

other members of the team at Suter's Tavern. Such knowledge can only have been rudimentary, though, not only because of L'Enfant's secrecy but because, at the end of April 1791, after three months in Washington, Banneker returned ailing to Maryland and was replaced by one of the younger Ellicotts. Banneker's intrinsic significance to the Federal City was not his arguable accomplishments as Major Ellicott's assistant but the symbolism of his presence: he was the gifted black man in attendance at the creation of a city whose past, present, and future is as much the cynosure of black as it is of white destiny in America.

When the survey lines of Washington were drawn a small population of blacks lived in the area. Very few, if any, were free (Virginia law forbade their residency six months after manumission and there was scant encouragement for them to live in Maryland's Georgetown) and fewer, if any, were property owners. Cultured, free Benjamin Banneker must have presented an incredible spectacle to the few score slaves who watched him at work and puzzled over rumors of his residency and common meals at Georgetown's finest hostelry. After Banneker, no blacks dined at Suter's, but in the rolling terrain and marshes along the Potomac hundreds cleared roads and hauled limestone from Aquia Creek quarry to build William Thornton's Capitol and James Hoban's President's Palace. Nine years later, in 1800, when the government's records arrived at the navy yard from Philadelphia, Washington's slave population had grown to more than five hundred and its free blacks to 123. The city's total number of inhabitants was 3,244. In Georgetown and its environs 1,449 slaves toiled while 277 freedmen eked out a precarious existence. Foreign labor, what there was of it, suffered grievously in Washington's insalubrious climate; domestic white labor merely trickled into the city during the early years because of the low wages made possible by slavery.

Congress preferred to ignore the dilemma of slavery in the capital of a republic. In the early 1790s, it had decreed that the laws of Maryland and Virginia governing the commerce and liberties of Africans should prevail in the District of Columbia.

After the 1808 Constitutional prohibition on importation of Africans into the United States took effect, Washington became one of the principal slave markets in the nation. Just for a moment, in 1805, there had been the faintest glimmer of humanitarianism when a resolution to manumit all slaves at age twenty-five in the District of Columbia failed adoption in Congress. Thereafter, decade by decade, Washington's black codes harshened.

In 1812, the city council quadrupled fines for participation in "nightly and disorderly meetings" and prescribed six-month jail sentences for free offenders unable to pay and forty lashes for slaves; in addition, free persons of color were required to carry at all times a certificate of freedom. In 1827, annoyed by the rising clamor of abolitionism, the council imposed a blanket curfew, increased fines, and augmented the cost of the freedman's bond from $20 to $500 plus the requirement of two white signatories. The following year, Congress forbade the presence of Africans on the Capitol grounds other than for reasons of "business." In the wake of Nat Turner's insurrection in Virginia, Georgetown strengthened its black code (in 1832), punishing with particular severity any person of color possessing abolitionist literature. Again, in 1836, after a relatively mild "riot" the preceding year, Georgetown and Washington City forbade Africans to operate taverns and eating establishments, increased the cost of freedmen's bonds to $1,000 in addition to five white signatories, required that all dances and assemblies have prior approval of the mayor; banned bathing in the river, carrying of guns, patronizing gambling or tippling houses, and using foul language. The 10:00 P.M. curfew was to be strictly enforced and those arrested for crimes, whether slave or free, could be auctioned to compensate the municipality for expenses incurred during their incarceration. That same year Congress adopted the "gag rule," prohibiting discussion of slavery. While all these measures were being conceived to "manage" the black population at home, the American Colonization Society, founded (1816) and headquartered in Washington, was laboring to solve the problem by "repatriating" blacks to Africa.

Thomas Jefferson lamented slavery with an eloquence born of

deep travail. "I tremble for my country when I reflect that God is just," he confessed, "and that His justice cannot sleep forever." Nevertheless, Jefferson left the problem to his successors and to the deity. Introspective President Madison deplored the slave traffic in the capital and was much pained by the ironic comments of foreign ministers, but he was helpless against the congressional power of the slaveocracy. The neglected Mall and the area around the President's Palace became the principal emporia of the traffic while Pennsylvania Avenue and South Capitol Street served as the causeways of coffle, the trains of bound slaves. "See there! Ain't that right down murder? Don't you call that *right down murder?*" a black passerby shouted at the Englishman Jesse Torrey who had paused, horror-stricken on Pennsylvania Avenue, on his way to a congressional debate. It *was* murder, Torrey replied.[4] It was also the way of life of the place. The auction block, the lash, and the manacled gangs on their way to the Deep South were as much a part of Washington as the steamy climate, the malaria, the marshes, and the dust.

Yet, despite repressive codes and thriving commerce in human chattel, Washington City was comparatively benign. Laws affecting blacks were never rigorously enforced; even if they had been they were less punitive than black codes elsewhere in the South. Washington was exceptional in its tolerance of private elementary educational institutions for blacks. Between 1807 and the beginning of the Civil War, more than fifteen academies for people of color were operated in Georgetown and Washington. Periodic toughening of the black code was due in part to municipal malaise over the decennial doubling and trebling of the nonwhite population. Such was the rapid increase in the city's free population, through migration, mitosis, and manumission, that it outnumbered enslaved blacks by almost eight hundred in 1830. By 1840, there were 4,808 free to 1,713 unemancipated blacks in the city. In 1850, slaves had increased to a mere 2,113 while the freedmen numbered 8,158. White population amounted to 29,730. The Georgetown census for

4. Jesse B. Torrey, *American Slave Trade* (Westport, Conn.: Negro Universities Press, 1971), p. 56.

that year was 6,080 whites, 1,561 free blacks, and 725 slaves. The pattern was similar in Alexandria—4,903 whites, 1,488 slaves, and 836 freedmen in 1810; 5,758 whites, 1,627 freedmen, and 1,064 slaves thirty years later. Before L'Enfant's death in 1825, the racial if not the architectural character of his city had become irreversibly fixed. Ignored, despised, and oppressed, blacks were already as permanent a feature of the federal capital as its grids and radii; one hundred fifty years later they were to become its dominant group.

In *Our Capital on the Potomac,* patrician Helen Nicolay muses about the sophistication of the local blacks and surmises, "As the proportion of free negroes [*sic*] in the District of Columbia was unusually large, the colored population may have been mentally above the average." If the city's blacks were "mentally above the average," it was because, above all else, they prized formal education. In 1804, Washington established a superintendency for white education, assessing a head tax of one dollar for white male adults. Forty-four years later, the city amended its education law, replacing the dollar assessment with a property tax. Free blacks were denied public revenues for elementary schools, but, in 1807, three free notables, George Bell, Nicholas Franklin, and Moses Liverpool, opened the first school for black pupils. A nominal tuition was required and, "to avoid disagreeable occurences," an early announcement emphasized, "no writings are to be done by the teachers for a slave, neither directly nor indirectly, to serve the purpose of a slave on any account whatsoever." Great caution was essential; Mayor Robert Brent, sympathetic to their endeavor, had barely succeeded in quashing a council resolution to ban the instruction of free blacks.

After the establishment of the Bell school, free black academies followed pell-mell. Mrs. Mary Billings of Georgetown opened her school on Dunbarton Street in 1810, moving to H Street in Washington City eleven years later. America's first black historian, George Washington Williams, wrote that "many of the better educated colored men and women now living . . . received the best portion of their education from her, and they all speak of her with a deep and tender sense of obligation." [5] One of her pupils, Henry Smothers, established· a school in Georgetown in 1820, later moving to Fourteenth and H streets, N.W., in Washington, where some one hundred students were enrolled. When financial reverses compelled Smothers to relinquish control, John Prout became the school's director, changing the name to Columbian Institute and charging twelve cents monthly. Columbian Institute was an exceptionally fine academy, entirely comparable to the best white schools of the period. One of its graduates, John F. Cook, Sr., a prominent Presbyterian minister, succeeded Prout in 1834 and renamed the institution Union Seminary. When the senior Cook died in 1855 his son, John, and, two years later, his brother, George, continued the school until the Civil War. Meanwhile, the audacious venture of establishing a female high school had been undertaken, in 1851, by a frail, white New Yorker, Miss Myrtilla Miner. Ridiculed and intimidated by the white citizenry, highstrung and unwell, Miss Miner succeeded in establishing, with the aid of Harriet Beecher Stowe, an institution that offered, according to Constance Green, "a better education than that available to most white children." [6]

The colored population was not only literate, it could be craftily contentious, as the 1821 circuit court case involving the respected bank messenger, William Costin, and the corporation of Washington demonstrated. Through his mother, Costin was related to Martha Custis Washington. Of impeccable character, and bearing himself with natural dignity, he was the acknowledged leader of the city's free colored community. When the municipal government tightened restrictions on all blacks in 1821 (requiring personal appearances before the mayor with freedom certificates and the depositing of a twenty dollar bond guaranteed by a white citizen), William Costin astonishingly claimed that the city had no right under the Constitution to impose restrictions upon nonslaves. "All who are not slaves are equally free," he contended before the distinguished Judge Wil-

5. Rayford W. Logan, *Howard University, the First Hundred Years, 1867–1967* (New York: New York University Press, 1969), p. 10.

6. Constance M. Green, *The Secret City, A History of Race Relations in the Nation's Capital* (Princeton, N.J.: Princeton University Press, 1967), p. 51.

liam Cranch. "They are . . . equally citizens of the United States." [7] Costin won his case but lost the principle. Justice Cranch reversed the lower court's fine of Costin for refusing to furnish his bond because the 1821 ordinance was not retroactive, but also ruled that the municipal corporation had the power to restrict any group's liberties in the interests of the larger society.

While free blacks resisted as best they could the steady paring away of their precarious freedoms, the plight of Washington's slave population remained as lamentable as ever. The English vistor Jesse Torrey, in *American Slave Trade* (1817), presented Washington as a place of enraging iniquity and brutality. Slave-pens and auction blocks spilled into the backyard of the White House and ringed the Smithsonian Institution on the Mall. The local jail was crowded with slaves being kept for auction and transfer south, Torrey claimed. Free blacks were there, too, frequently re-enslaved to cover penal upkeep costs and fines. Occasionally, there were kidnappings of manumitted blacks on the city streets.

One such case became a cause célèbre when a female slave, torn from her husband and children and awaiting makeup of a Georgia coffle, flung herself from the attic window of the burning F Street, N.W., tavern where she was confined. Hearing of the incident three weeks later, in early January 1816, Torrey visited the tavern. He found the woman languishing under fetid blankets, badly maimed but lucid. Securing a writ of injunction against her removal from the city, Torrey then sued for her freedom. Since the woman had been given to the tavern owner in payment for her medical and lodging fees, the suit was disallowed. But Torrey's sleuthing revealed that two of the unfortunate woman's attic companions were free blacks who had been abducted in Delaware. Eccentric, slave-owning John Randolph rushed to the Englishman's support, denouncing Washington's slave commerce:

> You call this the land of liberty, and every day that passes things are done in it at which the despotisms of Europe would be horror-struck

7. Green, *Secret City*, p. 26.

and disgusted. . . . In no part of the earth—not even excepting the rivers of the coast of Africa—was there so great, so infamous a slave market as in the metropolis, in the seat of government of this nation which prides itself on freedom.[8]

Other members of Congress spoke out. General Van Ness, one of the city's wealthiest notables, headed the list of trial fund subscribers and three distinguished local attorneys (among them Francis Scott Key) donated their services. Torrey's kidnap victims were set free, but the slave markets and the F Street tavern increased their business in the years that followed.

The architect of the Capitol, Dr. William Thornton, reposed complete confidence in his slave, Peter, who was sufficiently literate to understand his master's instructions in iambic tetrameter when on errand:

> To Peter.
> If anyone you chance to meet,
> Stay not to talk, but pass and greet,
> And neither give nor take a treat.

But could it have been loyal Peter whose alleged attempt to murder Widow Thornton caused the race riot of 1835? The identity of the assaulting Thornton slave, or slaves, is uncertain, but the deed's infamy caused an explosion of white wrath on August fifth which left the fashionable property of the mulatto restaurateur, Beverly Snow, in shambles as well as William Wormley's school for free blacks. No lives were lost in the "Snow Riot," and despite the passage of a city council ordinance a year later banishing blacks from ownership of commercial businesses, Snow's restaurant was reopened within a year or so by another mulatto, Absolom Shadd, who was able to liquidate his business for $25,000 twenty years later.

As it has always done after an interim of acrimony and clumsy repression, the city put the memory of the riot behind, returning to the tried ways of casual racial constraints and ami-

8. Federal Writer's Project, Works Progress Administration, *Washington: City and Capital*. American Guide Series (Washington, D.C.: Government Printing Office, 1937), pp. 69–70.

able hypocrisy. A few blacks were able to secure positions as clerks and messengers in government agencies. Solomon G. Brown was the chief messenger in the Patent Office in the 1830s. The litigious William Costin held an honored menial post in the privately owned Bank of Washington. Perhaps a half-dozen free blacks, like Messrs. Jones, Shadd, Snow, and Wormley, possessed a net worth in excess of $20,000. For the great majority of the free population, employment meant work as bricklayers, carpenters, oystermen, livery-stable hands, hackmen, blacksmiths, cobblers, cooks, hairdressers, tailors, and common laborers. Very few manumitted blacks were hired by the arsenal or navy yard. The Typographical Union, a thriving industry in a politicians' town, rejected nonwhites.

In the early days, much of Washington had been built by hired slave labor, a practice that continued during the reconstruction of government buildings after the British invasion of 1814. The arrival of Irish immigrants in the early 1830s rapidly led to the displacement of black laborers, slave and free, so that the bulk of the work on the Chesapeake & Ohio Canal was performed by whites. With slaves cut off from the remote chance to lay by money to purchase their freedom and freedmen displaced from or denied their livelihoods, by the late 1840s Washington had become for all classes of blacks a pressure cooker over a low but slowly rising flame. Yet Washington in the late 1840s was not unlike Washington a century later, a city sloping toward a radical racial readjustment. The signs had long been unmistakable, though subtle.

William Lloyd Garrison's *Liberator* had troubled the solons of Georgetown sufficiently to be mentioned in the city's 1836 black code as an extreme example of literature "calculated to excite insurrection or insubordination among the slaves or colored people." Year after year the petitions to Congress for the abolition of slavery in the District of Columbia had grown in volume and stridency, despite the 1836 gag rule and its subsequent amendments. Year after year, old Congressman John Quincy Adams, the former president, braved the censure of the House to call attention to them. On one occasion, in 1837, he boldly presented a petition from twenty-two slaves. In

1844, Adams triumphed; Congress repealed the prohibitions. Congressional petitions and abolitionist propaganda to annul slavery in the District rapidly increased. Primarily because of the need for state financing of the Alexandria Canal, but also because of anger and alarm over abolition, the leaders of the Old Dominion mounted a successful 1846 campaign for the retrocession of Alexandria to Virginia, thereby reducing the District's total area from one hundred to sixty-nine square miles. The planters of Virginia must have thought they had acted not a moment too soon, for two years later the abolitionist, Dr. Gamaliel Bailey of Boston, moved to Washington and began printing the *National Era*.

The Pearl Affair

News had recently arrived that the French had deposed their uninspiring king, Louis-Phillippe, and proclaimed a republic. Washingtonians jubilantly poured into Lafayette Square to acclaim the first of the revolutions that would sweep Europe during 1848. All the rhetoric that April Sunday was fiery, intoxicating, but the panegyric of Sen. Henry S. Foote of Mississippi, one of the most intemperate voices of the slaveocracy, transported the crowd in front of the White House. The February Revolution in France, the senator thundered, held out "to the whole family of man a bright promise of the universal establishment of civil and religious liberty." [9]

Three colored men listened spellbound as Foote's peroration, prophesying that "the age of tyrants and of slavery was rapidly drawing to a close," brought a roar of approval from the citizenry. Suddenly, one of the three, Daniel Bell, began shouting with the crowd. Paul Jennings shushed him, anxiously whispering, "Why, what are you doing, Daniel? Anybody would think you were one of these white people the way you're carrying on." Bell apologized as the trio hurried from Lafayette Square: "That man made me forget my color the way he talked, and if

9. Daniel Drayton, *Personal Memoir of Daniel Drayton* (Boston: Bela Marsh, 1855), pp. 26–27.

he didn't mean it for me, it sounds good all the same." The third friend, Samuel Edmonson, understood: "You are right, Daniel, I feel that way, too." [10]

The sequel to this incident is a matter of important though forgotten public record. By singular good fortune the words and deeds of Bell, Edmonson, and Jennings have been faithfully transcribed by one of their descendants in a remarkable little book, *Fugitives of the Pearl*. On their walk home from the square, we know that Jennings, the most intelligent and aggressive of the trio, confided that at that very moment a sailing vessel from Delaware was putting into Washington's White House Wharf, that he, Jennings, had met a Capt. Daniel Drayton of the *Pearl* the month before while accompanying his master, Sen. Daniel Webster, to Baltimore. Drayton had outlined a careful plan for the escape of nearly one hundred blacks from the city. Producing the note from Drayton, Jennings explained that he had kept silent until then to avoid betrayal. Edmonson, almost as white as his Brent forbears and a butler in one of Washington's grander households, hesitated before agreeing. Bell, a free man with a robust carpentry trade, fairly leapt at Jennings's plan. His wife and eight children had been manumitted by their deceased master, but the white heirs were contesting the will. In the two days before sailing time the three men recruited seventy-five passengers.

The *Pearl*'s mid-fortyish captain was an unlikely emancipator. He belonged to no abolitionist society, was not a religious fanatic, did not even come from Boston. Daniel Drayton was a New Jersey sailor, and apparently less than an expert one, since he occasionally ran his ships aground and had made such a poor living from sailing that he gave it up, only to return to the sea on the advice of his physician. Until he began sailing in southern waters, Drayton had never questioned the prevailing lore about blacks. He believed "the negroes [*sic*] as only fit to be slaves." Soon, astonishingly, he learned from firsthand experience that the blacks were neither docile nor stupid, that "they

10. John H. Paynter, *Fugitives of the Pearl* (Washington, D.C.: Associated Publishers, 1930), p. 23.

had the same desires, wishes, and hopes as myself.'' And what they wanted most was freedom. "No sooner, indeed, does a vessel known to be from the North anchor in any of these waters,'' Drayton's *Personal Memoir* relates, "than she is boarded, if she remains any length of time, in hopes of obtaining a passage to the land of freedom.'' [11] The *Pearl*'s captain may have informed northern abolitionists of his intention to sail a large number of blacks from Washington, but it is fairly certain that the conception and execution of the escape was entirely his. Drayton's sole co-conspirator, besides his two-man crew, was probably Daniel Webster's man, Paul Jennings.

It is a fair speculation that when the notables of Georgetown and Washington awoke the morning of April sixteenth to find fires unstoked, breakfasts unmade, and baths undrawn, their bewildered consternation must have been only slightly less desperate than if they had been South Carolinians discovering the insurrectionist plot of Gabriel Prosser. That they had vanished without trace—seventy-seven respected, privileged blacks, many of them free or soon to be—afforded the abolitionist foe a devastating propaganda weapon. Slavery was supposedly defensible on humanitarian grounds and the District of Columbia was reputedly the best place in which to be a slave: Captain Drayton's fleeing cargo was an unanswerable refutation of such beliefs.

Gentlemen gave orders and mounted saddle to lead posses aimlessly into the countryside. Merchants and their tutting customers watched from canopied storefronts the backing and filing of horsemen and worried about the angry mood of sunbaked Irishmen drifting into central Washington from their Swampoodle ghetto. In congressional boardinghouses, such as Abraham Lincoln's on First Street, S.E., politicians exchanged opinions on the significance of the escape. Meanwhile, "reliable'' blacks were being ferreted out and questioned by vigilantes.

No one thought to question Paul Jennings, Drayton's indispensable accomplice. On the eve of the flight, Jennings had given Aunt Rachel, Senator Webster's housekeeper, a letter and

11. Drayton, *Personal Memoir*, p. 21.

told her he would be absent from the city for a few days. His letter is a fascinating document, revealing the contradictory emotions uniting and dividing black and white in the world made by the slaveholders. "Honored Friend," Jennings wrote,

> A deep desire to be of help to my poor people has determined me to take a decided step in that direction. My only regret is that I shall appear ungrateful in thus leaving with so little ceremony one who has been so uniformly kind and considerate and has rendered each moment of service a benefaction as well as a pleasure. From the daily contact of your great personality, which it has been mine to enjoy, has been imbibed a respect for moral obligations and the claims of duty. Both of these draw me towards the path I have chosen.
>
> Jennings [12]

Late that evening, Jennings helped the *Pearl*'s seventy-seven passengers aboard. Afterwards, he returned to Daniel Webster's, had Aunt Rachel return his farewell letter, and went home as the *Pearl* weighed anchor. A tortured sense of probity stopped Jennings from following his friends. He was within two hundred dollars of gaining his freedom; twenty-five months of eight dollars each remained. He decided, finally, that Daniel Webster, a man whom history remembers as constantly demanding of his clients that they "freshen" his retainer, deserved this sacrifice.

Meanwhile, the *Pearl,* sailing from its berth at 10:00 P.M., headed for Chesapeake Bay, anchoring till daylight off Alexandria; then, catching wind, it moved along toward the mouth of the Potomac. Once into the bay, Drayton's fugitives would be safe. By late evening, still the sixteenth, the ship was within sight of Chesapeake Bay when it was suddenly buffeted by violent winds. Sayres, the navigator, strongly counselled taking shelter for the night at Cornfield Harbor below Port Lookout. Reluctantly, Drayton agreed. The risk of being overtaken was exceedingly remote since they were about 140 miles from Washington.

12. Paynter, *Fugitives*, p. 34.

At Washington's City Hall one hundred posse riders, under the command of one Mr. Cartwright and utterly indecisive as to which direction to gallop, impatiently slapped their riding crops. It was then that the hackman, Judson Diggs, yawed towards them behind his mule. Colored folks in Washington had never quite trusted Judson Diggs, their consensus being that "the very best way to put white folks 'next' to anything you were about to do was to let Judson into the secret." [13] That day Judson Diggs was ready to be especially co-operative. Not long before, he had been haughtily rejected by one of the Edmonson sisters (Judson was a roly-poly black man; the Edmonsons were comely mulattoes) who were passengers on the *Pearl;* moreover, one of the escaping families, carting a large, deadweight trunk, had offended him with an inadequate tip. To Cartwright's queries came ceremonial evasion; then, after a suitably menacing order, Judson divulged the truth. "I ain't goin' to tell yer no lie," he oozed, "kase I's mo' anxious den you is ter see 'em ketched. Now dem horses is all right on lan', but dey ain't no good on water, an' I specs dem niggers is a hunnerd miles down de ribber by dis time. . . ." [14]

A steam-powered vessel belonging to the Georgetown Dodges (three of whose slaves had fled) was commandeered. A boat putting into Alexandria identified a ship fitting the *Pearl*'s description. The chase was on. It would have been too late and Judson Diggs's perfidy of no avail but for the decision to anchor the *Pearl* for the night. Drayton and his crew had fallen into an exhausted sleep. "I knew nothing more," the captain recalled later, "till, waking suddenly, I heard the noise of a steamer blowing off steam along side of us. . . . The black men came to the cabin and asked if they should fight. I told them no." [15]

The jailing of Drayton in Washington on the eighteenth, the narrow escape from destruction of Gamaliel Bailey's *National Era* offices (Bailey was thought to be in collusion with Drayton), and the punitive selling of the seventy-seven blacks (men,

13. Paynter, *Fugitives,* p. 9.
14. Paynter, *Fugitives,* p. 72.
15. Drayton, *Personal Memoir,* p. 32.

women, and children) to Georgia and Louisiana agents were cause for jubilation in the white District of Columbia and throughout the white South. Abolitionist societies in New York and Boston sprang to Drayton's defense, attempting unsuccessfully to secure Daniel Webster for counsel (his fee was too high) and finally retaining Horace Mann, the Massachusetts educator and politician, and William Seward, New York's former governor. Mann was resourceful and eloquent, but Judge Crawford ruled there would be no mention of slavery in his court, not even to illuminate the unsuborned motives of the defendant. The guilty verdict and a sentence tantamount to life imprisonment were formalities. The plight of the blacks aroused even more antislavery passion than Drayton's trial. Jacob Astor ransomed one of the Edmonson boys before he could be shipped to New Orleans. Emily and Mary Edmonson, the sisters whose affection Judson Diggs had maladroitly sought, were repurchased from their New Orleans masters. Several others were similarly manumitted, but the funds raised at rallies in Boston's Faneuil Hall and by the New York Antislavery Society were not always immediately adequate to meet the elevated prices of slavers who preferred, for political as well as horseflesh reasons, to keep their merchandise.

The better sequel to the *Pearl* affair would have been for northern philanthropy to have rescued all Drayton's charges. A cynical opinion, however, might maintain that they were probably of more value to the abolitionist cause transported to the notorious New Orleans slave market and to the Georgia heartland. Unless they were hardened Negrophobes, few northerners could fail to be moved by the letter of Congressman John Slingerland describing the departure of some of the seventy-seven blacks for Georgia, a letter widely reprinted in the northern press. At the railroad depot scarring L'Enfant's Mall, the congressman had chanced upon a monster coffle:

A majority of them were of the number who attempted to gain their liberty last week. About half of them were females, a few of whom had but a slight tinge of African blood in their veins, and were finely formed and beautiful. The men were ironed together and the

whole group looked sad and dejected. At each end of the car stood
two ruffianly-looking personages, with large canes in their hands,
and, if their countenances were an index of their hearts, they were
the very impersonation of hardened villainy itself.

In the middle of the car stood the notorious slave-dealer of
Baltimore, Slatter, who I learn, is a member of the Methodist
Church, 'in good and regular standing.' . . . While observing this
old, gray-headed villain . . . the Chaplain of the Senate entered the
car—a Methodist brother—and took his brother Slatter by the hand,
chatted with him for some time, and seemed to view the
heartrending scene before him with as little concern as we should
look upon cattle.[16]

Drayton's trial and the pathos of the *Pearl*'s blacks troubled
Congress. In the House, Rep. Joshua Giddings rose to denounce
slavery in language that would have delighted John Randolph.
In the Senate, New Hampshire's John Parker Hale verbally
fenced with South Carolina's Calhoun and flung at Senator
Foote the latter's French Revolution speech in Lafayette Square.
Senator Foote's parliamentary riposte was to invite his colleague
to Mississippi to be lynched. But the Giddingses and the Hales
were now on the offensive. Before the Edmonson sisters returned to Washington, Mann and Seward would be elected to
the Senate, where they would soon be joined by the courtly antislavery militant, Charles Sumner. And in January 1849, the
rail-splitting congressman from Illinois, Abraham Lincoln, introduced a bill to abolish slavery in the District of Columbia. If
the confluence of Whig politics and abolitionist morality riled
southern politicians, the wiser southerners, like Henry Clay,
realized that the life-and-death matter of introducing slavery into
the new territories of the Southwest compelled compromise.
That compromise came in 1850, one of whose provisions conceded the end of the slave traffic, though not of slavery, in the
District of Columbia. Drayton received a presidential pardon
two years later.

Thus, in a roundabout and painful way, the *Pearl* achieved its

16. Drayton, *Personal Memoir*, p. 59.

purpose. Although it had not been a vehicle of freedom for most of its passengers, its impact had been greater than that of an earlier ship, the *Amistad,* whose crew of insurgent slaves had been freed by the New York Supreme Court. The *Pearl* had had a regnant influence upon the great Compromise of 1850 and had brought about the dismantlement of Washington's shameful slavepens. Its greatest significance, though, was to be felt indirectly through the pen of Harriet Beecher Stowe. When Mrs. Stowe gathered material for her novel, appearing first in serial form in Washington's *National Era* during 1851–1852, one of the mainsprings of inspiration and plot was the *Pearl* and its fugitives. The *Pearl* had been a small battering ram in the abolitionist flotilla; *Uncle Tom's Cabin* was a dreadnought.

From Emancipation to Segregation

Probably nobody saw more of wartime Washington—unofficial, real Washington—than Walt Whitman, who served as a volunteer medical orderly. Slightly more than a year after Congress had enacted legislation freeing all slaves in the District, Whitman wrote his mother (June 30, 1863) describing the calibre of the new black soldiers.

> I am where I see a good deal of them. There are getting to be many
> *black troops.* There is one very good regiment here black as tar;
> they go around, have the regular uniform—they submit to no
> nonsense. Others are constantly forming. [17]

Seventeen years before, Mary Bowen, the wife of the mayor who would be elected with the help of black votes, had written to a friend that surely, "No sane-minded man acquainted with the black population South could wish them liberated and allowed to remain in the States." [18] Yet, before the close of the Civil War, the discipline and valor of Gen. Ben Butler's "contrabands" had won grudging respect from white supporters

17. The Wound Dresser, *A Series of Letters written from Hospitals in Washington during the Rebellion* (Boston: Small, Maynard & Co., 1898), p. 92.
18. Green, *Secret City,* p. 44.

of the Union. Blacks everywhere, but especially in the District of Columbia, were proud of their brothers in uniform and expected, as they have after each war, that the nation would gratefully remember their services. If Washingtonians had been aware only of former slaves efficiently shouldering muskets, future race relations would have been more promising; but white and black citizens alike were increasingly apprehensive of the migration of thousands of plantation blacks, destitute, ignorant of urban ways, and swamping the meager relief provisions provided by the federal government and private charity organizations.

In March 1862, prominent Washingtonians joined with northern philanthropists to establish the Freedmen's Relief Association, through which clothing, housing, jobs, and rudimentary instruction in literacy were offered. Meanwhile, a "Contraband Department" was created by the government to register escaped or liberated slaves, provide rations, and to facilitate their resettlement in the North and West. In April 1862, owners in the District of Columbia were compensated for the compulsory manumission of their slaves. In July, Congress legislated immunity from repossession or sale for all slaves in the federal territory. In January of the following year the Emancipation Proclamation was issued. The result was a black avalanche: first, a trickle rising to about four hundred and living on Capitol Hill in what was called "Duff Green's Row" behind the present Library of Congress; then, by the end of 1862, nearly four thousand in the Contraband Department's "Camp Barker," near what is today Logan Circle in Northwest Washington. By the spring of 1863, more than ten thousand had swarmed into "Murder Bay" between the President's Park (the Ellipse) and the infested Canal, and into Foggy Bottom below Georgetown, while others lingered on Capitol Hill. When hostilities concluded at Appomattox, some forty thousand ex-slaves had found their way to the District since 1861. The special census of 1867 recorded a total area population for whites of 88,327, for blacks of 38,663 with 31,937 living in Washington City.

With more than 30 percent of the population black and with the Augean makeshift in which the freedmen lived, enormous problems and terrible tensions, such as the following were inevitable: Of Murder Bay, the police superintendent reported,

> Here, crime, filth, and poverty seem to vie with each other in a career of degradation and death. Whole families . . . are crowded into mere apologies for shanties. . . . During storms of rain or snow their roofs afford but slight protection, while from beneath a few rough boards used for floors, the miasmatic effluvia from the most disgustingly filthy and stagnant water . . . renders the atmosphere within these hovels stifling and sickening in the extreme.[19]

Inducements to move at least as far as the relatively unpopulated Anacostia region across the river or to migrate to the North or to the open lands of the West succeeded in displacing but a few thousand of the ex-slaves from the heart of Washington. In the minds of these simple folk Washington was surely the Promised Land. When one poor resident was asked why he settled in the District in the early twentieth century, his answer might as readily have come from a contraband of the 1860s: "I wants to stay around where the President lives. I figure if he eats, I'll eat." [20] A great number, unfortunately, ate almost nothing and died. By one account, nearly one-third of the total of immigrants between 1862 and 1866 went to their graves in the Potomac Beulah Land, encouraging some Washington Negrophobes to predict to an English traveller the disappearance of "the whole colored race in the next fifty years" from immorality, disease, and destitution.[21]

But blacks were not fated to become like the Powhatan Indians, and what was done locally to better their conditions would become, for a time, the pattern followed elsewhere. For more than a decade after the beginning of the Civil War, Washington, as it would do in the 1950s, pursued an uneven but steadily improving course of racial uplift. Interestingly, there

19. Green, *Secret City,* p. 82.

20. Haynes Johnson, *Dusk at the Mountain, the Negro, the Nation, and the Capital* (New York: Doubleday and Co., 1963), p. 39.

21. Green, *Secret City,* pp. 81–82.

were leaders like Frederick Douglass who expressed concern that the federal government might sap black initiative through the welfare programs of the Contraband Department. Douglass's concern was shared by the Lotus Club, a generally light-skinned and elite group of established black males antedating the white Oldest Inhabitants Society by two years. On one crucial issue, though, elite blacks and radical Republicans were wholly agreed—the urgency of public education. Congress complied in May 1862 by passing a law requiring the three jurisdictions in the District, Washington City, Georgetown, and the county, to open schools for blacks, assigning 10 percent of black property taxes for their support.

The first black public elementary school opened in Ebenezer African Methodist Episcopal Church on Capitol Hill in early 1864. A rough estimate of black real estate in the District had given the sponsors of the public education law the impression that more than $3,000 in revenue would be available. However, the city fathers of Washington and Georgetown and the judges of the county's levy court in their wisdom appropriated the parsimonious sums of $265 in 1862 and $410 in 1863 for Washington, and for Georgetown nothing in the first year and a mere $70 in 1863. The second public education law of 1864 sought to remedy the disparity in monies between white and black schools. Henceforth, funds were to be apportioned on a population basis. But until 1867, the three white trustees of the black school systems found themselves powerless to tap public funds beyond pittances and constrained to rely upon local and northern philanthropy. In summer 1866, Congress took matters forcefully in hand. Ten thousand dollars was appropriated for erection of black public schools in the county, empty military barracks were turned over to blacks for schoolhouses, and three lots in Washington were deeded to the trustees for black schools. The clout in the 1866 law, however, was the provision that the trustees could sue the District corporations for the unpaid 10 percent property tax appropriation.

The sequel to the public education battle, more complicated in its particulars than it is useful to recount, has an instructive contemporary resonance. Mayor Richard Wallach of Washington and Mayor Henry Addison of Georgetown commissioned a special census in 1867 to ascertain the respective educational needs and revenues of blacks and whites. This nine-hundred-page-plus document is a veritable X ray of social and economic conditions, and a primer for educators. If, as Constance Green states, it exaggerated the level of black literacy and glorified the achievements of black Washingtonians, the 1867 census was exactly true to the mood and ambitions of the District's thirty-eight thousand or more nonwhites. Reluctantly, the corporations of Georgetown and Washington paid over a sizeable portion of the withheld proportional revenues. A further development was the order of the secretary of the interior requiring that two members of the trustees of black schools must be black and empowering the trustees to hire a superintendent. But even with the aid of Congress, black educational progress was difficult, and the slackening of northern philanthropy made the ascent harder.

So long as the systems remained separate, whatever the well-intentioned legislation of the Reconstruction Congress, black education would be penalized by racism and skimpy property revenue. The people living in Washington's Fourth Ward presented a petition to Congress which, if approved, would resolve the dilemma: Fifty-seven white and twenty-eight black heads of households asked Congress to integrate the two systems. Mayor Sayles Bowen and several aldermen thought it a good idea. But many Washington blacks were opposed, preferring a separate system over which their control was complete if financially handicapped to a unitary structure diluting their power. For white radicals and a small number of blacks, equality in education represented the best solution. Sen. Charles Sumner introduced an 1870 bill to integrate fully the District school system. Ultimately, Sumner's proposal foundered in the acrimony over Mayor Bowen's costly city welfare and renovation programs benefitting black laborers and in the politicking over the new territorial government. Then, for a moment, northern philanthropy seemed to vindicate those who argued for black educational autonomy. In 1870, some nine years before creation of a comparable white institution, sufficient funds in honor of Myrtilla Miner were raised to start a black public high school in the basement of the Fifteenth Street Presbyterian Church. This Fifteenth Street School, the predecessor of the elite Dunbar High School, was a fine pioneering effort, establishing high standards for black education, but it did little to slow the lopsided appropriations in the years to come.

Nevertheless, the black community made maximum use of what there was. The Freedmen's Bureau, created in March 1865 as the successor to the Contraband Department, reported in January 1866 that some one hundred teachers of both sexes were teaching fifty-six hundred blacks in fifty-four day schools, while some twenty-three hundred pupils were receiving instruction from five hundred Sabbath school teachers. There were also eight or ten self-supporting schools staffed by black teachers offering courses to five hundred students. "Most of the teachers were poorly prepared," historian Rayford Logan writes, "and the physical facilities were generally not conducive to study." [22] Yet this testimony to faith in advancement through learning exhibited by thousands of impoverished peasants whose erstwhile masters had said were happy in their ignorance and wholly incapable, in any case, of formal instruction, was truly impressive.

During the controversy over public education, another, quieter but no less momentous, development in Negro education was occurring. In 1867, Gen. Oliver Otis Howard, head of the Freedmen's Bureau and an upstanding Congregationalist, requested and received from Congress a charter to incorporate Howard University. Its first students were five white girls who were daughters of trustees and faculty members. By 1871, a small number of white and black physicians were being graduated from the medical department, following the footsteps of its first product, James T. Wormley. At the same time, the law department, guided briefly by the mulatto Oberlin graduate, John Mercer Langston, began turning out practitioners, among the earliest of whom, James A. Cobb and Robert H. Terrell, soon proved themselves distinguished jurists.

22. Logan, *Howard University,* p. 11.

Meanwhile, in the political arena, strides being made by Washington's blacks threatened to break into a gallop. Until the end of the Civil War, Lotus Club patricians, as distressed by the tidal wave of peasant migration as upper-class whites, had confined themselves to genteel proddings of congressional allies for equal franchise rights and for the banning of discrimination in public places. They were so averse to charges of appearing "pushy" that when Frederick Douglass announced his intention to attend Lincoln's second inaugural reception and called for company, only a plucky Mrs. Dorsey agreed to go along. The appearance of the magnificent ex-slave at the White House was a triumph of personal diplomacy, with Douglass blustering his way beyond politely obdurate guards into the presence of the president, who generously made the most of the occasion by humbly asking Douglass's opinion of the inaugural address. Washington's blacks agreed that they were proud and concealed that they were also mightily relieved.

The assassination of Lincoln changed the climate of Washington's politics overnight. With the ascendancy of radical Republicans in Congress—men who came to suspect the new president of southern sympathies, who wished to make the South pay for its waywardness, and who believed that Washington's white notables were Copperheads—the speedy advancement of local blacks became the touchstone for a program of national Reconstruction. The vindictive, widely circulated speech of Congressman George Julian of Indiana reflected the extremism of Republican hardliners.

> I have argued that the ballot should be given to the negroes [*sic*] as a matter of justice to them. It should likewise be done as a matter of retributive justice to the slaveholders and rebels. . . . The rebels here will recoil from it with horror. . . . To be voted down by Yankee and negro ballots will seem to them an intolerable grievance.[23]

In January 1866, Congress debated a bill for the immediate enfranchisement of Washington's blacks, irrespective of length

23. Green, *Secret City*, pp. 78–79.

of residency or literacy. One-third of the population was now black and such was the fear of its nascent electoral power, one congressman deplored, that much of the white citizenry was "willing to surrender their own rights rather than to respect the rights of others." [24] Literacy amendments and proposals to abolish local government failed, however, and in January 1867 the electoral rolls were opened to all who demanded registration.

Eighty-two hundred blacks and ninety-eight hundred whites registered to vote in the spring municipal elections of 1867. Sen. Charles Sumner and other radicals urged blacks to field at least one candidate. To politically neurotic whites it seemed as though the day of Armageddon had arrived. Instead, because of the discipline of the churches and the fraternal orders, a congenial administration devoid of blacks and headed by conservative Mayor Richard Wallach was elected. Blacks had offered a dramatic good faith demonstration of sanguine forbearance. This strategy failed. Mayor Wallach's regime stymied black education progress by stealth and by official conduct. It had little concern for the armies of freedmen unemployed, disease-ridden, and starving in the settlements along the old canal and invading the Northeast Irish settlement at Swampoodle. Confederate sympathizers like William Corcoran, who had fled the city with a million in bullion at the outbreak of the war, were being welcomed home as heroes while Copperhead merchants were allowed to display Confederate trinketry. Small wonder, then, that, as Wilhelmus Bryan notes, "the negroes [sic] flushed with the strong showing made by their vote in 1867 and conscious of the backing of Congress, changed their attitude, and before the day of the [next] city election began to put forth their claims to at least an equal share of the offices and of the city contract work."

Sayles J. Bowen was swept into office by a black plurality in 1868. Two blacks, John F. Cook, a tax clerk, and Carter Stewart, a barber, were elected to the aldermanic board and the common council, respectively. During his tenure as postmaster of

---

24. Constance Green, *Washington: Village and Capital, 1800–1878* (Princeton, N.J.: Princeton University Press, 1962), p. 333.

the city and one of the three trustees of the colored school system, Bowen had proven himself an aggressive friend of Washington's blacks. The new mayor was immediately confronted by two serious dilemmas—black poverty and a white groundswell to move the national capital from a southern-minded milieu to a more central and more cosmopolitan locus somewhere in the North or Midwest. Mayor Bowen rightly saw both problems as being cut from the same cloth: employ black laborers to rebuild the city and the two dilemmas would dissipate. During the two years of his administration, Bowen created work for hundreds of freedmen, but at the politically suicidal price of overwhelming the city with debt. Two years later, Washington's debt had doubled to $2.4 million, but an earnest beginning in black public education was underway, sewers and lighting were being installed, and the civilized world's worst arterial slough, Pennsylvania Avenue, was being surfaced.

The choice of wooden blocks to pave the avenue was bizarre. Earlier experiments with this material had shown the results to be smooth, quiet, and quickly disastrous. Smooth as a "parlor floor" when completed in February 1871, within a year the grand roadway was a plane of rotting splinters; by then, however, Mayor Bowen (who may have conceived the avenue as a perpetual public works project) had been ousted. "He was not very popular anyway," Helen Nicolay tells us, "having the interests of the colored race too much at heart to please his pro-Southern townsmen." Before his electoral demise, though, blacks had induced the city council to enact the civil rights ordinances of 1869 and 1870, respectively fining hostelries refusing accommodations to well-behaved blacks and prohibiting discrimination against them in restaurants, bars, hotels, and places of amusement. Several leaders in the black community, convinced of the inevitability of racial progress, wondered aloud about the need for the 1870 law. Their confidence should have been shaken by the racist policies of the Typographical Union, the Bar Association, and the Medical Society of the District of Columbia. In March 1869, Drs. Alexander Augusta and Charles Purvis had applied for membership in the local medical society. Despite considerable support among the society's members and a congressional threat to repeal the charter, the black physicians were rejected. The rebuff was dismissed as a passing aberration.

The half-decade after 1868 was the Golden Age of black Washington. With a black president of Jesuit Georgetown University (Patrick Healey), a black public school system that Congress had decreed must be given subvention on a pro rata basis, two centers of higher learning (Howard University and Wayland Seminary) underway, dozens of blacks hired as messengers, clerks, and even a handful as officials in the federal and municipal bureaucracies; with James Wormley (staked by two or three radical Republican friends) opening the city's finest hotel; and with Frederick Douglass and the Reverend Sella J. Martin launching the impeccably edited newspaper, *New Era*—with all this, black Washington's future seemed as assured as the Confederacy's defeat. Out of Foggy Bottom, Murder Bay and Swampoodle came thousands of black laborers to dig Bowen's sewers, to lay fifteen miles of roadway and sidewalk, to erect hundreds of lampposts, and to set those costly wooden blocks into Pennsylvania Avenue while the city debt piled up. There were a few merchants so out of tune with the times as to refuse black patronage; they were made to feel the teeth of the city's civil rights ordinances. All references to race vanished from official records. Elegant whites and blacks greeted one another in exclusive surroundings as though nothing could be more natural.

In Wormley's Hotel gathered the *crème de la crème;* in early 1879, one such gathering inaugurated the Metropolitan, one of the city's, and the nation's, most exclusive social clubs. When Vice-President Henry Wilson died, Douglass and Wormley were among the official pallbearers accompanying the remains to their resting-place. At the second inaugural ball of President Ulysses S. Grant, in 1873, black representatives and senators waltzed with their wives in the swirl of diplomats and dignitaries, all of them apparently unmindful of the special courage and mission assumed by Frederick Douglass less than a decade before on a similar occasion.

Black political power was still far more potential and symbolic than real, but the potency of the symbols already distressed much of the local white citizenry and not a few conservative observers on Capitol Hill. They would have abolished Washington's government outright because of the size and ambition of the black population. There were other political forces favoring the abolition of the city's charter: congressional radicals wanting to punish the southern-oriented white population; intimates of President Grant, indifferent to the blacks and unembittered by Copperheads, who were determined to save Washington from itself and from its powerful regional enemies. Then there were followers of Sen. Charles Sumner honestly laboring to guarantee both the civil rights of the blacks and complete independence for the District. By the end of the 1860s it had become apparent that federal control of the district, but with a semblance of local autonomy, was the ideal compromise. While Congress pondered their destiny, Washingtonians voted for Matthew Emery as mayor, an honest stonemason who found himself compelled to honor Mayor Bowen's bloated contracts. The new mayor oversaw the completion of the wooden paving of Pennsylvania Avenue and grappled helplessly with the municipal debt. Nine months later, in February 1871, his government vanished with the congressional reorganization of the District of Columbia. Matthew Emery would be the last of Washington's elected mayors for more than a century.

Alexander Shepherd was the architect of the District's new government, although the official sponsor was Sen. Hannibal Hamlin of Maine. Shepherd's tactic was intended to turn the 1868 expiration of the city charter (twice extended) to the optimal advantage of all the parties: Capitol Hill, the business community, and even the local citizenry—black as well as white. Washington's future boss intended to scuttle the local establishment, to streamline the city's chain of command so that the inspired commands of a single organizer would be obeyed with a minimum of taxpayer interference. This was, he believed, the quickest way to pacify congressional fears or vindictiveness and to defuse hostility between local whites and blacks. Above all, Shepherd's scheme virtually guaranteed a lightning reconstruction of Washington that would silence those who were demanding the removal of the national capital to a more central location. William Maury puts the calculation bluntly:

> In seeking to retain the Capital, Shepherd and his cohorts needed to satisfactorily quash the three major objections of the removers. The piebald governmental system had to be replaced with something more effective. The City had to be made more palatable physically. And an effective and legal way of allaying fears of a black takeover had to be found.[25]

When, in May 1870, the Senate passed a Charles Sumner-inspired bill offering the District a territorial government all but tantamount to statehood, Shepherd organized his forces. The Sumner bill provided for a popularly elected governor and council, a nonvoting congressional delegate, and, *mirabile dictu,* annual appropriations from the federal treasury, proportionally computed; and with a final touch of federal largesse, a provision that the charters of Georgetown and Washington could not be annulled without approval of the majority of voters. What transpired between the Sumner bill and the one signed by President Grant has never been entirely clear. Profound misgivings about black-influenced municipal government, persuasive arguments by Maine's Sen. Lot Morrill for total abolition of local government, urgency about proposals to move the capital—all played their role. But what was decisive was Shepherd's unusual influence with Grant's administration; and the final legislation was superbly tailored to Shepherd's requirements. The annoying fixed federal appropriation had been traded for a presidentially appointed board of public works empowered to assess property owners for the costs of rebuilding Washington. To handicap opponents of runaway municipal grandeur even more, there was a three-member board of health, gubernatorially appointed, which could quarantine neighborhoods out of existence. The governor, of course, was appointed by Shepherd's ally in the White House, as were members of the council. The people of George-

25. William Maury, "Alexander R. Shepherd and the Board of Public Works," *Records of the Columbia Historical Society,* 1971–1972 (394–410), 397.

town, Washington City, and the county were not entirely stripped of their rights, however. An elected house of delegates was created, but it was hardly a match for the governor and his council. The board of education was also elective.

Washington's blacks had never looked upon Alexander Shepherd as a friend; they remembered his active opposition to Mayor Bowen. But their misgivings about the new territorial arrangement were rapidly dispelled. Three of the council's members were black—a caterer named John A. Gray, the miller Adolphus Hall, and the venerable Frederick Douglass. In the house of delegates two seats were won by blacks in the 1871 balloting—the government messenger Solomon Brown and the capable James A. Handy, bishop of the African Methodist Episcopal Church, a representation probably intentionally limited lest already uneasy whites be further alarmed. The urbane John Mercer Langston was appointed to the board of health. Four hundred appointive offices, mostly filled by loyal white Republicans, now handled business formerly managed by 160 city and county officials. Little had changed in terms of real power. Black office holders were, nevertheless, symbols of a frightening potential to influence decisively the affairs of the District. When Councilman Frederick Douglass limned Alexander Shepherd as the American Baron Haussmann and even compared him to Pericles, when he airily explained away charges of malversation against the board of public works in the *New York Graphic* ("Of course, whenever a large amount of money is to be expended in a short time, small quantities are likely to go astray.") [26]—the old settlers and Copperheads sniffed; but they shuddered, too, at the thought of the majestic Douglass and his forty thousand sons of Ethiopia loyally in step behind Boss Shepherd, crunching through Georgetown and leaving behind a cumulonimbus of debts and high taxes. No government at all was better than "nigger" rule: an opportunity which came when the depression of 1873–1874 destroyed Governor Shepherd's fiat.

26. Cited in Alexander R. Shepherd Papers, Library of Congress.

In June 1874, Congress suspended the three-year-old territorial government and created a three-man board of commissioners (presidentially appointed) to rule the District. Henceforth, none of the District's officials would be elected. "To arch-Southerners in Washington," Constance Green explains, "disenfranchisement represented a safeguard against a city government partly manned by Negroes, and many a big taxpayer . . . had seen advantages in a regime free of pressure from non-propertied 'riff-raff'." [27] Although it passed the Civil Rights Act of 1875, a legacy of the deceased Charles Sumner, congressional signs of an end to local and national black advancement were imminent. The passage of the 1878 Organic Act confirming the District's status as a congressional fiefdom provided compelling further proof. Many years later, the matter was expressed with repugnant candor during a Senate exchange between ex-Colonel (C.S.A.) John Tyler Morgan of Alabama and ex-Colonel (U.S.A.) John James Ingalls of Kansas:

>Morgan: 'To burn down the barn to get rid of the rats—'
>Ingalls: 'Yes, to burn down the barn to get rid of the rats, and that is what was done in this case, the rats being the negro population and the barn being the government of the District of Columbia. . . .' [28]

Although exceptional men like Blanche Bruce, Frederick Douglass, Henry P. Cheatham, John Langston, and John R. Lynch became small stars in the federal firmament, holding such reserved honorifics as recorder of deeds, auditor of the treasury, marshal of the district, paymaster general, and ambassador to Haiti, white conduct made it patently clear that one had to be a Douglass or a Langston to be assured restaurant service or hotel rooms. In a discrimination suit during the early 1880s, the victorious black plaintiff was awarded one dollar in damages. The crushing blow came in 1883 when the Supreme Court ruled that private acts of discrimination against individuals were

27. Constance Green, *Washington: Capital City, 1879–1950* (Princeton, N.J.: Princeton University Press, 1963), p. 5.
28. Johnson, *Dusk at the Mountain,* pp. 24–25.

not prohibited by the Thirteenth and Fourteenth amendments. "It would be running the slavery argument into the ground," the court pronounced,

> to make it apply to every act of discrimination which a person may see fit to make as to the guests he will entertain, or as to the people he will take into his coach or cab or car; or admit to his concert or theatre, or deal with in other matters of intercourse or business.

Some small solace remained to District blacks, nevertheless, for, in ruling the Civil Rights Act of 1875 unconstitutional, the justices reserved judgment as to the act's legality in territories under federal jurisdiction. At a reunion in Washington's Lincoln Hall in late October, Douglass's voice, annealed by the fiery indignation of his abolitionist youth, thundered that the decision "presents the United States before the world as a Nation utterly destitute of power to protect the rights of its own citizens upon its own soil. . . . . In humiliating the Colored people of this country, this decision has humbled the nation." [29] "Once upon a time," Mary Church Terrell's *Colored Woman in a White World* sighed, "Washington was called 'The Colored Man's Paradise.' " By the end of the century, if it was not quite a hell, Washington was surely a black man's purgatory.

The temptation to draw the picture too bleakly must be resisted. Culturally, the city was described as having "the most distinguished and brilliant assembly of Negroes in the world." Blue-veined descendants of the old colored families of Boston, New Orleans, and Philadelphia may have deemed such an appraisal slighting, but it cannot have been a gross overstatement. Where else in America was a black opera company to be found, one which performed at Lincoln Hall and several times at Ford's Theatre during the early 1870s? Where else would a black performance of Samuel Coleridge-Taylor's *Hiawatha* trilogy, conducted (in 1903) by the Anglo-African composer himself before a dazzled audience of blacks and whites, occur? What other city could boast of the American Negro Academy, established in

---

29. Letitia W. Brown and Elsie M. Lewis, *Washington in the New Era, 1870–1970* (Washington, D.C.: Smithsonian Institution, 1972), p. 7.

1897, before which the most brilliant minds of the race read and debated papers on a vast array of topics? Its first president, the Reverend Alexander Crummell, rector of Saint Luke's Episcopal Church and graduate of Queen's College, Cambridge, was a firebrand of modern stripe, proclaiming that blacks constituted a distinct nation—a premise to which neither his fellow academy members nor his parishioners unanimously subscribed. There was the peerless high school, founded in 1873 and subsequently renamed for Paul Laurence Dunbar. With the research facilities afforded at Howard University and the Library of Congress, what other city could accommodate so well the needs of Harvard alumnus Carter G. Woodson's Association for the Study of Negro Life and History, founded in 1915?

The following year appeared the first number of the association's pioneering *Journal of Negro History*. There was the Bethel Literary Association, organized by Bishop Daniel A. Payne of the African Methodist Episcopal Church well before the turn of the century. In the early 1900s, the Mu-So-Lit (musical, social, literary) at 1300 R Street, N.W., came into being. Almost exclusively Republican and exclusively male, the presentations of its distinguished speakers were far more often political than musical or literary in content. At about the same time, Sigma Pi Phi (the Boulé), then as now black America's most prestigious professional fraternity, organized its Washington chapter. Later would come the still active What Good Are We, begun by local well-to-do alumni of Howard University.

But despite these accomplishments and more, conditions worsened for District blacks. Many of the employment gains won during Reconstruction were to be lost during the first quarter of this century. The screws of segregation were painfully tightened during President Wilson's administration: separate working areas and eating facilities were decreed and the handful of decorative black appointments abolished. With rare exceptions (such as the Library of Congress, Justice Department, Internal Revenue Service) only the lowest positions were open to blacks—custodian, typist, messenger. Once again, though, perspective is needed. Of the 23,144 federal employees in Washington during the early 1890s, 2,400 were black. Lowly or not, government positions were relatively secure and provided retirement benefits. If the skilled trades and the navy yard had shut tight against black labor after the 1870s, service occupations such as barbering, catering, draying, and taxiing were largely in black hands. Tidy sums were earned in the catering business. "The Washington caterer is a curious character," the *Cleveland Leader*'s correspondent, Frank Carpenter, wrote.

> He is usually a colored gentleman, who supplies families and single boarders with meals at so much a month. Twenty dollars per person is the average price. For that he will bring you breakfast and dinner in a square tin box to your rooms, every morning and evening for thirty days.[30]

There were also the inspiring examples of Wormley's hotel and the Capitol Savings Bank, major and successful enterprises by any measure. James Wormley was also a charter member of the Board of Trade, to which Dr. Charles Purvis, director of Freedmen's Hospital, George Cook, superintendent of colored schools, and the future municipal judge, Robert Terrell, were elected in the mid-1890s.

Socially, the city's blacks were exceptional. There were families, like Cobb, Cook, Cardozo, Grimke, Syphax (descendants of Martha Washington), and Wormley, who refused to admit to being much ruffled by loss of political influence and the fastening on of segregation, and who paced their lives to equable and cultured cadences. There were the mestizo families like Bruce and Pinchback, whose unique achievements (senators on the family tree) and white demeanor commanded lingering and surprised obeisance from whites. One of the Pinchbacks, the numinous Jean Toomer, has left to Fisk University Library reminiscences of those times and families; both were special and in many ways better than much of what has followed, he says. But the supremacy of such families rested, in large part, upon one of the most scrupulously concealed taboos among modern blacks, that of color prejudice within the race. Allusion to Washington's historic pride of pigment usually produces ap-

---

30. Frank Carpenter, ed. *Carp's Washington* (New York: McGraw Hill, 1960), p. 6.

palled silence punctuated by outraged splutters. The subject may cause chagrin, but the refusal to recognize it is a much greater enormity. Washington shared with Charleston and New Orleans, and other cities of the South, a quasi-caste system based on color.

"I don't know how many castes of Negroes there were in the City at that time," Duke Ellington ruminates in *Music Is My Mistress,* "but I do know that if you decided to mix carelessly with another you would be told that one just did not do that sort of thing. It might be wonderful for somebody, but not for me and my cousins." Constance Green identifies three black strata: the blue-veined aristocrats, of antique lineage and affluence derived from banking, law, medicine, real estate, and genteel preaching, and numbering no more than a hundred families; the middle class, "derived mainly from the District's 18,000 mulattoes," becoming browner but prouder, and gaining its livelihood from government jobs and service occupations; and the rest, the lower classes, darker and poor, whose children seldom rose above a high school education. The lines were by no means as clearly drawn as Constance Green believed. Distinguished families like the Alexander Crummels and the Kelly Millers were not at all white in appearance. Nevertheless, churches, parties, marriages, college admissions, and Greek letter societies were influenced by color. The black-owned newspaper, the *Washington Bee,* kept close surveillance on what it called the "Four Hundred," publicly chastising them when they slipped maritally or socially. Washington was a city where many mulattoes strove to speak only to octoroons and the octoroons only to whites—when they could.

Generally, these conundra of color were haughtily ignored by local whites. By the turn of the century, not even Frederick Douglass could have dined in a downtown restaurant. In July 1919, a five-day race riot racked the city, ignited by rumors of black men attacking white women. Blacks fought back, importing weapons from Baltimore, and mulatto veterans in officers' uniforms circulated in white areas to gather intelligence. Blacks were proud of their solidarity and whites were sobered by it.

But racial repression went along unabated. James T. Wormley, son of the hotel owner, had long since been dropped from membership in the powerful Board of Trade, as had the names of the handful of elite black families from the *Social Register*. Throughout the 1920s, southern congressmen plotted to fasten upon the District antimiscegenation laws, streetcar segregation, banishment of blacks from all government employment, apartheid residential ordinances, and separate facilities at Rock Creek Park. It was little short of a miracle that they were less than completely successful, given the Supreme Court's postwar annulment of the Civil Rights Act of 1875 even within federal jurisdictions.

Perhaps no event was more representative of the nadir in race relations in Washington than the 1922 dedication ceremonies for the Lincoln Memorial. A roped-off section, separated by a dirt road, was assigned to blacks, and from that section the distinguished educator and successor to Booker T. Washington, Dr. Robert Russa Moten, trudged to the speakers platform to address the crowd.

The ordinary arrangement of the races was as though they lived on separate continents. Sixty years or more after the Civil War ended, had Daniel Bell, Samuel Edmonson, and Paul Jennings, the men of the *Pearl,* been able to spend a day in their city they would have found white dominion as absolute as in the 1840s. The slaves were gone, but, since 1830, they had always been a minority of Washington's black population. For the descendants of the free people of color, the lucrative activities of catering, hotelkeeping, and barbering had become more difficult when not impossible because of segregation laws. A much larger percentage now worked for the government, but, exception made for the odd judgeship (Robert Terrell) or assistant district attorney (William H. Lewis) appointment, more federal jobs merely meant more messengers and janitors. Southern congressional influence, generally approved by the white citizenry and seldom protested by northerners, sought to banish even the physical presence of blacks from the federal capital. "As a colored woman," Mary Church Terrell lamented,

I may walk from the Capitol to the White House ravenously hungry
and supplied with money to purchase a meal without finding a
single restaurant in which I would be permitted to take a morsel of
food if it were patronized by white people, unless I were willing to
sit behind a screen. And in some places I would not be allowed to
do even that.[31]

Towards Visibility

W. M. Kiplinger's *Washington Is Like That* decrees, "You
cannot know San Francisco without knowing its Chinatown,
you cannot know New Orleans without its French quarter, and
you cannot know Washington without knowing its black islands." Kiplinger was writing in 1942 when blacks comprised
about 30 percent of a total population of 663,091. In the year of
the nation's bicentenary, the percentages have been reversed. In
1976, Washington, with a population of about 724,000, was 76
percent black, and the racial islands were white. Many forces
have prevailed in the history of the District of Columbia. No
force, however, has been more dominant than race. Down the
decades white Washingtonians have agonized over the menace
of black Washingtonians. Typical of the more genteel Negrophobia were the reflections of Theodore Noyes, co-owner of the
Star, in his 1932 book, *Political Equity for the District of Columbia,* which pleaded for the right to vote in presidential elections and for full-fledged representation of the District in the
Senate and House. Local government was another matter, however. "About one-third of the inhabitants of Washington are
colored," Noyes lectured those who would pry open the Pandora's lid of self-government. "In addition to the permanent
colored element, an army of recruits would be attracted by elections to the city from the farms of Maryland and Virginia, to be
used as voting material by political 'bosses,' and to be supported as loafers. . . ."

A phalanx of retired army and navy officers, business mag-

31. Mary Church Terrell, *A Colored Woman in a White World* (Washington, D.C.:
Ransdell Inc., 1940), p. 384.

nates on the Board of Trade (Washington's de facto government), real estate brokers, congressmen invested with committee seniority because of the South's one-party system, the Army Corps of Engineers with decisive planning power through its presidentially appointed district commissioner—all comprised a brotherhood of distinguished bigots consorting to enforce upon the city the strictures of men such as Noyes. Segregation was a sacrosanct principle for them and local government an unspeakable heresy. For all its pretensions, the colored elite of a generation ago was more powerless than ever. Not even Mary Church Terrell could arrange for a position as page in the Library of Congress for Langston Hughes. No political or economic reasons existed to make Congress, the commissioners, or, in the final analysis, even the superintendent of education responsive to the wishes and needs of the black community. Since 1901, an appointed white superintendent had run the school system, theoretically assisted by the black assistant superintendent. In fact, the superintendents seldom consulted either their assistants or the biracial board of education. "The Board has nothing to say. That is done under the table," Howard University President and board member Mordecai Johnson once remarked when asked about decisions affecting budget and teacher placement.[32] In the humiliation of its civic impotency, it is hardly surprising that many of the Negro cave-dwelling families (the local term for old families) retreated into a world of fantasy and caste prejudice.

It was ironic that the grandson of the man whose administration had promoted the politics of Boss Shepherd and Frederick Douglass was the architect of a master plan of racial segregation, a final solution—Ulysses Grant III. Grant, as head of the National Capital Park Planning Commission, was empowered to design a Washington free of slums, striated with roads and highways, and generously provided with federal temples. In 1947 General Grant unveiled a proposal calling for the massive

32. Joan C. Baratz, "A Quest for Equal Educational Opportunity in a Major Urban School District: The Case of Washington, D.C." (Syracuse, N.Y.: Syracuse University Research Corp., 1974), p. 42.

removal of the city's black population away from central Washington—from Foggy Bottom, Southwest, and Georgetown—to the farthest regions of Anacostia. Neat, simple housing complexes surrounded by belts of green—Potomac Bantustans— were Grant's solution to the problems of black demography. Grant's master plan delighted the more reactionary members of the Board of Trade and the military misanthropes in mufti who were simultaneously proposing fixed menial occupations for the black population. Washington was on the verge of becoming a model for the nation of racial and residential repression.

Despite the appearance of unassailability, the coalition of reactionary white interests soon encountered stiff opposition. The war against European fascism had changed national attitudes. Voices were raised in protest against the scandal of segregation, slum housing, and unequal education in the capital. Grant's redevelopment plan was unsympathetically scrutinized in Congress and when his term as commissioner expired in 1950, the Redevelopment Land Agency radically amended the Anacostia Bantustans plan and concentrated instead on the massive renewal of Southwest Washington.

Meanwhile, responsive to the new mood of racial fair play, President Truman had appointed a Committee on Civil Rights whose October 1947 report deplored the shame of a segregated capital. A little more than a year afterward came the omnibus survey of Washington's race relations, *Segregation in Washington,* prepared by University of Chicago Professor Joseph Lohman under the auspices of a stellar, ninety-odd member National Committee on Segregation in the Nation's Capital, comprised of private citizens and underwritten by the Julius Rosenwald Foundation. *Segregation in Washington* made shocking reading, laying aside the curtain separating the two races to reveal the existence of two cities, the black one cripplingly disadvantaged in every respect.

None of this was news to the city's Negroes. Those who did not read ponderous studies knew what life was like because they lived in the conditions now reduced to statistics and academic prose. Those affluent blacks who read had already known much of the details through the Washington edition of the *Pittsburgh*

Courier or Howard University's *Journal of Negro Education.* In 1947, the latter revealed that the discrepancy in pupil expenditures between black and white was increasing—$161.21 for white pupils and $120.52 for black. White classrooms averaged 34.5 pupils; black, 38.8. One thousand eight hundred and fifty-one unused spaces existed in white schools; black schools, whose absolute capacity had been filled, were accommodating 2,234 surplus black students. Columbia University Professor George D. Strayer's 1949 report, authorized by a concerned House District Appropriations Committee, confirmed what blacks knew. Black public education in Washington, with the exception of unique Dunbar High School, was bad and getting rapidly worse. Forty-three percent of the student population was nonwhite.

In 1933 blacks had begun to take matters into their own hands. The new Negro Alliance organized that year had considerable success in persuading blacks to withhold patronage from white businesses located in their neighborhoods. The alliance moved from boycott triumph to triumph—small Jewish stores in the U Street area, the A & P food store chain, etc.—until the Sanitary Grocery Company (Safeway, Inc.) obtained an injunction from the district court. Peoples Drug Store also fought back, refusing to hire blacks or to integrate its soda fountains even after fifteen months of picketing. These were temporary setbacks for the alliance, more costly to the apparent victors than to the momentarily defeated. In 1938, the Supreme Court overturned the Sanitary Company injunction and the threat of black pickets encouraged many businesses to integrate rather than incur the sizeable losses suffered by Peoples Drug Store.

One of the major achievements of the New Negro Alliance, in union with the NAACP and the Brotherhood of Sleeping Car Porters, came in 1941. The New Deal had done practically nothing about black housing conditions and little enough about jobs beyond some relief for unskilled labor through the WPA. When, despite the wartime transfusion to the economy, civil rights leaders realized that hiring discrimination would be maintained in defense industries, they rallied to A. Philip Randolph's call for a protest march of fifty thousand on the capital. The threat was sufficient. President Roosevelt issued Executive Order 8802 requiring fair hiring policies wherever defense contracts were involved.

The landmark victory of Washington blacks came in 1953. The Supreme Court had mutilated and finally destroyed the Civil Rights Act of 1875, but the local civil rights laws (those of 1872 and 1873) had never been overturned. The Coordinating Committee for the Enforcement of the D.C. Anti-Discrimination Laws, formed in 1949, chose Thompson's Restaurant as a test case. Doughty Mary Church Terrell, chairperson of the co-ordinating committee, and her friends were refused service by the restaurant. They sued. In 1953, the Supreme Court declared the 1872 and 1873 laws still in force. The following year, in May, the historic Supreme Court decision of *Brown* vs. *Board of Education,* to which an earlier District case, *Bolling* vs. *Sharpe,* had been joined, was handed down. Segregation—if not yet integration—was over in Washington. A few months later, Mary Church Terrell died.

3

Vignettes—Characters
and Culture

*L*IKE the nation itself, Washington has been far more notable for its reverence of power than for its respect for culture. In this sense, it has been one of the most distinctly American of all major cities. Old families, black or white, have little of the social leverage of their counterparts elsewhere; they are generally left unobserved to meet, marry, and multiply in their own worlds. Performing artists are appreciated, but never as they have been in Boston or Philadelphia. Literary and theatre personalities attract readers and audiences, but never with the sustained, rapt attention possible in New York. Academics are imported to dispense wisdom for the enlightenment of congressional bodies and government agencies, but, five (now six) large universities notwithstanding, the voice of scholarship in Washington echoes far less resonantly than that of senior bureaucrats and junior congressmen. The reason for this has not been primarily a lack of culture but, rather, the lack of a compelling importance of culture in a city consecrated to the single industry of politics. "Washington is the town of the politically triumphant," Helen Nicolay wrote. "Better be dead than out of office, if you belong to a political set." [1]

1. Helen Nicolay, *Our Capital on the Potomac* (New York: Century Co., 1924), p. 253.

Another characteristic of Washington has been the homogeneity of the citizenry. Gallused, tobacco-spewing southern congressmen or picaresque, yarn-spinning, prairie politicians once bestowed a certain raunchy charm, but most Washingtonians, black or white, have always been resolutely middle-class and southern in behavior. In the government bureaucracy and the private professions, unorthodoxy and eccentricity, whether of manner or mind, have been the discouraged exceptions to a regnant blandness. To be sure, a stratum of its black population has always infused Washington life with the sound and color of transplanted Africa. Yet differences of race, class, or geographic origin considered, mainstream Washington nevertheless reflected rather more the stamp of its historic purpose than its southern or black background. In 1942, out of a population of 665,000, some 276,000 worked for the federal government. Several thousand more were municipal employees. These people were restricted from engaging in partisan politics by the Hatch Act—hardly necessary, since Washingtonians were denied the right even to elect the lowest city official. What all this did was to reward plodding steadfastness rather than innovation and ambition in work—advancement in grade came through seniority rather than competition. When Congress took the ballot out of his politics, the Washingtonian took on the mentality of the colonial—circumspect, docile, and resigned. Leadbelly chided him in song:

> He's a bourgeois man,
> Livin' in a bourgeois town,
> I got the Bourgeois blues,
> An' I'm sure gonna spread the news.[2]

So, until the 1970s, Washington presented the paradox of a town where politics mattered above everything else, but where the people have been impotent politically since the mid-1870s

2. THE BOURGEOIS BLUES
Words & Music by Huddie Ledbetter
Edited with new additional material by Alan Lomax
TRO—© copyright 1959 FOLKWAYS MUSIC PUBLISHERS, INC., New York, N.Y.
Used by permission.

DISTRICT OF COLUMBIA

A photographer's essay by Don Carl Steffen

Photographs in sequence

Lincoln Memorial at midnight.
Worker sandblasting at the Joseph H. Hirshhorn Museum.
Thomas Jefferson Memorial.
Watergate Outdoor Theater steps.
Window washers.
Fishing in the Tidal Basin under the cherry trees.
Cyclist with Woodrow Wilson and Arlington Memorial bridges in
    background.
Arlington Memorial Bridge. Lee's mansion and Arlington National
    Cemetary seen through the trees.
Playing chess on permanent table in Lafayette Park.
Farragut Park at lunchtime.
V Street, N.E., a black neighborhood.
Georgetown.
Mall area, including the Reflecting Pool, Washington Monument, and the
    Capitol.
Georgetown "eight" on Potomac River. Watergate hotels and offices,
    Washington National Monument, and John F. Kennedy Center in
    background.
Visitors at Lincoln Memorial.

and where culture was a concern of rather low priority. There were other reasons for the shabbiness of the city's cultural attainments. The major local fortunes, those of the Blair, Corcoran, Custis, Dodge, Riggs, and Peter families, were inadequate to mount the grand civic philanthropy disbursed by the plutocracy of New York, Boston, or Philadelphia. Banking was big in Washington, but never titanic; commerce throve, but fairly modestly; of industry, there was practically nothing. There were great fortunes represented in Congress, certainly. Du Ponts, Harrimans, Stanfords, and Guggenheims claimed their senatorial birthright, but they left their eleemosynary deeds at home. The greatest example of nineteenth-century philanthropic largesse to the city was not even American but the quirk of a bastard English nobleman's generosity—Mr. Smithson's $500,000 bequest which Congress bumblingly and ten years later released to build the Smithsonian Institution.

It was, of course, unthinkable that Congress itself might adorn the capital with museums, theatres, concert halls, dramatic groups, and an orchestra. The notion was still anathema during the 1960s when the appropriations debate over the Kennedy Center for the Performing Arts raged. In local matters involving outlays from the treasury, Congress has always been meretriciously faithful to the dogma of laissez-faire. President John Quincy Adams was not even given a serious hearing when he proposed the establishment of a national university in the District of Columbia. Culture was always a purely private affair.

Far out Northwest above Georgetown had been the manor house of Joel Barlow, "Kalorama," where, from 1807 to 1811, the author of *Hasty Pudding* and the *Columbiad* held sumptuous court. A Yale graduate, a man at home in radical circles in Europe, rich and gracious, Barlow imagined himself the poet laureate of the Republic, and the society he kept outside Washington City was probably the most sophisticated after Monticello. At the noble Octagon House on New York Avenue, George Washington's good friend, Col. John Tayloe, relieved the social drabness with dinners and dances that put Washingtonians on their best mettle. Near the President's Park was the palatial Van Ness mansion (built with the dowry of the daughter of the early landholder, David Burnes), unique for its hot and cold running water, where the cotillions were lively and the conversations more artful than usual. President Madison was reputed to be distinctly antisocial, but when Dolley hosted a ball, ably assisted by her retainer, "French John," the Octagon (occupied while the scorched White House was under repair) and the White House shimmered with a gay urbanity redolent of the courts of Europe. In the 1850s, the fortunate journeyed to Georgetown for an evening with the Baron and Baroness Bodisco, a hearth noted for its authentic Old World posh. The baron had married a girl young enough to be his daughter; after retiring as the czar's ambassador, he settled permanently in Washington and became one of its most distinguished social fixtures. Yet, however glittering the soirées in a half dozen grand houses, a prevalent note of despair was sounded by the refined residents. "My God," a French diplomat was heard to exclaim, "what have I done to be condemned to live in such a city?"

Bad as it was, the city was not entirely devoid of artistic release. The marine band gave concerts at the Capitol. There were the more rewarding performances at the Washington Theatre on Louisiana Avenue between Fourth and Sixth streets, N.W. In 1821, a new theatre opened on the site of the earlier establishment of the same name. The following year, Washingtonians saw Junius Booth there in *Hamlet, Richard III,* and *The Iron Chest.* The favorite playhouse of the citizens was Carusi's, a crowded, scruffy place where Charles and Fanny Kemble and Edwin Booth, Junius's second son, performed. Although the Washington Theatre was enlarged, in 1831, to seat one thousand, the house lights were extinguished forever only five years later when, as the renamed American Theatre, it folded under competition from the new National Theatre, founded in 1835. In the years thereafter, the National had a checkered career. Destroyed by fire and rebuilt on the same site in 1850 under the name New National Hall, converted into a circus shortly thereafter, then rebuilt as the New National Theatre in 1855, it continued to give performances until 1922 in the same building. In that year the present building was erected.

Except for the circus hiatus, the 1850s were golden years for the National. Jenny Lind arrived in 1851, under the management of P. T. Barnum, and official Washington dropped its business to pay call at Willard's Hotel on the famous Swedish opera singer. Groups of congressmen filled trays with calling cards. Daniel Webster obtained a private audience. President Fillmore strolled over from the White House for a chat. On opening night in New National Hall, Secretary of State Lewis Cass was present. "I detest music," Cass said afterward. "But I wanted to see her. I'd a lot rather have talked to her at Willard's." [3] Eight years later, the divine Adelina Patti sang at the National. It is not recorded that President Buchanan meandered over to Willard's, but there would surely have been a pride of congressmen at her debut as bemused by her singing as Secretary Cass and equally desirous of "talking to her at Willard's."

Although Congress could not be persuaded of the utility of a national university or of the funding of the arts, it demonstrated more sagacity in the matter of the sciences. Thomas Jefferson successfully prevailed upon the lawmakers to establish a coastal survey, whose work became a permanent part of the federal budget, attracting scientists to the District of Columbia. Funds were also appropriated for an astronomic observatory, under the direction of the Navy Department. Georgetown University had already erected one of the earliest observatories in this country, in 1843. Thus, Washington became the stargazing center for the nation. There was also the Library of Congress, established in 1800, destroyed by the British in the War of 1812, and reborn through the purchase of Thomas Jefferson's personal library, also later destroyed by fire. Cramped in its room in the Capitol, neglectfully funded and erratically used by Congress, its first head, George Watterson, heroically made the best of a deplorable arrangement. The great days of the Library of Congress were more than half a century in the future, under the assiduous stewardship of Ainsworth Rand Spofford.

By default, the real librarian of the Republic was the remark-

3. Garnett Laidlaw Eskew, *Willard's of Washington, the Epic of a Capital Caravansary* (New York: Coward McCann, 1954), p. 23.

able printer and, later, Federalist mayor of the city, Peter Force. Force came to Washington in 1815 where he founded, eight years later, the *National Journal,* a mouthpiece for the second Adams administration. "Mayor Force," William Tindall's *Standard History of the City of Washington* tells us, "was one of the first American collectors of manuscripts and documents, and was untiring in securing files of Washington papers, army orders, and other published records of American affairs, thus preserving unbroken successive historical information." Much of what we know today of Revolutionary America is the result of Peter Force's seven-volume *American Archives* and his papers, available in the Library of Congress.

Unsurprisingly, there were no strictly literary or society publications in the District. It was to *Harper's Magazine* that a prosy young notable took his memorable description of a Bodisco ball, not to a local journal. The District's newspapers were political, even ideological. The earliest, the *Alexandria Gazette,* appearing in 1792 and extant today, has been southern and highly conservative. The second, the impartial *Observer and Washington Advertiser,* a four-page weekly, had a short run after its 1795 founding. The third, the *Washington Gazette,* survived for two years, folding in 1798; its international format garnered too small a readership to sustain it. In 1800, Samuel Harrison Smith transplanted his paper to Washington, where it became, as the *National Intelligencer,* the major newspaper for nearly seven decades. In 1812, William Seaton acquired part ownership. Seaton succeeded Peter Force as mayor for a decade (1840–1850) and the *National Intelligencer* adopted a militant Whig philosophy which infuriated Congress to the point that it seriously debated legislation to abolish local government.

The real estate speculator, Duff Green, began his *United States Telegraph* in the late 1820s, a paper which was first abrasively anti-Adams, became quickly disenchanted with Jackson, and then successively partisan to Henry Clay and John C. Calhoun. For the abolitionist minority, there was Gamaliel Bailey's *National Era,* whose debut barely survived an avenging mob inflamed by the *Pearl* escape, certain that Bailey was in collusion with the fugitives. The roster of the *National Era* contributors makes it one of the most prized collections of American journalism. Whittier, Lowell, Sumner, Edward Everett Hale, and Salmon Chase, Henry Stanton, Alice Carey, Wendell Phillips, and Harriet Beecher Stowe were among its contributors.

Anne Royall's Journalism

There are several fine documents on early life in the District of Columbia—not the territory of frustrated architects, fustian politicians, and self-conscious levees, but of working people and ordinary events. For the very early period, there is Christian Hines's memoir, *Early Recollections of Washington City;* then there are Helen Nicolay's *Our Capital,* Samuel Busey's *Personal Reminiscences* and Perley Poore's *Reminiscences.* But it is in those unread volumes of Anne Royall, *Sketches of History, Life, & Manners in the United States* and *The Black Book,* that the sights, sounds, and personalities of the District leap out from the page.

John Greenleaf Whittier called her the "Old Hag," which was much kinder than the language reserved for her in congressional cloakrooms and in Capitol Hill boardinghouses. Samuel Clagett Busey, the District's leading physician, charged that she blackmailed congressmen and intimidated prominent citizens in order to support her newspapers. Ainsworth Spofford, the librarian of Congress, believed the untrue story of her childhood abduction and rearing by Indians mainly because it seemed to explain "a certain flavor of wildness to her conduct and writings." [4] She was, said Edna Colman's *Seventy-Five Years of White House Gossip,* "the mother of yellow journalism." A rare sympathetic assessment of Anne Royall was uttered by John Quincy Adams, who said she was "a virago errant in enchanted armor." [5] Anne Royall knew that she was unpopular,

4. Ainsworth Spofford, "Washington in Literature," *Records of the Columbia Historical Society* (43–64), 47.
5. Bessie Rowland James, *Anne Royall's U.S.A.* (Brunswick, N.J.: Rutgers University Press, 1972), p. viii.

that when she descended to Pennsylvania Avenue from her Capitol Hill rooms, the city emptied before her as though she were the bearer of pestilence, "for whenever it is known I am in the Avenue the news flies like a whirlwind." [6]

Anne Royall was as much ridiculed as hated. Her contemporaries have succeeded in dismissing her to posterity as a "common scold," a judgment, until recently, seldom questioned by the few historians who have bothered to notice her. The normally meticulous Spofford wrote of her career with a subdued levity that allowed for several inaccuracies perpetuated by chroniclers of early Washington. She was not "tall and angular with a hard-featured but not unkind face," but short and a bit dumpy.[7] Spofford confused Anne with her constant companion, Sally Dorret. Nor was she kidnapped by raiding Indians. Anne Newport was born in June 1769 in a Maryland hamlet near the Pennsylvania frontier, the daughter of a haughty, illegitimate male offspring of the Calverts. In 1797, she married Capt. William Royall, a well-to-do, scholarly Virginian who had served with distinction in the Revolutionary War. They lived well and owned slaves, and, although the captain drank too much and was occasionally violent, Anne was a loyal and not discontented wife. Captain Royall died in 1816 or 1817, leaving his estate to his wife. Royall relatives contested the will; Anne won the first round of litigation in 1817 and set off with three slaves to see the country while the case went up on appeal. While she was in Florence, Alabama, she received the news that the court had invalidated William Royall's will and awarded his estate to the captain's nephew. That was in 1823.

Anne Royall's fortune was finished, but her picturesque vocation was launched. A life of travel and journalism followed. She voyaged tirelessly during the next decade or so and wrote prolifically for the rest of her life. Much of what she wrote concerned the District of Columbia, and her first observations were about Alexandria, no longer a bustling port city but a racially piebald

6. *The Black Book or a Continuation of Travels in the United States,* 3 vols. (pub. and date obliterated), 3:148.

7. Spofford, "Washington in Literature," *Records,* pp. 47–48.

place in a stasis of charming desuetude. "The slaves of this place bear every mark of good treatment," she observed, but the "white people of this place lack a great deal of being dressed equal to the blacks of Huntsville [Alabama] or Lexington [Kentucky]." She noted also, with a disconcerting acerbity, the rampant miscegenation which prevailed everywhere in the South but which seemed especially advanced in Alexandria. "To see a man neither black nor white, with blue eyes and a woolly head, has something in it at which the mind recoils," she jotted in her notebook after her morning's constitutional. "It appears that these people, instead of abolishing slavery, are gradually not only becoming slaves themselves, but changing color." They were not only melding colors; Anne Royall believed that Alexandria's males were being debilitated by their decaying environment. "They are children compared to our men of the west," she noted, and though handsome, "they will not do, too effeminate." [8]

So much for the declining population of the District's second largest settlement. She moved on from M.E. Clagett's Hotel, where, trading on her husband's freemasonry membership, she had stayed rent-free, as would Mrs. Trollope a decade afterward (Clagett was generous to unaccompanied ladies). Her next stop was Richmond. There, Anne hoped to find evidence of her husband's military service, his war records having been destroyed by fire. Her ultimate destination was Washington, where she intended to petition the War Department for the captain's pension. She did not reach the capital until the following year, on July 24, 1824, arriving at dawn by steamboat from Fredericksburg. Docking in Potomac Creek, she took in the vista that few visitors failed to be moved by—the Capitol, "the eighth wonder of the world" and the President's Palace, rivalling "the snow in whiteness."

L'Enfant, with a few months to live, would have been pleased by her initial pleasure with the city, but he would not have answered for the citizens. Anne Royall quickly took their mea-

8. Anne Royall, *Sketches of History, Life, & Manners in the United States* (New Haven, Conn.: 1826), quotes from pp. 100–101, 106.

sure. She found them arrogant, impudent, and proud, and their diction perfect, "the most correct and pure of any part of the United States," an attribute that has persisted to the present despite the lamentable accretion of bureaucratese to the language. In her enumeration of the classes of citizens, Anne eliminated the transient congressmen. There were four types, she said, "whose pursuits, interests, and manners differ as widely as though they lived on opposite sides of the globe": the owners of boardinghouses and the "subordinate officers of government"; the laboring classes; the "better sort"; and the free Negroes. In modern terms, the business community and the bureaucrats, the blue-collar workers and menial employees, the professionals, and the blacks. But whether ignorant, impudent, or proud, Anne Royall also concluded, with a still compelling veracity that "if you are poor, you have no business in Washington." [9]

Some things have changed, at least superficially, since Anne Royall's arrival. The vice that she saw everywhere—the boozing and the harlotry—has become less overt and less crude. "It is certainly not to be expected that the metropolis of the United States should be exempt from evils common to every large city," she deplored, "but I will venture to say that no city . . . has kept pace with it in vice and dissolute manners."

"Near to the very door of the Representatives' Hall," was a liquor concession, an elaborate and large "circular apartment, lighted with sky lights." It may have been from there that splenetic John Randolph ordered his mug refilled while sitting booted and spurred, his dog at his feet, in the House. Hawking of alcohol within the Capitol and epidemic drunkenness were not the worst offenses, however. More than a decade before her arrival, Benjamin Latrobe had worried about what would become of the surplus of unattached women in Washington. Anne Royall could have told him. "But of all the sights that ever disgraced a city," she protested, "one which most astonishes a stranger, is the number of abandoned females, which swarm in every room and nook in the Capitol, even in daylight." [10]

9. Royall, *Sketches,* p. 157.
10. Royall, *Sketches,* p. 160.

Leaving Anne Royall's pages for a moment, rifling those of another journalist of a somewhat later period, and relying upon knowledge of recent history, it seems that Washington has both greatly changed and remained much the same. The surplus of females remains, although it has declined since its apogee in the 1940s and 1950s. Booze is still consumed in titanic quantities; more of it is purchased locally per capita than in any other city in the nation. Trollops are still seen in parts of the city, especially the Northwest area below Logan Circle. Graceless assignations in dark congressional corridors are a thing of the past, although the 1976 trystings of powerful senior congressmen show the constancy of legislative pecadilloes. The appearance of sobriety and probity has become de rigueur in Washington. These are fairly recent changes, however. When Frank Carpenter's daughter published his recollections as a Washington journalist stretching back to the 1870s, he dubbed the place "sinful city":

> There are more of the demimonde in Washington now than ever before. No law is put into force to stop them. They parade Pennsylvania Avenue in scores every bright afternoon, dressed in their sealskins and silks, either walking or driving in some of the best looking turnouts in the City. They even enter the galleries of Congress . . . the private galleries reserved for the members' families, where a member of Congress must have furnished a ticket for their admission.[11]

The arrogance of Washingtonians has also become much more muted since Anne Royall's time. If "impudence and pride" were once the "decided traits in the bulk of the citizens," perhaps it was because Washingtonians were surer of their city's imperial destiny then, unshaken by congressional miserliness, undaunted by regional covetousness, and still confident of controlling their own affairs. Whatever the explanation, impudence and arrogance went out of the citizenry long ago, to be replaced by an anodyne parochialism and passive pride. Only during the last thirty years—the last decade,

---

11. Quoted by James Kirkpatrick Flack, Jr., "The Formation of the Washington Intellectual Community" (Ph.D. diss., Wayne State University, 1968), p. 21.

really—have Washingtonians begun to experience again the confidence of being inhabitants of the "metropolis of the United States."

Anne Royall remained six months during her first visit, the Dorrett family on Capitol Hill having obligingly provided a free room. After breakfast her first day, she adjusted her poke bonnet and went off to find the secretary of state. She and John Quincy Adams got on well instantly, the secretary buying a subscription to her forthcoming *Sketches* and promising assistance in the pension matter. There was another distinguished acquaintance to be made. The Marquis de Lafayette was being honored at that moment; it was his first visit to the city of his old commander-in-chief. Anne sought him out and, according to her account, the marquis remembered her husband, graciously chatted at length, and then penned a letter to his fellow Masons confirming Captain Royall's military service. Armed with Secretary Adams's good will and General Lafayette's document, she settled in for an unsuccessful siege of the War Department. Then early in 1825, Anne left Washington temporarily for New York and Philadelphia.

When she returned to the city three years later, she came in triumph. In return for her literary support, the Masons had underwritten her three years of travel. She was now author of four books, *Sketches,* the popular and controversial *Black Book, Mrs. Royall's Pennsylvania,* and *Mrs. Royall's Southern Tour.* Masons praised *The Black Book* because it battered the Roman Catholics who were just then leading a nationwide attack on freemasonry. Businessmen and high-tariff politicians acclaimed it because it scolded Americans to do without foreign goods. When she had departed three years before, a Georgetown University Jesuit, pitying her despite her anticlericalism, gave her money to buy clothing. In 1828, she entered the Capitol on the shoulders of applauding senators, the first woman ever allowed on the Senate floor.

Washington soon got to know her well—too well, many thought. With her poke bonnet and her game leg (a permanent injury sustained in the cause of freemasonry at the hands of an irate innkeeper), Anne Royall was ubiquitous. Did she really stalk John Quincy Adams during his early morning swim in the Potomac and sit on his clothes until the president gave her an interview on the United States Bank controversy? "Come here!" Anne reportedly shouted to Adams. "I'm sitting on your clothes and you don't get them until I get an interview." [12] It might have happened that way; the technique was certainly pure Anne Royall and explains why some have credited her with pioneering the presidential press conference. The story, nonetheless, is probably apocryphal.

Men who did not hate her were strangely devoted to this frumpy haridan. One of the Maryland Carrolls, a good Roman Catholic, gave her lodgings. William Brent, the Supreme Court secretary, a Carroll relative and also Catholic, arranged for her to stay in the deserted Brick Capitol, the makeshift structure erected on the present site of the Library of Congress after the burning of Washington by the British. John Quincy Adams continued to work for her pension petition after leaving the White House, which may explain why it was stymied by Andrew Jackson's appointees. A warm friendship developed between Anne and John Randolph. But those who feared or detested Anne Royall were in the majority. "All the Congressmen call on me," she boasted to P. T. Barnum.

> They do not dare do otherwise. Enemies and friends all alike, they have to come to me. And why should they not? I made them every devil of them. You know how I look, ragged and poor, but thank God I am saucy and independent. The whole government is afraid of me, and well they may be. I know them all, from top to toe—I can fathom their rascality. . . .[13]

From her next abode, the Bank House on Capitol Hill (formerly headquarters of the Bank of Washington), she waged raucous combat with the neighborhood preachers. "Capitol Hill is a den of blackcoats," she cried. Every Sunday, members of a Presbyterian congregation worshipping in the fire station across

---

12. Quoted in Edna M. Colman, *Seventy Five Years of White House Gossip* (New York: Doubleday and Co., 1926), p. 141.

13. Quoted in Irving Wallace, *Nymphos and Other Maniacs* (New York: Simon & Schuster, 1971), p. 262.

the street prayed for her soul under her window after services. Anne countered with imprecations which became, Sunday after Sunday, increasingly salty. Finally, she went too far, calling Deacon John Coyle a "damned old bald-headed son-of-a-bitch." Stones were thrown at the Bank House and a suit brought against her in May 1829. An ancient law punishing "common scolds" with dunking in the Potomac served as the plaintiff's charge. Distinguished Justice Cranch presided. The case became another of Anne's many *causes célèbres*. The Jacksonians, with whom she had not yet broken, rushed to her defense. Secretary of War John H. Eaton, whose future wife, Peggy, Anne would befriend, testified that Mrs. Royall had always behaved like a lady. She was fined ten dollars and ordered to post a fifty-dollar bond to assure good behavior for one year.

What was it about her that stirred aversion and controversy? Her childlike contumacy was part of the reason. Mainly, though, it was probably that Washington was supremely a man's town, the place where the frilly cultural diversions in older cities of the East took a distant backseat to the *macho* business of politics. Nowhere has the presumption that the role of talented women should be confined to hostessing and to ministering to careers of ambitious spouses been more rooted than in Washington. Anne Royall was a threatening anomaly, an accomplished maverick in skirts whom men resented and ridiculed. But Anne Royall was not merely a political busybody— she founded two newspapers in the capital to espouse her opinions. She was not the first female American journalist, as some historians have recorded, but she was surely one of the best.

First, came the inappropriately named *Paul Pry,* a Saturday weekly launched in 1831. Congressmen risked sprained ankles cantering across Pennsylvania Avenue to avoid her. Merchants found themselves on the receiving end of high-pressure sales pitches. Her subscription *Blitzkrieg* completed, Anne published the first issue of the four-page *Paul Pry* on December third. "Our course will be a straightforward one as heretofore," the first editorial proclaimed, the same firmness which has ever maintained our pen will be continued. To this end, let it be understood that we are of no party. We will neither oppose nor advocate any man for the Presidency. The welfare and happiness of our country is our politics. To promote this we shall oppose and expose all and every species of political evil and religious frauds without fear, favor or affection.

Enlightened though she was on most matters, Anne defended slavery against the abolitionists. Abolitionists were to be "exterminated." Dirty old men should also beware. Bachelors and old maids ought to marry as soon as possible. The remainder of her editorial degenerated into silly wickedness and gave her numerous enemies ammunition.

Her politics, however, were never silly. She revered Andrew Jackson and was more radical than the administration in calling for the destruction of the national bank, an issue over which she soon broke with Jacksonians because of their lack of speed in destroying Nicholas Biddle's institution. Outmaneuvered on the Capitol's steps or trapped between the editor and an impassable pool of rancid water on Pennsylvania Avenue, congressmen were browbeaten into giving those interviews which should make Anne Royall a constant subject of instructive attention in journalism schools.

The *Paul Pry* was more than erratically censorious. It was a pioneer in ecology and municipal planning. It recorded the regular inundations from the Potomac River and inveighed against the municipality's indifference to "fetid water" and malarial marshes, which were the cause "of annual bilious fever." Whatever they thought about its editor, *Paul Pry* worried about the health of congressmen, who, "are too valuable to be killed off as rapidly as they are by the unsanitary conditions here at the capital city." [14] Her newspaper also advocated public schools, betterment of the condition of wage earners, an unfettered press, and justice to the Indian. She was an avenging angel in matters of nepotism and corruption. Her special offender was one

14. Sarah Harvey Porter, *The Life & Times of Anne Royall* (Cedar Rapids, Iowa: Torch Press, 1909), p. 154.

Burch, the clerk of the House of Representatives. Anne demanded his dismissal for trafficking in offices.

Paul Pry ceased publication in late 1836; in December its successor appeared. The weekly *Huntress* continued the investigative journalism and the personal interview pioneered by *Paul Pry*. Her last editorial contained the prayer that "the Union of these states may be eternal." A few weeks later (October 1854), Anne Royall died at age eighty-five. Washington lost not only an innovative journalist but one of its most pertinacious reformers. She was a rarer specimen than she should have been. Incorruptible, brash, and outrageously prying, her legacy was the priceless one of treating politicians like the errant potentates they have always been prone to emulate, but for a free, aggressive press.

The *"Five of Hearts"*

When Henry Adams arrived in Washington in 1868 he believed that he was discovering a city that time had ignored. "No Bostonian had ever gone there," he exaggerated.[15] "Everywhere, except in Washington, Americans were toiling for the same object," Henry believed. "Every one complained of surroundings, except where, as at Washington, there were no surroundings to complain of." To him the village seemed unchanged. "Had he not known that a great war and eight years of astonishing movement had passed over it," Henry wrote, "he would have noticed nothing that betrayed growth."[16]

The quality of life Henry Adams sought was utterly beyond post-Civil War Washington. Nevertheless, he enjoyed his sojourn; he was a bachelor and an Adams, and he suddenly found himself being received as a "young duke," after years of polite indifference in London. "Washington was a mere political camp," he decided, "as transient and temporary as a camp-meeting for religious revival."[17] His friend, William Evarts,

15. Henry Adams, *The Education of Henry Adams* (New York: Random House, 1931), p. 243.

16. Adams, *Education,* p. 245.

17. Adams, *Education,* p. 256.

the attorney general, presented him to President Andrew Johnson, "not the sort of man whom a young reformer of thirty, with two or three foreign educations, was likely to see with enthusiasm." [18] Later, though, after he had met President Grant, Henry reflected that at least Johnson "sat in his chair at his desk with a look of self-esteem that had its value." Grant was another matter. The president's classic remark to a travelled lady that "Venice would be a fine city if it were drained," (today, Italian engineers might agree) made the young journalist twitch to avoid a burst of hilarity. The Venice remark was about sufficient to condemn the president, but when Grant opined that the "best way to treat a bad law was to execute it," Adams visibly paled and resolved never to attend a White House function thereafter. He liked the informality of Washington, loved the manners of the women, but returned, after a season, to Boston to take the editorship of the *North American Review* and a lectureship at Harvard.

Ten years later, Henry and wife were back. "Home was Washington," he decided. Harvard was a bore. Grant was out and Adams's friend Evarts was the new secretary of state. John Hay, another friend, was the assistant secretary. The Grand Old Man of American historians, George Bancroft, had returned from his Berlin ambassadorship to settle in the city not long before.

Years ago Henry had abandoned any notion of active participation in politics. The taunt of the family's Irish gardener ("You'll be thinkin' you'll be President, too") had stayed with him. Perhaps he might become "stable-companion to statesmen, whether they liked it or not," Henry mused. [19] Although it was no longer true, as Henry had written in 1868, that "the value of real estate had not increased since 1800" (Boss Shepherd's "honest graft," as Adams called it, had sent values skyward), his and his wife's income of $25,000 was still more than adequate to establish a household of restrained luxury. "Lafayette Square was society. . . . Beyond the Square the

18. Adams, *Education,* pp. 245–246.
19. Adams, *Education,* p. 317.

country began,'' so of course the Adamses leased on H Street, first at 1501, and two years later, at 1607, a former Corcoran residence that gave them a direct view of the White House across the square.

"Stable-companionship to statesmen" was not meant to include the presidents across the park. There was a good word for Grover Cleveland, but Adams remained convinced that presidents were a bare cut above the average congressman of whom a friend had once said "You must take a stick and hit him on the snout!" Henry's and Marian's haughty world excluded chief executives. E. L. Godkin of the *Nation* was welcome at H Street; Carl Schurz, the learned German emigré and secretary of interior was a regular; Zachary Taylor's son, Richard, was an intimate, as were attorney general and Harvard man Charles Devens, mordant Mississippi Sen. Lucius Q. Lamar, and the bubbly Aristarchi Bey, the Turkish minister. Bancroft, of whom Frank Carpenter wrote, "It is more of an honor to have his company at dinner than that of the President," was an occasional guest, interrupting his writing and the perfecting of his creation, the American Beauty Rose, to come from his H Street home. But of all their callers, the Ohio millionaire and historian, John Hay, and Clarence King, director of the newly formed United States Geological Survey, were the most constant. So much so that, in 1884, the Hays and Adamses built adjoining mansions on H Street (at 1601 and 1603) and formed, with Clarence King, the capital's most exclusive informal group, the Five of Hearts. To be invited to dinner with the Five of Hearts was, for many, the ultimate imprimatur of culture. Henry James, who spent the 1882 season with the Adamses and who found Washington "too much a village—a nigger village," repaid their hospitality by lampooning the Adamses' snobbery in a short story, "Pandora," in which Bonnycastle (Adams) airily suggests to his wife, "Hang it, there's only a month left; let us be vulgar and have some fun—let us invite the President." [20]

20. Ernest Samuels, *Henry Adams, the Middle Years* (Cambridge, Mass.: Belknap Press, 1958), p. 168.

In 1868, Henry had dismissed Washington as a city "without a club." A decade later, this was no longer true. Strictly speaking, it had not been true in 1868, for, since the 1850s the "Scientific" or "Saturday Club" (also known as the "Washington Scientifics"), composed of astronomers, geodesists, mathematicians, and physicists, had held Saturday meetings. In March 1871, its members, meeting in the Regent's Room of the Smithsonian Institution, adopted a constitution, changed the name to Philosophical Society, and elected the distinguished scientist, Joseph Henry, president. Three years later came the first issue of the society's publication, the *Bulletin of the Philosophical Society of Washington*. Among the distinguished members gathering twice monthly at Ford's Theatre in evening attire to hear learned papers were Stephen Vincent Benét, Salmon Chase, Montgomery C. Meigs, and Gen. William Tecumseh Sherman. There was also a naturalists' club, the Potomac-Side Naturalists, organized in 1858, but it fizzled during the Civil War.

Another club, informal and fluid in membership, was launched shortly after Henry's first visit under the careful patronage of former Postmaster General Horatio King, a self-made man of considerable means. "There had been literary groups at the Capital before," James K. Flack, Jr., Washington's cultural historian records, "but . . . King's was the first to consider the quality of its members a sine qua non." [21] Participants came by invitation only and one distinguished widow was dumbfounded when she was told by King that his home was too small to allow her to be present.

While a select few discussed literature at King's (Lew Wallace and Millard Fillmore participated), a larger and more enduring group was being established, The Literary Society of Washington, later known simply as "The Literary," and guided by its three female founders, Esmeralda Boyle, Sara Carr Upton, and Olive Seward. In 1875, John George Nicolay, Lincoln's private secretary, drafted a constitution for The Literary, limiting membership to thirty (later increased to forty). Its roster of speakers was impressive: Thomas Nelson Page, Rich-

---

21. Flack, "The Formation of the Washington Intellectual Community," p. 48.

ard Hovey, Edward Gallaudet, and George F. Kennan, among others. James A. Garfield headed The Literary during his year in the White House, although to many members it seemed that Admiral John A. Dahlgren's widow, the formidable Madeleine, had the final say in the society's affairs. Despite Mrs. Dahlgren's aggrieved discouragement of politics, politics did ruffle the composure of the meetings, as when I. Edwards Clarke blamed poverty on exploitation and Edward Gallaudet blamed it on sloth. One of the most memorable of such discussions was that of George Kennan and Samuel Clemens on the need for revolution in Russia, leaving Mrs. Dahlgren horror-stricken.

Too stuffy for their tastes, the Danish minister and his beautiful, American-born wife, Lillie Hegermann-Lindencrone, joined with Carl Schurz and Horatio King, in 1879, to form a competitor to The Literary, the National Rational Dining Club. It sparkled while it lasted, but lasted briefly. There was another significant social entity hovering in the background during the sixties and seventies. With the advent of the Civil War and the departure of the southern elite, a cultural void (insofar as the southerners had culture rather than manners) was created which the Republican newcomers and a few of the old settlers attempted to fill by organizing a men's club of intellectually uncertain but exclusive social character. Meeting at Wormley's Hotel, in October 1863, the club's twenty-six members elected John B. Stephenson, the librarian of Congress, president, and George Riggs, the banker, treasurer. Before its meetings were suspended in late 1867, its roster of prestigious names included General Grant, financier Jay Cooke, and Supreme Court Chief Justice Salmon Chase. A majority of the membership was military, however, giving the club the aura of today's Army and Navy Club. Five years later, a nucleus of members met at Riggs's home to reconstitute the club, bestowing upon it the name "Metropolitan." William W. Corcoran became the new president and George Bancroft its most distinguished member. Today, the Metropolitan Club continues to be the proudest preserve of cave-dwelling Washington, an institution too "steeped in sociability," as Flack writes, to wish to tax itself with a weighty intellectual program, the Potomac counterpart of the English gentleman's club.

Friends and acquaintances of Henry Adams belonged to The Literary, the Philosophical Society, and the Metropolitan Club. Not Henry. His club was his home, and conversation on H Street was both more profound and more scintillating than at the Smithsonian or Ford's. He condescended to one exception; when the Cosmos Club was organized in 1878–1879, for "the advancement of its members in science, literature, and art," Adams was among the charter members. A few steps down H Street from his home, the Cosmos barely measured up to Henry's standards; friends Clarence King and John Nicolay belonged, and recruitment of membership was national as well as local. The scientific bent of the Cosmos also appealed. Although not incorporated as a scientific body, the Cosmos was very early monopolized by scientists. If the literati showed a distinct preference for the more congenial milieux of Boston and New York, America's scientific community increasingly discovered Washington as an oasis of great potential—a discovery which continues into the present. Had there been a first-rate university in the city, instead of four struggling, sectarian institutions (Columbian, Catholic, Georgetown, and Howard), Washington might have become the nation's greatest science center. But Harvard's President Charles William Eliot lobbied effectively against John Quincy Adams's national university proposal when it was resurrected during the 1870s.[22] Even so, the Smithsonian's Bureau of Ethnology, the Patent Office, Naval Observatory, Army Medical Museum, and the new Department of Agriculture were magnets to scientists.

Then came, in 1879, in part due to the lobbying of Clarence King, the uniting of the coastal surveys into one department, the United States Geological Survey, briefly headed by King himself. John Wesley Powell's geological exploration of the Rocky Mountains and Clarence King's of the fortieth parallel, contained in his brilliantly written *Systematic Geology* (1878), fired

---

22. Constance Green, *Washington: Village and Capital, 1800–1878* (Princeton, N.J.: Princeton University Press, 1962), p. 378.

imaginations. Dozens of scientists arrived to accept commissions in the new geological survey. No scientist himself, Henry Adams was deeply influenced by King as he labored toward a "scientific" theory of history. In the company of the Cosmos Club geodesists and physicists and at home on H Street, Henry sifted and imbibed the principles of energy conservation and entropy which were to lace *The Education,* his finest book. By the time his and Hay's joint mansions rose on Lafayette Square, it was no longer fair to speak of the capital as a cultural backwater. Its southern tempo and softmindedness persisted, certainly, but Washington, by the mid-1880s—thanks to Shepherd's unmonitored planning, to the new class of moneyed northerners and Ohioans capturing the White House, and to the army of engineers and scientists—was becoming a fairly modern metropolis and a considerable center of culture. The addition, during the decade of the 1880s, of anthropological and biological societies and the National Geographic Society confirmed this trend.

Meanwhile, Henry Adams pursued his labors. Secretary of State Evarts, as well as his successors, granted free rein among the documents in Mullett's grandiose and costly new State, War, and Navy Department Building next to the White House. From H Street, there was a steady flow of major works: *Life of Albert Gallatin* (1879); the then-scandalous and anonymously published novel of Washington society, *Democracy* (1880); *John Randolph* (1882); *History of the United States from 1801 to 1817* (1889–1891); the splendid *Mont Saint-Michel and Chartres* (1904); and his ultimate statement, *The Education of Henry Adams* (1906). Adams's neighbor was also prolific, finishing the monumental *Abraham Lincoln: A History* in collaboration with Nicolay (1890), and, with Adams's encouragement, anonymously authoring the popular, antilabor novel, *The Breadwinners* (1894). "So that between them," Henry wrote near the end of his life, "they had written nearly all the American history there was to write." Marian Adams's death by suicide in 1884 left Henry badly bruised; it has also left the city the exquisite and enigmatic Saint-Gaudens statue to Marian in Rock

Creek Church Cemetery. Clarence King's extended absences exploring the California vastness made Henry's social life somewhat less rich. There was personal tragedy and much loneliness, but by any measure the Five of Hearts had lived lives of exemplary intellectual radiance. *The Education* reflected upon their achievements:

> Hay and Adams had the advantage of looking out of their windows on the antiquities of La Fayette Square, with the sense of having all that any one had; all that the world had to offer; all that they wanted in life, including their names on scores of title-pages and in one or two biographical dictionaries; but this had nothing to do with consideration, and they knew no more than . . . Saint-Gaudens whether to call it success.

Yet, despite those notable accomplishments, as the paragraph's *dénouement* shows, Adams was not sure what was the value of his learning, books, and renown. "Thus, neither Hay, King, nor Adams knew whether they had attained success," Henry complained, "or how to estimate it, or what to call it." [23] Perhaps, after all, Hay had a better idea. In 1897, President William McKinley summoned him to the embassy in London, and the following year, Hay became secretary of state, a post he discharged brilliantly under McKinley and Roosevelt. Henry was left alone on the square. "Only the Lodges and the Roosevelts remained, but even they were at once absorbed in the interests of power." [24] Henry resisted this unexpected intrusion of the real world. But when neighbor Theodore moved across the square into the White House in 1901 (McKinley had been assassinated and daughter Alice had danced for joy), Henry was constrained to enter the White House for the first time since Grant's tenure. He bore the ordeal bravely, but it was a disaster. The new president "lectures me on history as though he were a high school pedagogue," he grumbled. Roosevelt might be a Harvard man and a patrician, but Henry contemptu-

23. Adams, *Education,* pp. 326–327, 328.
24. Adams, *Education,* pp. 355–356.

ously described the president's behavior and policies as like watching "a monkey up a tree with a chronometer." [25] He was almost ready to decamp for Fiji again.

King died in 1901, Hay four years later. Adams survived, querulously, until 1918. Washington forgot that he was there, and few today remember that he is buried near Saint-Gaudens's statue. His presence in the capital had considerably boosted the formal and casual efforts of its finite intelligentsia to organize and disseminate a bit of art, literature, and science. Sadly, nevertheless, Henry Adams never really understood Washington and never knew just how limited his comprehension was. His Cosmos fellow, Lester Frank Ward, author of the influential *Dynamic Sociology,* could have enlightened him, as could the men he most despised, Senators James G. Blaine and Roscoe Conkling, or the Marshal of the District of Columbia, Frederick Douglass, a specimen of what Adams called an "archaic race."

Henry had arrived on the scene at the very moment when almost none of his perceptions of Washington was any longer valid. Easterners might persist in dismissing the place as a village and a cultural desert well into the twentieth century, but Washington in 1878 was well on the way to becoming a metropolis, slower, more African, and rawer than her eastern sisters, but a hub of power, nonetheless, where the long-range possibility of culture taking root was less and less unthinkable. Henry recoiled before the aggressive corruption of Grant's administration and he witnessed sadly what he called the "degradation of the democratic dogma" by successive presidents and Congresses; he was made to sense acutely that his "stable-companionship" was not widely desired by the country's elected leaders, that he was an oddity. He saw that his class, the Brahmins, was being shunted aside by new men from new places, with newer and greater wealth, just as the plantocracy of the South had fallen before the financial superiority of his own kind. But Henry tended to take the phenomenon personally and to see it in purely negative terms.

25. Ernest Samuels, *Henry Adams, the Major Phase* (Cambridge, Mass.: Belknap, 1964), p. 253.

His best-selling novel, *Democracy,* for all its trenchancy, bespoke Henry's bewilderment by the Washington scene. The heroine, the beautiful, brilliant and morally exacting Madeleine Lee, recently arrived in Washington, falls in love with Republican Sen. Silas P. Ratcliffe of Illinois, "the Prairie Giant from Peonia." Ratcliffe, who is a composite of James Blaine and Roscoe Conkling, spiritedly explains that an unsavory quid pro quo was necessary to keep the government "out of rebel hands." No matter the urgency and ultimate high purpose of Ratcliffe's motives, Madeleine sends him away, sighing, "I want to go to Egypt, democracy has shaken my nerves to pieces. Oh, what a rest it would be to live in the Great Pyramid and look out forever at the polar star."

But political brokering had always been the vital fluid of the city and the country. The first Adams president had swamped the federal judiciary with midnight judgeships on his last day in power. Now, the game was rougher and grander; the stakes were railroads, mineral resources, and banking trusts, and upstarts named Cooke, Fiske, and Gould were the winners. What Nietzsche described as the "miasma of Social Darwinism" was enveloping America, and Washington was naturally one of the places where pollution was greatest. Adams's refinement and learning blinded him to the predestined and oblique beneficence of the race to riches. Society may have stopped beyond Lafayette Square, but the American world began at its frontier. It watched covetously the goings-on along H Street, and when it eventually swept over the square it absorbed a bit of the culture of the Five of Hearts.

Mary Hundley's Dunbar

Mrs. Mary Hundley, professor of Latin and French in Washington's Dunbar High School, was one of those regal and vanishing anomalies of the color line for which places like Charleston, New Orleans, and Washington were famous: auburn hair (just beginning to streak) gathered into a bun; aquiline features and clear pigment betraying no trace of African antecedents; a bygone purity of diction whether in English or French. To meet

Mrs. Hundley was to learn with an absolute certainty that, despite a white-dominated board of education and rigid segregation, Dunbar must have been, all in all, an exceptional institution. Professor Hundley was one of those awesomely excellent preceptors whose petrified charges learned what was good for them and, years later, were grateful they had been good and learned. Mary Hundley still lives, but the type, if it survives at all, is an anomaly in today's District public schools.

But Dunbar itself was an anomaly. Its excellence derived from enforced inequity, from inviolable District policy that two public school systems should exist serving whites and blacks, with the former receiving a greater proportion of the funds appropriated for education. There were dedicated and qualified teachers serving the black schools but many were probably only half as good as those of the whites. Statistics in the 1949 Strayer Report showed this to be true. Consistently, blacks scored lower than whites on tests in the crucial areas of reading and math. In many places in the South there was a Dunbar equivalent (often private and affiliated with a black college or university), a unique institution where talented or advantaged students received quality instruction. Where such schools were public, white indifference or guilt allowed them to thrive quietly. Where private, the black bourgeoisie heroically assumed the burden.

White indifference and guilt and black elitism operated in collusion in the case of Dunbar High School. Bruces, Cobbses, Syphaxes, Wormleys, and Weavers were determined to perpetuate the standards of the old Preparatory High School for Colored Youth, established in the basement of the Fifteenth Street Presbyterian Church in November 1870. They were just as much resolved to make the school their special, exclusive domain, a crucible for the formation of unpoor, well-bred, and generally light-skinned clients. Between 1885 and 1950, its enrollment rose from 361 to 1,700, but Dunbar's philosophy and standards remained intact. It was the high school of the black cave dwellers. Still, it suffered the disadvantages of duality. In 1946, forty-five overworked instructors taught 1,529 students, and classes ranged from thirty-five to forty-five, with a few running as high as ninety. The official teacher-pupil ratio for the District was 1:28. Science equipment was usually insufficient and antique. Nevertheless, Dunbar somehow managed to excel.

"The college preparation a student could get at the Paul Dunbar High School," Constance Green records, "was unquestionably better than that obtainable in other cities with segregated systems." It was even better than that. According to Prof. Thomas Sowell, "as far back as 1892, Dunbar students came in first in citywide tests given in *both* black and white schools. Over the 85 year span, most of Dunbar's graduates went on to college, even though most Americans—white or black—did not." [26] Dunbar's excellence was so well-known that middle-class families moved to the District not only from nearby Maryland and Virginia but from the Deep South in order to place their children there. Regardless of neighborhood residency, Dunbar's students were admitted on the exclusive basis of entrance examinations. Conversely, there was no requirement that the school admit average students living nearby. Like Howard University, a private institution underwritten by public funds, Dunbar, recipient of funds from the city's treasury (however inadequate), was left alone to operate as a fiefdom of advantaged blacks. If there were protests within the black community against this arrangement, none have survived in the written record, nor would they have registered loudly with black assistant superintendents of education, most of whom had been either students or teachers at Dunbar.

When Mary Hundley published her history, *The Dunbar Story,* little more than a decade ago, the first black cabinet minister wrote the introduction. "The efficacy of this high school is certainly expressed in the successes of its graduates," Dunbar alumnus Robert Weaver stated, and the secretary of housing and urban development (HUD) assuredly knew whereof he spoke. "I went to Harvard College," Weaver continued, "where many of my classmates had been trained in some of the best preparatory schools in the nation. I found myself on the whole about as

26. "Black Excellence: A History of Dunbar High," *The Washington Post,* April 28, 1974.

well able to survive in college as they were." [27] Edward Brooke, the first black senator since Reconstruction and a Dunbar graduate, might have composed an identical encomium, as could William Hastie, the first black federal judge; Benjamin O. Davis, Sr., the first black general; or Charles Drew, the discoverer of blood plasma. The Dunbar degree was not always a guarantee of brilliant success but it was very seldom a passport to failure.

Dunbar's curriculum was rigorously collegiate. Initially, it consisted of English and the classics. Shortly, were added mathematics, astronomy, English grammar, composition, literature, U.S. history, and elocution. Then came foreign languages, mental and moral philosophy, and general history, drawing, penmanship, and bookkeeping. Technical instruction was added toward the turn of the century. To teach the growing diversity of offerings, Dunbar recruited an arresting galaxy of instructors. Miss Mary Jane Patterson was the first black female college graduate in America, holding an Oberlin College bachelor's (1862). Richard T. Green was the first black Harvard graduate (1870). The brilliant teacher and civic leader, Francis L. Cardozo, had obtained a degree at the University of Glasgow and pursued studies at the London School of Theology. The second black Harvard graduate, Robert H. Terrell, was a faculty member. Dunbar's list of stellar teachers runs on indefinitely into the twentieth century—Edward C. Williams, a Western Reserve University Phi Beta Kappa; Garnett C. Wilkinson, another Oberlinian; Howard's Walter Smith; and Harold Haynes of the University of Chicago, all principals and teachers of exceptional abilities.

White antagonism surfaced briefly during the beginning years of the 1900s. Booker T. Washington, solitary broker of black institutional fortunes, had proclaimed the inappropriateness of liberal arts studies for his people in 1895. Agriculture, simple technical instruction, and business education suited the Negroes'

27. Introduction to Mary Gibson Hundley, *The Dunbar Story, 1870–1955* (New York: Vantage Press, 1965).

livelihood and citizenship needs far better, said Dr. Washington. Quoting the Tuskegee educator chapter and verse, southern white leadership assaulted institutions consecrated to the training of black gentlemen and scholars. Liberal arts-oriented Atlanta and Fisk universities paid dearly in white philanthropy diverted to schools turning out farmers and skilled laborers, like Hampton and Tuskegee institutes. Anna Cooper, Dunbar's sixth principal (1901–1906), was told her school must be converted from a liberal arts to a trades school. Miss Cooper stubbornly refused and Washington's black bourgeoisie, arising momentarily from its inbred insouciance, rallied firmly to her support. Remarkably, the city capitulated. Dunbar was left alone to teach Latin, literature, and philosophy while the board of education grudgingly authorized construction of Armstrong Technical High School, in 1902, and later, in 1928, the creation of Cardozo Business High School.

Further evidence of Dunbar's elitist persuasion had been the extension, but a few years before the Anna Cooper crisis, of preparation from three to four years by the addition of electives. By the early twenties, Dunbar graduates were being admitted to Ivy League schools, especially Dartmouth, in increasing numbers. Dunbar was among the black high schools, numbering fewer than half a dozen in the nation, whose students were accepted into major northern universities without special examination. Alumni such as Sterling Brown, dean of black poets; Mercer Cook, French scholar and ambassador; and Rayford Logan, civil rights activist and Howard University historian, established brilliant collegiate records before going on to professional renown.

By the early 1950s Dunbar's uniqueness was beginning to falter. Its enrollment had grown beyond the saturation point as 47 percent of the District's school population became black and the pressures upon Dunbar mounted to admit a different class of student—marginally bright youngsters from deprived homes. The old building literally burst at the seams, its overworked teachers no longer able to keep up the standards or the individual attention of years past. Nor were the teachers as well-prepared. The occupational strides made by white-collar blacks, nationally, during and after the war, and the small but unprecedented number of worthwhile federal positions available in Washington siphoned off Dunbar's brilliant trickle of teaching talent. Black Amherst, Dartmouth, and Harvard Phi Beta Kappas now had more lucrative avenues open to them than high school teaching. After 1945, Dunbar's teaching staff began to resemble that of other black city secondary schools—recruits from the local teachers' college (although a nucleus of Mary Hundleys continued to conduct their business in the old ways of excellence). During the previous decade, Dunbar's Alumni Association had been exceptionally generous in its donations. After 1950, however, "only a gift from each class reunion of ten- or twenty-year alumni was left to remind the alumni of their brilliant renaissance in the 1940s," Mary Hundley writes.[28] Dunbar's PTA followed the same inexorable downward curve from exigent attentiveness to the curriculum and upward mobility of graduates to perfunctory meetings devoted to the specifics of materiel and parochial squabbling.

Brown vs. *the Board of Education* was the death blow. After 1954, Dunbar rapidly became simply another city high school. By the end of the decade, black families scrambled and saved to push their children into Washington's private academies, into Beauvoir, Saint Albans, Sidwell Friends, and the Madeira School. After a rather mild flurry of alumni protest in 1975, the city fathers have decided to authorize the razing of old Dunbar and the construction of a modern plant whose only tie with the vanished institution will be its name. When Americans converge on the capital during the bicentenary, an almost completed new Dunbar High School will be rising on First and N streets, N.W. It will be as remote from the history of old Dunbar's splendor as the Hay-Adams Hotel from the radiance of Lafayette Square during the intellectual reign of the Five of Hearts. Still, it must be conceded that Dunbar education, like Lafayette Square society, was the luxury of an era—meritorious, attractive, self-confident but necessarily transitory.

28. Introduction, *Dunbar Story*.

Arts and Leisure Today

Cultural diversity and enrichment, like home rule, have been a long time coming to Washington. If presidents and congressmen have seldom been so philistine as to utter publicly the apocryphal words of Reich Marshal Hermann Goering— "Whenever I hear the word culture, I reach for my gun"—until quite recently few ever made much effort to breathe life into local arts. Maestro Reginald DeKoven's plans for the Lafayette Square Opera House (better known as Belasco's) were a case in point. Shortly after the turn of the century, he organized a symphony orchestra, invited Jan Paderewski to play, and gave six successful concerts there. But the orchestra's second season of Friday concerts was spoiled when the White House announced, at the last minute, that Mrs. Theodore Roosevelt's teas would be held on that day. DeKoven's well-heeled patrons vanished. In Washington, the mighty did not reach for weapons on the eve of a cultural event; they consulted their political calendars.

For many years, the largesse of the Corcoran family remained a solitary example of what Washington sorely lacked— millionaires of the stripe of Henry Clay Frick or Andrew Carnegie whose philanthropy could upgrade Washington from a cultural backwater among the world's great capitals. When the foundation established by Elizabeth Sprague Coolidge donated a 511-seat auditorium to the Library of Congress, in 1925, music-starved citizens flocked to its free chamber music concerts. Their popularity was so great that a pavilion was donated, in 1935, through the generosity of the Gertrude Clark Whittall Foundation. There was also the Standard Oil tycoon, Henry Clay Folger, who incomparably enriched the city by his 1932 gift of the Folger Shakespeare Library and its Elizabethan theatre. Today, the Folger Theatre mounts some of the most exciting and unconventional dramatic productions on the East Coast, but for many years archaic fire regulations kept the small playhouse dark. Welcome and significant as these gifts were, there was need for much more.

In 1930, cavernous Constitution Hall replaced Belasco's as

the principal forum for the performing arts, 3,766 seats being added to the city's concert capacity. Ironically, Constitution Hall's most famous concert may have been the one its owners, the Daughters of the American Revolution, rejected. Denied its facilities because of race, the magnificent contralto, Marian Anderson, sang at the Lincoln Memorial before an Easter Sunday crowd of seventy-five thousand in 1939. When Constitution Hall performances were superior, it was almost always the case that the artists were visitors. The local National Symphony Orchestra, founded in 1931, performed at the hall regularly, achieving, under its second conductor, Dr. Howard Mitchell, a workmanlike competency that seldom ventured beyond the security of Fiedleresque classics. Another boost for the performing arts came with the concert series inaugurated in the East Garden Court of the National Gallery of Art in 1942. The opening of George Washington University's Lisner Auditorium, four years later, greatly expanded artistic facilities, although it did little to improve the fare. Then there was the durable National Theatre, one of the nation's largest, whose new 1,300-seat building was finished in 1922. The National filled the need for a municipal theatre, mounting touring Broadway plays and musicals for white audiences only and preferring to remain dark from 1948 to 1950 rather than to integrate. By the early fifties, there were seats aplenty in Washington, but there was almost nothing to see that was local and good in ballet, music, or drama, despite the sporadic labors of university groups.

The arts were affected, as was everything else in the city, by race relations. At Seventh and T streets, N.W., off Florida Avenue, music was alive and thriving at the beloved, bedraggled Howard Theatre. Audiences were black and the music was black—the blues and jazz. From its first curtain, in 1910, until the house lights were extinguished sixty years later (they glowed again very briefly in 1975), the Howard was in a class just below Harlem's Apollo Theatre as cradle and platform for black entertainment. From Handy to Henderson, from Miller and Lyle to Mabel Mercer, from Bojangles to Bessie and Basie, the music flowed and greats like Ella Fitzgerald and Pearl Bailey were discovered there until integration, affluence, and the declining neighborhood shut the theatre. During the late sixties jazz suffered a sharp setback when white audiences were intimidated by black hostility and many blacks were frightened away by crime. The 1968 riots were nearly fatal. But Duke Ellington's hometown is unthinkable without jazz. Today, it is more popular than ever, appealing equally to blacks and whites. There are the mainly black nightspots like Ed Murphy's, La Zambra, Pigfoot, and pulsating Manny's Lounge across the Anacostia River; salt and pepper clubs like Mr. Henry's Upstairs, Harold's Rogue and Jar, and Top O'Foolery; and fairly white watering holes like Georgetown's well-known Blues Alley and Arlington's Potomac River Jazz Club.

At long last, in the era of Camelot, the performing arts really began to flourish in the city. When the incredible happened in 1968—a local production moving to Broadway—it marked the beginning of the end of the capital's cultural torpor. Nor was *The Great White Hope* to be merely a splendid achievement *sans* sequel of Zelda Fichandler's repertory company, for Arena Stage went on to excel itself by mounting and exporting *Indians, Raisin,* and *Moonchildren.* In April 1976, Arena Stage received the first Tony awarded to a theatre outside New York City. The smaller and newer Kreeger Theatre behind Arena Stage presents more specialized dramatic productions.

If the success of the now-defunct Washington Theatre Club (initially directed by the voluble Davey Marlin-Jones and sustained by Hazel Wentworth) was confined to the metropolitan area, its repertory pluck and polish were nonetheless outstanding. The South African play, *Blood Knot,* one of its early productions, and the black drama, *Ceremonies in Dark Old Men,* one of the last, were memorable efforts that attracted capacity crowds of blacks and whites.

Among the oldest and most rewarding of the community theatres is the Black Alley, a small, underfunded operation whose brilliant young black director, Douglas Johnson, has transformed it into an uneven but extraordinary experience. For all the annoyance of ad hoc scheduling and frequent miscasting, when the Back Alley succeeds (as with its *Native Son*), it does so superlatively. Although all of the District's universities have long had amateur drama groups, the 1970 opening of Catholic University's new Hartke Theatre confirmed a standard of experimental drama possibly unexcelled in the area. Ford's Theatre, one of the last major houses to open (closed since Lincoln's assassination) has offered varied fare since 1968, much of it historic, under Frankie Hewitt's direction. With its two uproarious successes, *Me and Bessie* and *Your Arms Too Short To Box With God,* Ford's, like the National, has also discovered Washington's well-heeled and enthusiastic black theatre-goers.

The floodtide of Washington's cultural renaissance swept in with the opening of the John F. Kennedy Center for the Performing Arts in 1971. To celebrate the occasion, a *cordon bleu* audience laced with New Frontier royalty assembled on the evening of October 8, 1971, for the premier, commissioned performance of Leonard Bernstein's ambitious *Mass*—a work whose antiwar sentiments made the Nixon White House churlishly uncomfortable. This $72 million Carrara marble matchbox on the Potomac, with its acoustically perfect concert hall, opera house, and theatre, and its classic film cinema, endowed the city with a temple to the muses portending the displacement of New York as the nation's performing arts capital. Ballet, which had been virtually an underground activity in Washington, surfaced in a *tour en l'air* that becomes ever more dazzling, even though the hardworking National Ballet Company was compelled to dissolve after a 1974 season of great critical acclaim but disappointing receipts. The local black company, the Capitol Ballet, has yet to appear at the Kennedy Center. It is a going concern, though, and if its supporting dancers are sometimes amateurish, the Capitol Ballet's prima ballerina, Sandra Fortune, and its visiting male lead, Sylvester Campbell, are superior by any measure. But while Washington awaits the sustained success of local dancers, there has been an avalanche of visiting talent. Alvin Ailey's dance company, the Joffrey Ballet, Fontaine and Nureyev, Eric Lund, and the Bolshoi pirouette before capacity crowds at the Kennedy Center.

Like sap rising after the spring thaw, all the performing arts are flowing vigorously now. Marcel Marceau makes himself known of a season at the Kennedy, and Pearl Bailey needs almost a season to say farewell. The best of Eugene O'Neill and Tennessee Williams and the jolliest of British dramatic productions offer Washingtonians some of the richest and most diverting theatre anywhere. Local opera, mainly that of the Washington Opera Society, is improving, but, as in the case of ballet, it is the visiting talent—the Bolshoi, the Metropolitan, the Berlin, and soon La Scala itself—which causes the swamping of the Kennedy Center box office. While local ballet and opera temporarily bask in the reflected aureole of foreign performances, the National Symphony, now domiciled at the center, seems well along to becoming an unsurpassed organization after its exacting tutelage under Antal Dorati and James DePriest. Under the baton of its future conductor, Mstislav Rostropovitch, the promise of the National Symphony Orchestra is spectacular. The Center's American Film Institute (AFI), although small and makeshift, has become one of the country's premier film centers. Prefaced by learned (and sometimes much-too-long) lectures, the best and the rarest of D. W. Griffith, Erich von Stroheim, Howard Hawkes and William Wyler, and a cornucopia of works of other screen immortals are available to the cinematic cognoscenti.

Although the Kennedy Center has helped Washington discover itself culturally, it has come in for sharp criticism in many quarters. There have been murmurings about the proconsular powers of its patrician manager, Roger Stevens. Without Stevens's will and skill Washington might still be awaiting the funds to finish the Kennedy Center for the Performing Arts. His detractors charge, however, that he has done his job too well, that his dual role as center manager and impresario amounts to a conflict of interests. Many Washington artists also believe that the management is much more concerned about making the Kennedy Center a sort of international Cape Canaveral of the arts than it is about launching local talent and local citizen appetites. There is playbill proof, though, that ragtime, jazz, and soul music have not been slighted; nor has drama that appeals to the majority population. Annually, the dedicated Robert Hooks's D.C. Black Repertory Company has presented its best in the Eisenhower Theatre. All in all, it is probably true that, so long as its productions are superior, the Kennedy Center's artistic elitism will prove to be as salutary locally as nationally.

The best time for the Kennedy Center or almost anything else is spring and early summer, before the onset of Washington's killing heat and humidity. It is then that citizens and the twenty million annual tourists discover the full advantages of the District, for it is one of the few East Coast urban centers where thousands of people, by foot, bicycle, car, or bus (and $5.5 billion Metro) can enjoy the city together on a May weekend and find amusement without having to behave like jittery prospectors racing and snarling to stake out a blanket's worth of grass. "The city of Washington," Louis Halle's *Spring in Washington* reminds us, "has never had the praise it deserves from those of us who do not give ourselves altogether to city life. Unlike New York, it makes room for nature in its midst and seems to welcome it." [29] Washington lives under an umbrella of trees—three hundred and fifty thousand of them. It is covered with seven hundred parks—from riverine and slightly ragged Anacostia Park with the best kiddie amusement park bargain in the town after Memorial Day; to elegant and formal Dumbarton Oaks or adjacent Montrose Park with its tennis and footpaths, both in Georgetown; to the cycling delights of the Chesapeake & Ohio Canal trail; or to the heavily used East Potomac Park peninsula with its golf and fine riverside prospects of southwest and the geyser at Hains Point.

For those, like Louis Halle, with a woodchuck's view of Washington, "There is Rock Creek Park, with its forests and fields, which wanders through Washington and remains uncorrupted. . . . You may see a hawk circling over the trees, or a kingfisher following the stream." [30] Rock Creek Park is equally treasured by those who would not recognize a Carolina wren if it pecked them. Another expanse of trails, trees, flowers, fish, and birds is the National Arboretum. For those Washingtonians who crave action in order to recharge, there is football, soccer, and polo on the Mall. The spectator sports are unevenly per-

29. Louis Halle, *Spring in Washington* (New York: Atheneum, 1967), p. 5.
30. Halle, *Spring,* p. 6.

formed but enthusiastically supported—the top-class Redskins in football along with the hard-driving Bullets in basketball. Then there are the Diplomats in soccer and the Capitals in hockey.

No longer a slumberous and strangely rootless town—a place of transient elected officials, aides and military officers, and of grey bureaucrats and unobtrusive blacks—Washington has wrenched free of its demure and conventional past. In taking on life of their own, Washingtonians have turned the city into a playground and theatre for themselves, rather than allowing it to remain the tourist center and history museum of the past in which citizens were content to serve as the ushers. The feel of the place before the sauna of July is exciting in a low-key way. The sidewalk cafés on upper Connecticut Avenue and along Pennsylvania Avenue are the next best thing to being in Paris.

Dressed and out on the town, the Washingtonian has a fair amount of varied nightlife from which to choose, and it is getting better yearly. It is one of the bluegrass centers of the United States, thanks to the legions of clerks and secretaries working for the federal government. If it is rock music for the evening, Washington has places whose decibel levels compare respectably with the best in London. For the less frenetic in quest of entertainment, the range is nearly as broad as a national party platform. On the steps of the Capitol or at the Jefferson Memorial, the military band concerts are a free delight, as are the doings at Fort Dupont Park in Southeast, where Dizzy Gillespie has been known to appear, or the D.C. Black Repertory, or the African Heritage Dancers and Drummers to donate their time. The Mall may be the most exciting place in the city because of the annual Festival of American Folklife held during late June and early July. Cajuns and Lumbees, Appalachians and rural blacks, Indians, Africans, and Chicanos, folk musicians of every variety and masters of forgotten or disappearing crafts— all congregate in the shadow of the Washington Monument for an ethnic jamboree lasting daily till sundown. In addition, the Mall's outdoor Sylvan Theatre offers an annual Shakespeare festival.

But many night-outers are drawn out of the city to Columbia,

Maryland's Merriweather Post Pavilion for jazz, folk, pop, and classical concerts. Almost as far is Virginia's Filene Center at Wolf Trap Farm for the Performing Arts, a gift of Mrs. Jouett Shouse, and aptly described by Thierry Bright-Sagnier's *Washington At Night* as "an open-air Kennedy Center." Ringed by picnic areas and a terraced greensward for reclining spectators, the superb roofed auditorium is a setting for every kind of musical experience and some theatre, although classical music, opera, and dance prevail. A little farther away is the new, ultramodern Capital Centre in Largo, Maryland, which alternates between a menu of sports and pop music. The same distance away is Rockville, Maryland's Shady Grove Music Theatre with a theatre-in-the-round bill of comedy, jazz, rock, country, and soul. Deep in the Maryland countryside, there is the large, rustic Olney Theatre, going back more than a generation.

For many of Washington's teenagers there is just one place to go on a summer evening—Carter Barron Amphitheatre adjacent to Rock Creek Park. Carter Barron was once a sylvan setting for opera and ballet. When it became clear that the amphitheatre would become black, private funds quickly materialized to build suburban outdoor centers. For a time Carter Barron was too risky even for older and affluent blacks. Rock and rocks drove them away. But a sprinkling of well-dressed blacks and adventurous whites was in evidence during the 1975 summer season and the National Capital Parks Service even intends to sponsor again classical music and a Shakespeare festival.

Music and theatre are not adequately nourishing for many of those seeking more visceral pleasures. And Washington has a vast population of unattached and generally young nighthawks. There are still more single women than men in the city, and from Friday night to Sunday morning it sometimes seems that all the singles are out in search of one another in Georgetown, at Capitol Hill, or along M Street between Connecticut and Pennsylvania avenues. The proliferation of singles bars and clubs is so great that it would require an appendix in order not to omit some group's favorite lair. Georgetown's Clyde's, slightly pretentious The Guards, and L Street's folksier Fran O'Brien's are among the well-established spots giving a faster and freer pace to the city's life after dark. Down-at-the-heels Charing Cross, chic, pricey Nathan's, and bogus old-fashioned Jenkins Hill are also singles watering holes on the most-favored list. Ventuno 21, the sort of egregiously posh and polychromatic den that a son of Hugh Hefner would have conceived, is probably the *ne plus ultra* in singles clubs. For the certifiably raunchy—conventioneers, servicemen on pass, itchy tourists and locals, and the occasional college student—Washington provides a few rather tame strip joints and several enduring topless go-go clubs. Baltimore was better for stripping and New York is much superior in the topless go-go line, but the Gold Rush and The Silver Slipper for the former, and Archibald's and Erik's for the latter, are far from stale examples of both genres.

Washington's discothèques lag far behind those of Chicago or New York in *éclat*, but a night of wriggling at Rive Gauche's Boccaccio, Le Club Zanzibar, or Raphael's is worth a one-time effort. At the end of an evening, if the celebrant is black, is affluent, and has a membership card, the sartorially exacting Foxtrappe Club is a congenially elegant place to booze, dance, chat, and make connections. For the slightly older bunch, jawing about business and politics around the famous Ebony Table at Billy Simpson's restaurant has been a traditional cap to a night. Chitterlings, ribs, and collard greens at the long-established Florida Avenue Grill are potent hangover antidotes at the shank of the evening.

For the sexually gay, Washington affords almost as much pleasure as Capri in its heyday. There are places and even neighborhoods where *le vice anglais* has been fully domesticated. Again the list is too long to risk the offense of omission. Mr. Henry's on Capitol Hill appears to have become straighter, perhaps because of the fame brought to it by the singer Roberta Flack. Mr. Henry's Georgetown remains finely balanced between two clienteles. The newest center of gay life nests between Capitol Hill and the new Southwest, in a sparsely populated corridor of railroad tracks, defunct light industry, and marginal auto repair garages. In this no-man's-land are Pier 9, a discotheque, Grand Central, offering male go-go dancers, The Lost and The Found Restaurant, a good, well-appointed eatery just behind Waay Off Broadway, the city's most risqué theatre.

A Washington where artists, intellectuals, dilettantes, and eccentrics feel at home is a new development and may well be a national portent. As in London, Paris, or Rome, mingling of political and other talents may become the rule rather than the exception. The local attention to the care and feeding of media superstars and the growing colony of "beautiful people" is a recent trend that will probably endure. There will always be a majority of civil servants, lawyers, lobbyists, and politicians whose lifestyles and professional concerns will continue to give the city its special character; one that is cautious, traditional, business-for-pleasure, and occasionally fustian. But if Americans no longer regard Paris as the perfect urban setting—the place where, as Jefferson is reputed to have said, good Americans go after death—and if they have recently become disenchanted by New York City, Washington is now well underway to winning a place in their hearts as the scaled-down and much-improved model of Manhattan. Increasingly, the city offers bits and pieces of the best of New York with (for the present) only bits and pieces of the liabilities. It seems inevitable that the capital at long last is destined to become one of America's major cosmopolitan centers.

4

Behind the Marble Mask

NTER any large American city, especially an older one in the East, and the two primal realities of racial diversity and economic disparity leap out. Boston and Baltimore are not melting pots but ethnic pressure cookers. Each group—Italian, Irish, and Jew, Afro-American, Slav, and WASP—warily accepts the necessity of coexistence only so long as none attempts to intrude upon the other beyond a given political and residential limit. Chicago and Newark have become reverse Potemkin metropoli where poverty, instead of being camouflaged or confined, is so graphically and ubiquitously displayed that it obscures whatever impressive urban renewal there is. Pittsburgh has been better managed by its industrial magnates, but the Balkan character and blight of its neighborhoods envelop the visitor as he moves away from the area behind the Point. Philadelphia's decay and misery appall. Then there is New York, which perfects, when it does not invent, conditions of ethnic and economic hyperbole.

Washington is different, the rare exception—a city of moderate disparity, rather than of heartless extremes of wealth and poverty. True enough, in Northeast, above Benning Road, and in far Southeast, on either side of Martin Luther King Avenue in Anacostia, there are hives of destitution—black destitution—that beggar powers of description, exhaust compassion for the impoverished, and bewilder faith in ultimate social justice. These are the real slums. And there is more poverty elsewhere—

again, mainly black—off H Street, N.E., Fourteenth Street, N.W., and above and below Florida Avenue, N.W., in the Howard University area. But, as the *Washington Post*'s Nicholas Von Hoffman discovered after a reportorial sortie, these areas (and they are more properly not slums but working-class neighborhoods) are "nothing like North Philadelphia or Harlem where thousands of people are packed into each block." [1]

Washington's slums and poor neighborhoods are, in the main, demure, relatively habitable (population density here is among the nation's lowest), and, in many instances (those on either side of Sixteenth Street, N.W., for example), arrestingly antique in their decay. The capital's imperial grandeur has been democratized, so that even the poor and the marginal live better here than elsewhere. Statistics bear this out. Black unemployment here is a third less than the black national average. The national median income of black families in 1974 was $7,810; for the Washington metropolitan area it was $11,000, which is $2,360 less than the national median for whites. And in a city which has become, since 1950, the blackest of all major American cities (from 32 percent then, to the present 76 percent), overall conditions have improved somewhat.

The city is wealthier than ever, with a per capita income of $6,566, which is 30 percent above the national average (although poorer than ever in relation to its neighboring counties), and middle-class blacks are better off than ever, anywhere. More are represented in the local federal bureaucracy (27 percent of the total force) and more are employed in the upper grades (14 percent in grades twelve through eighteen) than elsewhere. The migrant black who chose Washington on the bet that, where the president ate well, he mightn't do too badly himself was right after all. And despite the population decline as whites and now, in increasing numbers, blacks move to the Maryland and Virginia suburbs (down from more than eight hundred thousand twenty-five years ago to about 720,000 currently), Washington is not a moribund city, a place succumbing

---

1. "Cardozo," April 9, 1967.

to the terminal diseases usually accompanying racial displacement. Racially piebald but relatively placid, Washington appears to be, at least for the moment, more and more possible at a time in American life when, one after another, cities are faltering.

Superficially, at least, the city seems to be capable of achieving the elusive urban reality for which Americans have been questing, civility, confidence in the future, and unity in diversity. Life is not really so ideal, of course. Behind the marble facade, and away from tourist Washington, there is misery, racism, enormous wealth and social fragmentation aplenty. Gen. U. S. Grant III is nearly totally forgotten, but, whether by careful plan or the workings of natural selection, parts of the city remain tightly closed to all but a handful of blacks desiring apartments and homes. An uninformed visitor to Spring Valley or Cleveland Park or Glover Park would never imagine that Washington is, at least by population, a black city.

Generalizations of this sort are risky, however; what was true last year may have been nullified this year by the city's rapidly changing residential map, and the causes for a given circumstance may alter radically even though things remain the same. When the *Washington Post* revealed ten years ago that real estate agents in Northwest subtly discriminated against black buyers by offering whites better terms—negotiable purchase prices, lower down payments, referrals to savings and loan institutions—it was a shameful but hardly astonishing revelation. Although it seems unlikely that such practices have been entirely abandoned today, it is also probable that they are less widespread and that money rather than race now primarily determines who buys what and where. It is certainly possible for blacks to live "west of the park" today and a number are doing so, but the hundred-thousand-dollar purchase price limits the appetite.

The picture is uglier when the city's crime problem is addressed. President Richard Nixon foisted upon Washington a stigma from which it may not recover for a decade, that of being the "crime capital of the world." It was not a novel accusation. *Newsweek* claimed this distinction for the District as long ago as 1941. And three congressional investigations, one in 1950, another in 1966, and the last in 1969, attracted national attention to the problem. The findings of these committees, that the victims of local crime were mainly the poor and the black and that Washington was far more free of crime than an excited public believed, were either ignored or quickly forgotten. The truth was that, at the very moment Nixon was capitalizing on this issue, Washington ranked nineteenth in the nation among major cities plagued by crime.

Statistics have a way of being especially irrelevant in Washington. Murders, rapes, and armed robberies in Baltimore or Detroit (where they are much higher) or homicides in Alabama (which has one of the leading murder rates in the nation) are matters of local import. Millions of Americans make no annual pilgrimages to these places, as they do to the nation's capital. Riots and rape in Washington are scandals which outrage people in the Dakotas perhaps more than the citizens of the District of Columbia. The shooting of Sen. John Stennis of Mississippi, Sen. William Proxmire's feat of self-defense against teen-age assailants, the 1975 orgy of violence against white participants in Human Kindness Day on the Mall, or the blinding by pistol shot of a white hobo on the Ellipse behind the White House surpass the possibility of an appeal to data. Violence in Washington, like the shot heard round the world, resounds in the most remote hamlet.

Crime in Washington is also special because it reflects more graphically than is possible elsewhere racial desperation whose cause and solution few affluent Americans care to understand. The simplistic explanations are not invalid. More adequate police protection helps; expanded court facilities are useful; stiffer penalties may dissuade; welfare reform is a step in the right direction; better public education is vitally important. But crime in the District will survive all these stopgaps—even the sane and ultimately inevitable one of rigid gun-control legislation. For, whatever the individual motives, the black crime monopoly is rooted in social and economic disability, in the rampant reality of gaps in income, social services, and in the galloping appreciation of property values making the city the second most expensive place to live in America. Tocqueville said of the French Revolution that it occurred not because of hopeless repression but because of the frustration of rising expectations. Crime in Washington, where minority incomes are higher and ghettoes are less squalid, is Tocquevillian in origin. It is the frightening monitor of government failure to encourage social equity.

An important aspect of Washington has been ignored. If it is a city that melds its elements more successfully than most, in its own way it is still a heterogeneous metropolis—much less so than Boston or Milwaukee, but nevertheless significantly pluralistic. What is puzzling is that this fact has never been examined in a city bursting, since the New Deal certainly, with social scientists. There are at least seventy identifiable neighborhoods in the city, many of them separated by race, class, religion, and income, yet the local literature is virtually silent. National issues, residential transiency, and Negrophobia have served as collective barriers against hometown investigation of the hometown. Even Constance Green's two-volume history treats Washington's neighborhoods kaleidoscopically.

Many of these neighborhoods are annoyingly indeterminate by boundary—even some of the oldest or best known like rich, white-liberal Cleveland Park where oldtimers insist on narrowing the "real" limits to Lowell, Macomb, and Newark streets, or Capitol Hill, the strivers' Georgetown, whose Twelfth Street boundary is disputed, or Anacostia's century-old black settlement, Barry Farms, decennially nibbled and slashed since the 1940s first by white and now black housing developments. Others, like Buzzard Point and Greenleaf Point, are still on the city map but have become military or federal properties. Indeterminate or anachronistic, Washington's neighborhoods all have one thing in common, that they are perceived and tend to perceive themselves in terms of their location to Rock Creek Park, a 1,754-acre arcadia of bridle paths, bike trails, picnic enclaves, golf course, and zoo. Shaped like an upside-down sea horse running north to south almost the length of the city's middle, the park divides everything. "West of the park" is the District's equivalent of the *seizième arrondissement,* the quadrant of the white, the affluent, and the municipally well-served.

In a recent survey of area incomes, the *Washington Post* discovered that if two areas west of the park—Cleveland Park and Georgetown—were converted into counties they would be the richest in the nation, along with adjacent Montgomery County, Maryland, currently the richest. Life in the northwestern quadrant is very good indeed, as Sam Smith, the liberal, cause-committed editor of the *D.C. Gazette* discovered after the hassle of crime, children, and schools caused him to leave Capitol Hill for Cleveland Park. "We found the problems of urban living declining and the pleasures increasing," Smith confesses. "Everyone from the Post Office to the Sanitation Department to the local chain supermarket seemed to respond proportionately to the increase in our property taxes. It was nice to feel that you got something for your money. . . ." [2]

North, east, and south of the park is the rest of Washington where approximately 88 percent of the citizenry lives. Mostly, this is black Washington, but there are enough whites and others and sufficient variety in income and lifestyles, to make neighborhoods in the remaining quadrants enormously contrasting. Running due north from Lafayette Square is Sixteenth Street, bisecting Washington's upper triangle, and forming the park's eastern border. High up Sixteenth Street there is another neighborhood divide—Walter Reed Army Hospital—which looks on the city map like a flag descending to half mast on its Sixteenth Street staff.

Along upper Sixteenth Street and separated from the white Golconda west of the park lie two affluent black communities sometimes designated as the "Gold" and the "Platinum" coasts, separated by the flag-like configuration of Walter Reed Hospital. Immediately below the army hospital is the Gold Coast, an area of large, regal homes with scant space between. Here, most of Washington's oldest and richest black families reside. Above the flag are most of the rest, in homes generally smaller but more modern. Amid faint signs of revival, lower Sixteenth Street decays. Fine houses below Carter Barron Am-

2. Sam Smith, *Captive Capital, Colonial Life in Modern Washington* (Bloomington, Ind.: Indiana University Press, 1974), p. 132.

phitheatre announce by lawn and porch signs their conversion into temples of unusual religious sects or headquarters of Third-World-oriented organizations. Hispanics from the Adams-Morgan neighborhood fill the miniparks off the intersecting Columbia Road. Farther along is the architectural stereopticon effect of fortress-like churches and older, generally shabby-grand, embassies, one of them representing a country no longer extant (Lithuania) and another, a government not recognized by the United States (Cuba). Once ritzy apartment buildings occupied by lower-level African diplomats, bohemians, students, and un-poor white geriatrics follow. Then comes Meridian Hill Park (unofficially renamed Malcom X) and the imperial poverty spoken of earlier. East of Sixteenth Street, all the way to Howard University and below and beyond it, are the solid, deceptively dignified brownstone facades of the city's black poor.

South of the park—south, that is, of center city, of the Federal Triangle and the Mall—the bottom triangle begins, containing the remaining quadrants of Southeast and Southwest Washington. Renovated and pushily chic Capitol Hill and the depressed area of Capitol East (already a real estate agent's paradise) are there, and the well-designed new luxury high-rise apartments and town houses of Southwest; and across the Anacostia River (the area whose population has increased 22.6 percent over the last decade) lies the District's most neglected section. This is also a section of the city whose potentially best real estate, running almost half its length along the river, is being arrogantly husbanded by the Defense Department long after its military usefulness has ended. A move to transfer the Bolling Air Force Base property to the city for construction of low-income housing was sabotaged by a senior South Carolina congressman, Mendel Rivers, who objected to the land being used for the "social concoctions of some idiots around Washington." Rivers's 1969 bill prevented Bolling's use for civilian purposes until 1975. Quite recently, the Defense Department announced that the entire 920 acres were to be developed as a "Little Pentagon," a plan already completed to the extent of forty million dollars in military housing construction. Eventually, 1,055 housing units will be built at Bolling, the largest such undertaking since McLean Gardens in the 1940s and the New Southwest in the 1950s, but totally removed from any social or jurisdictional contact with the District of Columbia. The commanding general, in a 1975 interview, guardedly supposed that Bolling's families would send their children to nearby public schools— schools that are already straining to serve the children of area taxpayers. It remains to be seen whether this will be done or whether, as is more likely, the Little Pentagon will have its own schools, as it will its own shopping center and recreational facilities.

South of the Park

This is where the city began. Before it began, there were two small settlements already in existence within the borders of what was to become Washington City—Carrollsburg (Greenleaf Point) and Hamburg (Funkstown). Carrollsburg lay adjacent to and east of the future navy yard. Its eighteenth-century developers originally intended for Carrollsburg to challenge Alexandria as a commercial port, a scheme that quickly fizzled. In the early 1790s, after the miserable proceeds from two land auctions presided over by George Washington himself, the commissioners gambled on the scheme of the Massachusetts capitalist, James Greenleaf, and his Pennsylvania partner of reputedly fabulous wealth, Robert Morris. Greenleaf and Morris offered to buy three thousand lots at reduced price and to build twenty houses annually for seven years; in return, Greenleaf and Morris were to advance the commissioners $2,700 monthly until the Capitol and the President's Palace were completed.

Bankruptcy in 1797 aborted the scheme. George Gibbs's *Memoirs* describe the results greeting the astounded legislators arriving from Philadelphia in 1800: Greenleaf Point presented "the appearance of a considerable town, which had been destroyed by some unusual calamity. There are fifty or sixty spacious houses, five or six of them inhabited by . . . vagrants, and a few more by decent looking people; but there are no fences, gardens, nor the least appearance of business." Commercially, residentially, Carrollsburg was a complete failure, as was nearby Buzzard Point, which L'Enfant had identified as the city's ideal residential nucleus. Fort McNair has swallowed up much of Carrollsburg, and Buzzard Point, after two hundred years of neglect, may become the headquarters of a federal agency.

Few inhabitants would have agreed with the mordant Benjamin Latrobe that "a great[er] benefit could not have accrued to this city than the destruction of its principal buildings by the British." Still, there were definite benefits from Adm. Alexander Cockburn's barbarism. Despite the close vote in Congress to move the capital, in fact, much because of it, the city's friends rallied to rebuild Capitol Hill. Southeast Washington now began a period of development that seemed to foretell the realization of L'Enfant's hopes. For a while, the Treasury Building was a few steps from the Capitol, as was the city's largest bank. Taverns, hotels, and markets throve. Carroll Row, the massive, white structure located on the site of the Library of Congress, housed a number of famous hostelries through the years. There was Long's Hotel in the house at the north end of Carroll Row where the glittering inaugural ball for James Madison was held. The new president seems to have comported himself rather stiffly at the gala, but Mrs. Madison and the retiring chief executive, Thomas Jefferson, threw themselves into the occasion. "The crowd was excessive, the heat oppressive, and the entertainment bad," John Quincy Adams noted in his diary. But Jefferson, it is reported, palavered and danced until well past midnight. The row also housed the Queen Hotel, offering some of the best accommodations in the city.

Nearby, Pontius D. Stelle had put up his New Jersey Avenue hotel shortly after the government moved from Philadelphia. Stelle's rivalled Suter's in Georgetown. As the Washington summers approached, the House and Senate adjourned daily before 2:00 P.M., usually to Stelle's, where members were afforded a bibulous respite from weighty matters and oppressive heat. In the one hundred block of New Jersey Avenue, S.E., William Sanderson maintained a popular hotel, where Silas

Wright and John C. Calhoun boarded. Sanderson's place was demolished to make way for the extension of the Capitol grounds.

The hill also possessed two well-provisioned markets, one at First and East Capitol streets and the other at Seventh and K, S.E. A typical day at these markets was probably not unlike a shopping tour of Eastern Market today (the city's sole surviving old market), where, amid Hogarthian cheese vendors, eccentric poultry hawkers, and animated sausage merchants, a melee of families and singles nudge and natter, black and white, affluent and poor. For then as now (though more so then), Southeast was composed of all types, incomes, and of both races. In addition to the families Brent, Brice, Carroll, and Coombs, Gamble, Law, Prout, and Tingey, Tayloe and Smallwood, there were many free blacks and a sizeable white working-class community: artisans, mechanics, carpenters, and merchants, already numbering some five hundred in the early 1790s and greatly multiplying after the establishment of the navy yard. Michael French suggests that the hill is still peopled by a surviving group of families descended from the working-class community of the early nineteenth century. But if so, they are, for the most part, the few aged, poor whites who now lend a barely noticed folksy character to upper Pennsylvania and Maryland avenues, and who are being as doggedly pressured by the local real estate agents as are the long-established black homeowners.

Well into the 1850s, construction on the hill and the distinction of its resident families seemed to assure competitiveness with cosmopolitan Georgetown. Interviewed by the *Star,* old Col. James Tait, an institution on the hill and commander of the District militia, remembered how costly were the building lots. The large landholders confidently kept prices high through the years. Colonel Tait's father, not a poor man, was typical of the frustrated would-be buyers of the period. Slowly, then in a flood after the Civil War, families like the Taits moved to the Northwest. In the 1820s and 1830s, however, no one doubted the ultimate primacy of the hill. "Capitol Hill was *the* place," Colonel Tait recalled. "New Jersey Avenue, South of the Capitol, was the aristocratic part of town. . . . The City was expected to grow east." [3] If the physical amenities of Georgetown greatly exceeded those of Southeast in the early years, the social excitement was on the hill. The District remembered the consummate flirtatiousness of Baltimore's Elizabeth Patterson during her visits to the hill. Napoleon's brother, Jerome, was doomed to be smitten by her during his 1804 sojourn. By the time another Capitol Hill femme fatale began to charm and scandalize the city, the tragic Mrs. Bonaparte and her children had been declared nullities by imperial decree. Peggy O'Neale, the innkeeper's daughter, chose more wisely, marrying President Jackson's secretary of war, John Eaton. Neighbor and Vice-President John C. Calhoun's wife publicly announced that Mrs. Eaton was not welcome in her home. The Peggy O'Neale affair soon mushroomed into a viciously feline imbroglio polarizing Washington society and playing a considerable part in destroying Jackson's cabinet.

But surely and more rapidly, it became clear that the fine hotels and friendly taverns, the well-stocked markets and regal town houses, the delicious gossip and political repercussions of emancipated ladies' amours—and even the Capitol itself—could not keep the Southeast afloat. The elite families were either dead or gone by the end of the Civil War. The earliest available *Elite List* (1888), the city's blue book, contains only four hill names. The era had passed into oblivion when Southeast residents could look "down their noses at . . . even Northern Liberties, Hamburg, and Georgetown," Paul Herron's book, *The Story of Capitol Hill,* informs us. Southeast sank below the consciousness of establishment Washington, nor did the McMillan Commission do anything to reverse its decline. Lighting, sewage, paving, and streetcar lines flowed downhill and away from Southeast Washington. And with the coming of the Civil War, thousands of former slaves poured into the area, inundating Capitol Hill and spilling across the river into what was then called "Union Town." The area behind the Capitol took on the aspect of a teeming Brazilian *favella* or North African settlement.

3. "East Washington," *Washington Star,* May 3, 1883.

As early as the 1850s, property owners had begun to erect slave, servant, or rental quarters behind their houses. Access to these dwellings was along the service alleys. With the post-Civil War influx of blacks and poor whites, hundreds of property owners doubly divided their back lots permitting construction of other buildings whose only ingress was through secondary alleys connecting with the main rear approaches. According to an 1871 estimate, 81 percent of alley-dwelling households were black, the rest white. Even Congress began to notice the eruption, finally becoming sufficiently alarmed, in 1892, to forbid further construction. Although the most populous alleys were in Northwest and Southwest, some of the worst were across the street from the Capitol and behind other nearby streets. President Theodore Roosevelt included the alley problem in his 1904 message to Congress, in which he called for a special commission to study the problem.

The multivolume study, *The President's Home Commission* (*1908*), was widely discussed and then utterly ignored. But the problem itself certainly could not be filed, even though the home commission encouragingly predicted that the silent decline in alley population would continue. The decline persisted, but, as Charles Frederick Weller's *Neglected Neighborhoods* found, "the situation is worse . . . than in 1905." "Purdy's Court" at the foot of the Capitol, notorious "Willow Tree Alley" two blocks away, "Louse Alley" three blocks south, and "Navy Place" (the worst in Southeast) were Capitol Hill examples of Washington's "submerged population of sixteen thousand souls . . . unique, with few if any parallels in other American cities." Not all, perhaps not even the majority, of the people in the alleys (93 percent of whom were black) were antisocial indigents. The God-fearing, hard-working poor—husbands working as unskilled laborers and wives toiling as domestics—lived sardine-like with alcoholics, prostitutes, and criminals, and all of them had too many children.

In the minds of most citizens, though, all alley denizens were indistinguishable from those in "Murder Bay," a morass of hovels stretching from the old canal north along the Ellipse almost to Pennsylvania Avenue. An early newspaper gave the following description of this neighborhood where few strangers who entered came out alive and where bodies were routinely fished from the canal:

> It consisted of rows of little frame shanties occupied mostly by negroes [*sic*], but with a sprinkling of whites of the worst character. There were no pavements in this locality. The water soaking through from the canal kept the ground continuously wet, and the feet of the people passing churned the soft ground into black and odorous mud, making even the ground consistent with the depravity that existed there.[4]

But "Murder Bay" was not really an alley settlement, nor was it altogether typical. It lasted until construction of the Federal Triangle was begun in the late 1920s.

Once again, on the eve of World War One, there was a flurry of interest in the alleys because of Mrs. Wilson's concern. The first Mrs. Wilson was reputedly a hardboiled segregationist but her heart went out to the alley dwellers. Constance Green reports that "it was laughingly said that no one could move in polite society in Washington who could not talk alleys." On her deathbed, Mrs. Wilson sighed "I should be happier if I knew the Alley Bill had passed." In the autumn of 1914, it passed. It had virtually no effect. The number of alleys continued to shrink (by 40 percent in 1927) but mainly because the unfortunate dwellers somehow managed to escape or were crowded out, rather than because of municipal and federal benevolence.

At the beginning of the New Deal, another *frisson* of alley-mindedness passed over Washington. Eleanor Roosevelt returned to the haunts of Ellen Wilson and the establishment talked alleys anew. In 1934, Congress passed a new and much stronger act creating the Alley Dwelling Authority, empowered to compensate property owners and charged to clear the alleys by July 1, 1944. But on Christmas Day, 1945, a *Washington Post* reporter visited "Boxtown" in Southeast. The slum's grim mood was summed up by a Mrs. Watkins: "It'll be good when

---

4. Undated, unidentified article, Martin L. King, Jr., Memorial Library, Washingtoniana, Vertical Files ("Murder Bay").

the weather stops—then, maybe there'll be more work and, with enough to eat, I guess maybe we can forget Christmas." Litigation and Pearl Harbor altered the alley target date to 1955. It was not to be supposed that Congress, white Washington, or most American voters were reconciled to being billed for the housing costs of the poor. If Washington had finally become the national showcase by the mid-twentieth century, the showcase was partly submerged in detritus.

Meanwhile, most of the Southeast section of the city, white communities included, spiralled downward. Of this area's 54,000 people, 76.5 percent were white in 1936, and most of the whites were furious. By his choice of commissioners and from gossip about his off-the-record statements, President Roosevelt showed himself to be oddly indifferent about local conditions. Newspapers during this period are full of articles about citizen unrest. The *Herald,* for July 27, 1935, "Neglected Southeast," reports Minnesota's Sen. Henrik Shipstead charging that the Southeast is ignored because "there arc no millionaires in this section." On August 13, the *Washington Post* reported "Southeast Citizens Vote Protest to Roosevelt." Follow-up articles in the *Star* revealed that a garbage disposal plant in the heart of Southeast (at New Jersey Avenue and K Street) befouled the neighborhood, that the Pennsylvania Avenue bridge over the Anacostia (a rickety, narrow, forty-year-old structure) had recently dropped four feet, that no new schools had been built in decades, and that the infrequent placement of traffic lights was arbitrarily determined. In Anacostia, whites were seriously contemplating withholding their property taxes.

Southwest Washington was more neglected and more deplorable. In 1950, 43 percent of the 5,600 dwelling units in Southwest had outdoor toilets and 70 percent were without central heating. Twenty-one percent had no electricity, 44 percent had no baths. The 23,500 inhabitants (overwhelmingly black) subsisted on annual family incomes of less than $2,500. According to Daniel Thurz, an expert on Southwest, "the neighborhood had deteriorated to a point where it was cited as one of the worst housing areas in the United States."

This blight was monitored with growing alarm and repugnance by Washington's leading conservatives. Under the flinty direction of Gen. U. S. Grant III, the new Redevelopment Land Agency (RLA), established in 1946, drew up a master plan for the wholesale banishment of blacks from Capitol Hill and Southwest to the remote parts of Anacostia. Grant's relocation plan was certainly autocratic and racist and deserving of the surprisingly firm opposition it engendered. The Anacostians protested. New Deal liberals west of the park and progressive Congressmen attuned to the postwar spirit of tolerance denounced RLA's highhandedness. But all things considered, Grant's plan did have this to recommend it: it provided low-cost housing for the poor whose displacement, given the aesthetic, economic, and political realities of the nation's capital, was but a matter of time. RLA's plan was stymied for five years and then officially scrapped. "Time," a local punster remarked, "wounds all heels." But General Grant's wounds were superficial. After his retirement from RLA, the slums in Southwest were bulldozed, the blacks scattered, and Anacostia became the city's dumping ground after all.

The National Capital Planning Commission had wanted the Southwest area to become an enclave for low- and middle-income families, but it reckoned without the supersalesmanship of William Zeckendorf, president of the development firm of Webb & Knapp. In February 1954, Webb & Knapp presented appropriate congressmen and District officials with a plan to turn Southwest into "a monumental, cultural, and high-income residential center," to be designed by I. M. Pei. Zeckendorf's plan was truly Ozymandian. Three hundred and thirty of Southwest's 427 acres were to be redeveloped with federal, District, and private financing. An opera house, large convention hall, symphony hall, and a grand mall connecting with the center of the city were to be built. RLA endorsed the plan enthusiastically. Congress was enraptured. The Supreme Court struck down objections. "We do not sit to determine whether a particular housing project is or is not desirable," Justice William O. Douglas pronounced.

One hundred and eighty-five million dollars and five years later, Southwest was substantially completed. Over the debris had risen an architect's paradise of high-rise apartments balanced on concrete fingertips, colonial town houses in verdant culs-de-sac, Olympic-sized swimming pools, two theatres that would considerably upgrade culture in Washington, and a renovated waterfront whose proposed bridge (*ponte vecchio*) of shops and stalls has been regrettably scaled down to a narrow sterile promenade and a row of warehouse-elegant restaurants. As a gesture to postwar liberalism, RLA built several blocks of public housing at the edge of its white-collar ghetto, placing within range of mutual contempt people with $5,000 median incomes and those earning $24,000. Daniel Thurz estimates that about one-fourth of the original population remained in Southwest. The majority were dumped into the housing projects thrown up in Anacostia. Middle-class blacks have come to favor the area, however. Statistics on such a sensitive matter, if they exist, are unavailable, but several visits to the new Southwest inspire the confidence that well-salaried blacks are abundantly represented among the population. The area is probably a microcosm of what urban middle-class America may come to be, a place where income rather than race determines mobility.

Meanwhile, in Southeast, things were beginning to hum. An early signal of what was in store for Capitol Hill appeared at a meeting of the Southeast Citizens' Association, the Capitol Hill Lions' Club, and General Grant at Friendship House in May 1949. The group voted to request the widening of B Street, S.E. and N.E., to eliminate the bottleneck around the Capitol, to demand that a local high school not be assigned to blacks, and to request that their neighborhood be rezoned to eliminate businesses from much of the area. Adjourning inspired and resolute from Friendship House, the hill's notables efficiently set about the task of renovation. A year later, hill businessmen were offering a $2,000 prize for the best revamped town house. On April 30, the *Washington Post* carried photos of a painting bee in the 1200 block of G Street, S.E., where six houses had been transformed in one day by brush-wielding Eastern High School students. At about the same time, the Capitol Hill Restoration Society gathered signatures for a petition to the commissioners asking for a ban on public housing construction in the area.

Meanwhile, real estate agents and a growing number of home-owners continued to rip away wooden porches from brick fronts, to sandblast or paint, and otherwise to adorn brown-stones with shutters, massive doors, antique lamps, door-knockers, and grillwork. A really eye-catching feat of extensive restoration was the work done at Philadelphia Row on Eleventh Street, S.E., in the late 1950s.

Among the earliest remodellers were H. Curley Boswell and the Lendall Gays. After 1959, they were joined by hundreds of renovating residents and by real estate agencies such as those of Beau Bogan, Helen Carey, and Rhea Radin. By the early 1960s, Capitol Hill was fast becoming one of the most desirable neighborhoods in the District. Under the Kennedy administra-tion, racial integration began to be a fashionable ideal and the preservation of historic buildings an even more fashionable real-ity. It was chic to buy a rundown brownstone in the middle of a black block, to restore it and open it once a year for public viewing during the restoration tour, and to claim how much richer life was in a community where affluent whites and poor blacks, civil service families and homosexuals, old settlers and refugees from sterile suburbs harmoniously coexisted.

Hill propaganda was impressive; many of the well-meaning young propagandists believed it; some of it was even true; and with the important exception of some of the real estate agents and the businessman-dominated Capitol Hill Restoration Soci-ety, the motives were generally commendable. Nevertheless, most blacks and many of the older whites were less than ecstatic about the inrush of overly friendly, activist, young families and colorful gays. Until the late 1960s, occupants of renovated homes tended to annoy and embarrass their less fortunate neigh-bors with a superfluity of Peace Corps uplift. The nuns of Saint Peter's Roman Catholic Church fanned out across the neigh-borhood to instruct black mothers in dietetics, infant care, and sewing. One Marguerite Kelly galvanized the District's bureau-cracy and local block captains of the Democratic party into launching the Great Rat Purge of 1963. A special poison, Raticate, was distributed free to anyone willing to answer the door in a sixty-block area. Alleys were baited and rats (and maybe a few cats) succumbed by the thousands. When the Great Rat Purge ended, the restored blocks were free of rodents, but in time the survivors returned to those that were unrestored.

Then there was the bright promise of the Emergency Recreation Council (ERC), an aggressively liberal and scrupulously biracial organization that charged that the stodgy Capitol Hill Restoration Society could do no right. Members of the ERC opposed the exclusion of all-black Capitol East from the councils of community leadership, claiming that Capitol Hill extended beyond Twelfth Street (the generally agreed upon boundary) to the Anacostia River. The ERC's most important battle, which it won, was the fight to locate a community swimming pool behind Eastern Market, an area which merchants anticipated would eventually become a mini-strip of posh boutiques and galleries. The business community was horrified by the prospect of swarms of black children drawn into the neighborhood by the pool. The swarms of noisy youngsters are now a permanent summer fixture, but so are swarms of well-heeled shoppers. Although ERC was an exemplary experiment in biracial activism, blacks became increasingly dissatisfied with their white comrades. Indeed, by the late 1960s they had become so suspicious and hostile that the organization foundered.

Militant, white goodwill had not been enough. Statistics nullified rhetoric and occasional success. Sam Smith, who was both observer and participant during these years, tells us what really happened as a result of white influx. "Between 1960 and 1965," says *Captive Capital,* "the two census tracts closest to the Capitol gained 1,100 whites and lost 1,100 blacks. . . ." The *Washington Post* reported the purchases of mostly black homes for thirteen to nineteen thousand dollars and their resale, after renovation, for forty thousand dollars and up. Capitol Hill blacks have tried to organize against galloping renovation but their weapons are woefully inadequate to the combat, and those whites who were once their allies appear to have lost heart in the holocaust of 1968 and the ensuing climate of "benign neglect." It is a moot point whether or not an infusion of affluent blacks might help to stabilize the situation. It is also an academic question because those who could afford the inflated properties on the hill have, with rare exceptions, preferred other areas of the city or the suburbs. Today, Capitol Hill is still statistically racially integrated and varied by income, but culturally and socially, it has become a tale of two communities growing further apart.

East (and North) of the Park

East of Rock Creek Park comprises Northeast and a portion of the Northwest quadrant. It is the most varied of all the areas, architecturally, economically, racially. Five of the major academic institutions are in the area. Catholic, George Washington, and Howard universities, the new Federal City College, and Gallaudet College, the school for the deaf. Here the "other" ethnics are found, the few thousand Chinese, the suddenly multiplying Hispanics, and what remains of the once sizeable Jewish community. In addition to the Gold and Platinum coasts off upper Sixteenth Street, there is the middle-class black community of Brookland in Northeast, adjacent to Catholic University. There are the neighborhoods of Brentwood, Eckington, and Trinidad, where poverty runs from the matrifocal, welfare families in sleazy public housing and stained brownstones to the hardworking "mainstreamers," aspirants to the good life in neat, brick row houses, each with its own porch. Across the Anacostia River, a small wedge of far Northeast contains black neighborhoods such as Benning and Eastland Gardens—some of the worst slums in the city. Most of the whites are bunched around George Washington and Catholic universities, in the Adams-Morgan and Kalorama Triangle section, and in the Mount Pleasant enclave just below the Gold Coast, and are spottily located elsewhere.

Until the 1895 consolidation of the three jurisdictions, Washington City, Washington County, and Georgetown, the old Boundary Road (today's Florida Avenue) separated Washington City from most of the area east of the park. What there is of neighborhood history above the Mall during the first eighty-odd years was enacted upon a rather small stage. Where Massachusetts, Connecticut, and New Hampshire avenues joined was the sketchy roundabout called Pacific Circle. Rhode Island Avenue, Massachusetts Avenue, and Sixteenth Street intersected at the more ambitious Scott Circle. A little farther along, Massachusetts and Vermont met Fourteenth and M streets at Thomas Circle. A distance above, was Iowa Circle (now Logan Circle), formed by the confluence of Rhode Island and Vermont, P and Thirteenth. Truly local history emerged from these four nuclei, and nearly all of it was post-Civil War.

Marietta Minnegerode Andrews's *My Studio Window* evokes the mellow charm of Scott Circle in the 1870s, a necklace of mansions and of homes of middle-class black and white families. In those days, the color of one's neighbors mattered far less than their manners, and a cousin of the Virginia Lees could be on polite terms with the industrious and dignified Freeman family two houses away. Marietta Andrews respectfully remembered the Freemans many years later, the mother who "was a well-bred woman and her son [who] is now a leading physician. . . ." Across the circle was a hostess of color even more popular than Marietta, many of whose guests were frequent callers at the Andrews mansion. "Mamie the Mulattress" was Washington's most renowned clairvoyant. Life on Scott Circle, in spite of the wrenching changes wrought by Alexander Shepherd and the money-madness of the Gilded Age, was paced to a southern rhythm and was faithful to old habits and values. It was a world spiritually far removed from the plangent scandals of the Gold Trust and the Crédit Mobilier, business machinations plotted in New York and joyously participated in by President Grant's intimates a few blocks away. It is not recorded that the Henry Adamses ever visited the Scott Circle Andrewses. Probably not. But had they done so, there would have been a communion of tastes transcending political differences about the Civil War, for the view from Marietta's studio window, like that of Henry's on Lafayette Square, was aristocratically hazy though not wholly defective.

Marietta Andrews believed that her circle would survive. What she tells us about her home provides one of the most informative apostrophes to an almost vanished milieu:

Thus a little old-fashioned home of one's own becomes a landmark, especially if it remains unchanged through changing years—the same old oriental rugs, mellowed by the tramping of many feet, till the patterns are almost obliterated, the colors having melted into a pleasant neutral, while unaccustomed guests must be cautioned not to trip and break their necks in the worn places! The same old clumsy pullbells, which jangle discordantly in the kitchen when one needs a friendly hand to hook one up—the same old hot-air furnace, probably the only one left on Sixteenth Street, which may one day be exhibited in the National Museum; the same decrepit retainer to attend thereto, though time has taken toll of him, left his eyes too dim to see dust and his step too slow to answer the imperative front door.

Charming picture of a vulnerable and quaint decrepitude which the steady advance of hotels, embassies, and businesses up Sixteenth Street would eventually destroy as inexorably as it would the society on Lafayette Square.

Before that happened, though, there were to be years of congenial evolution along Sixteenth Street which seemed to assure its regnant position as the second-most important artery, and Scott Circle as the residential hub of avenues and streets on which much of marmoreal Washington would emerge. The splendid Spanish Embassy chose Sixteenth Street. At the nearby intersection of Connecticut and N Street was the British Embassy. The decision of Col. John B. Henderson to build his castle above Scott Circle on the Sixteenth Street axis delighted Mrs. Andrews. Henderson's castle was the *dernier cri* in baronial luxury. Old photographs show a sprawling, turreted structure, more Victorian than medieval and likely to take on a House of Usher aspect, as it finally did, once the enlivening spirit of its makers moved on. During the Hendersons' ascendancy, though, the castle was admired even more for the riches within than for its external majesty.

Contemporary newspapers fairly gushed over the appointments of the grand ballroom and the "priceless" art displayed in multiple rows throughout. A measure of Washington society's aesthetic education in those days is revealed by the auctioneer's catalogue when the castle's treasures were liquidated. There were dozens of works by M. F. Henderson, Chauncey Ives, and Lucian Powell, but not a painting valued at more than several hundred dollars nor a single old master or nineteenth-century French canvas. The days of the Mellons, Phillipses, and Kreegers had not quite arrived. Quality, though, is in the eye of the beholder, and those who were privileged to share the Hendersons' foyer departed grateful and smug. "Into her Castle," said the *Washington Herald*, "Mrs. Henderson brought only the great of Washington. In queenly fashion she ruled society, her word became law in modes and manners." [5]

The castle's master, Senator Henderson, one of Washington's most powerful politicians, was a fascinating contradiction. He had left the Democratic party because of his opposition to slavery and was the author of the Thirteenth Amendment. However, unlike Marietta Andrews, he did not care to have blacks in the neighborhood. The District commissioners were roused from their customary inanition to smite black property owners with eviction notices. Those who protested found their homes reassessed and were offered less than the minimal compensation originally stipulated. A mere matter of eminent domain was not to be allowed to trouble the Hendersons' grand design of transforming Sixteenth Street into the "Avenue of the Presidents," an endeavor enhanced by the laying out of Meridian Hill Park directly across Sixteenth Street. In 1910, $490,000 in federal and District funds were allocated to purchase Meridian Hill estate—probably a bargain, but not the gift most Washingtonians believed the Hendersons had made the city.

There was fierce competition between the Hendersons and Charles Carroll Glover, Sr., the latter equally determined to make Massachusetts Avenue the most prestigious residential stretch. So pertinaciously did Mrs. Henderson push her street that, as one of his last acts, President Taft decreed that it was to be called "Avenue of the Presidents." Her triumph was short-lived, for President Wilson's party owed no favors to the re-

5. April 26, 1937.

cently bereaved widow of the aged Republican senator. The Taft decree was immediately rescinded. In the early 1930s, Charles Glover provided the British with a choice piece of real estate for their new embassy on Massachusetts Avenue, permanently winning for the Glover roadway the unofficial title of "Embassy Row."

Gradually, Sixteenth Street lost its pre-eminence. Mrs. Henderson died in 1931, past ninety and querulous. The castle became an after-hours club, boardinghouse, hotel, and finally, a crumbling shell to be torn down in early 1949. Until the 1950s, Sixteenth Street remained one of the capital's most elegant thoroughfares. By then, however, the Henderson neighborhood had been flooded with luxury apartment buildings and outsized sectarian temples. Marietta Andrews's Scott Circle had become a business intersection where traffic plunges into an underpass above which the game bronze horse supporting obese Gen. Winfield Scott still looks tolerably fit.

A distance away from Scott Circle, but on the same axis, there is another roundabout. Sen. William Stewart purchased the property, in 1870, on what was then Pacific Circle, with a modest outlay of his Nevada silver mining riches. A decade before the Hendersons' mansion went up, "Stewart's Castle," a large, octagonal town house, rose near the square. Nearby, "Boss" Shepherd, heading pell-mell into bankruptcy, opened his lustrous mansion in 1875. Today, Pacific Circle is called Dupont. According to Gerald Zilg, a contemporary historian in the robust muckraker tradition, Rear Admiral Samuel du Pont's command of Union naval forces before Charleston harbor was an unmitigated calamity which a modicum of intelligence could have avoided. Samuel du Pont was compelled to resign his commission; he died of a broken heart on his Delaware estate. The du Ponts labored mightily but unobtrusively to rehabilitate their kinsman and the renaming of Pacific Square, in 1882, was a notable measure of the family's power to amend history. Two years later, Admiral du Pont's bronze effigy rose in the center of the rechristened federal real estate.

The 1972 brochure published by the Dupont Circle Citizens' Association (DCCA) commemorating that organization's fiftieth anniversary, proclaims that "by 1910, Dupont Circle was not only the acme of Victorianism, but was the winter residence of the wealthy, politically powerful, the diplomatic corps, the socially influential, and the cultured. A social directory of the Circle would have read like the *Who's Who* of the United States." Secretary of State James G. Blaine; Chief Justice Charles Evans Hughes; future Speaker of the House Nicholas Longworth and his peppery bride, Alice Roosevelt; Assistant Secretary of the Navy Franklin Roosevelt and the noble Eleanor; Lars Anderson, the diplomat; Frances Hodgson Burnett of *Little Lord Fauntleroy* fame; the composer Reginald DeKoven; and the newspaper owner "Cissy" Patterson were but a few of the Potomac nobility in residence.

The residents strove to place their cultural pretensions on sound footing by encouraging a Shakespeare Club, the Friday Morning Music Club (still extant), and the seminal Literary Society. Social obligations were dizzyingly heavy. Ladies were expected to give one "at home" per week and to make hundreds of house calls during "The Season." The burden was too much for one young congressional wife, who fled terrified through her kitchen during her first at home, re-entering through the front door to mingle with the scrutinizing guests and whisper that perhaps they ought to leave, since she knew the absent lady of the house to be "a rather odd sort of person." Then there were the neighbors who were bitter political enemies, like the Woodrow Wilsons, in residence on S Street after 1923, and the Cabot Lodges nearby, whom circle hostesses were careful never to commingle in intimate gatherings. No such complications pestered invitations to Secretary of Commerce Herbert Hoover and his popular wife, another circle area family.

Contrary to Henry Adams's haughty dismissal of the regions beyond Lafayette Square, by the early 1900s Dupont Circle, for architectural extravagance and social brilliance, had pulled well ahead of Adams's neighborhood. There was nothing on Lafayette Park like the forty-room neoclassical Lars Anderson House, built in 1905, which houses today the museum and records of the Society of the Cincinnati; and it would be to the vast Townsend House (of roughly the same vintage) that the Cosmos Club would move, in the early fifties, from its Lafayette Square quarters. Half-million-dollar mansions were springing up like mushrooms. None was ever comparable to that of Thomas Walsh, the Irishman from Colorado with a Midas touch, who settled in Washington and commissioned an $835,000 palace in 1901, embedding a hunk of gold ore from his mine in the entry. Walsh's daughter, Evalyn, was the last private owner of the fabulous Hope Diamond, whose curse had undone a string of wealthy collectors. The legend of the curse appeared to be true, for accidental deaths and insanity racked the Walshes, and also the McLeans, Evalyn's husband's family, from the sunrise to the twilight of their social reign. But Edward B. McLean, owner of the *Washington Post,* and his well-dowered Evalyn made the best of adversity in the father's sixty-room, beaux arts marble colossus at 2020 Massachusetts Avenue. Its present occupant, the Indonesian Embassy, has taken admirable care to leave its basic structure untouched.

If, for swank, nothing quite matched the Walsh-McLean House, for zestful eccentricity, few homes anywhere in America were comparable with the New Hampshire Avenue Christian Heurich Mansion. The style is defiantly eclectic. Often labelled Victorian, though clearly marked by Gothic influences, it is purely and simply an architectural sport which one writer says H. H. Richardson "himself would not have built." Of massive, rust-colored stone, festooned with catalogue-ordered gargoyles and unbalanced by a corner tower capped by a conical roof, the 1894 town house has somehow escaped demolition and appropriately serves now as the home of the Columbia Historical Society. Under the porte-cochère and through the portals, the occasional visitor is transported to another century, though which is not sure. A gilded, baroque front parlor with painted ceiling; a dining hall after the heart of Ludwig II of Bavaria, with intricately carved oak panelling on walls and ceiling; the music room with carved musicians' mezzanine; in the basement a "Germanic Victorian" *Bierstube* (well used by Mr. Heurich until his death at 105); on the staircase a filigree railing in brass and at the foot a newel post sprouting an *art nouveau* light fixture, one of many—the Heurich Mansion makes you laugh with rather than at it.

When the *New York Times* rediscovered Dupont Circle in a 1969 illustrated article, almost a half-century had unfolded since the days of its pre-eminence among the city's communities. The shuttered embassy of the last Romanov, the relocation of the British Embassy, the ravages of the Great Depression, and the arrival of a less ostentatious generation helped to take the bloom off the circle by the late twenties. Alice Roosevelt Longworth and President Wilson's widow maintained their *grandes dames* level of entertainment during the thirties as if nothing had changed. "Cissy" Patterson, too rich to notice the depression, lived on in regal anachronism in the forty-room marble hyperbole designed by Stanford White, the headquarters today of the Washington Club. Until the late twenties, Andrew Mellon resided in the McCormick Apartment House where his neighbor on the floor above, Lord Duveen, the art merchant, contrived to meet and interest the treasury secretary in conversation about old masters.

If the area was already beginning to slip, certainly the presence of a Mellon disguised the fact, as did the residency of Robert Woods Bliss, U. S. Grant III, and William D. Leahy. Upper Dupont Circle staved off the wrecker's ball, the luxury high-rise apartments, and the commercial buildings more successfully than the area in the circle's immediate vicinity. The circle itself, though still impressive, has been ringed by banks, hotels, and office buildings. The era of forty-room town houses steadily succumbed to the plethora of New Deal agencies requiring office space and to the city's wartime population explosion. Indicative of the altered state of the neighborhood was the needless destruction, in 1966, of the National Presbyterian Church at Eighteenth and N streets, and Connecticut Avenue, over the strenuous protest of the Dupont Circle Citizens' Association. Thus crumbled one of the city's finest examples of Romanesque architecture.

The author of the Sunday *Times* article also wrote of the upswing in circle restoration during the 1960s. The surviving great mansions are spoken for by embassies and staid societies, but along the cross streets (where dwellings were less palatial) four-bedroom houses were being snapped up for thirty-five thousand dollars and remodelled in the manner of Georgetown and Capitol Hill. On Corcoran Street, under the inspiration of families like the Emmanuel Levines and the Robert Meehans, restoration was virtually complete by the end of the sixties. And the trend continues.

There was another Dupont Circle during the decade—one which threatened to frighten away potential middle-class home-owners. Had the martial figure of Admiral du Pont not been removed in 1921 to make way for the present memorial fountain, he would have stared down upon scenes more humiliating to his dignity than the one in Charleston Harbor one hundred years before. The beginning of the invasion by the youth occurred early in the decade. As good a date as any is 1963, when one Eddie Hicks was arrested for playing his guitar under a tree in Dupont Circle Park. According to the *Washington Post*'s Leroy Aarons, newspaper accounts of Hicks's arrest caught the attention of the young and the park became a symbol of their revolt against conventions. They came in droves, summer after summer, remaining well into autumn. Each evening the decibel level rose higher as the cacophony of percussion and string instruments, accompanied by or competing with shrill voices, crashed into the avenues.

The circle became a national magnet for beatniks, hippies, gays, and runaways, freaks, flower children, and adults who were children. At first, the kids caroused harmlessly, the gays cruised candidly, and the drug of choice for most was pot. Otis Redding and Janis Joplin music set the mood of the crowds. Then the Vietnam War and the worsening racial strife changed the environment. Hard drugs, crime, political rallies, and confrontations with the police turned Dupont Park into a maelstrom of dissidence and violence. The storm has gone the way of the clash of generations and the war, and the park is being recaptured by middle-class singles and families. Despite the shabby end of the youth occupation, there are a few bar-stool radicals who somewhat regret its passing.

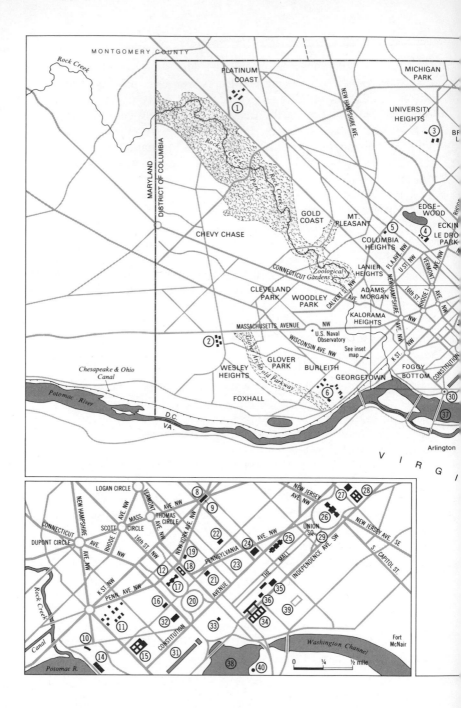

MONTGOMERY COUNTY

PLATINUM
COAST

MICHIGAN
PARK

①

UNIVERSITY
HEIGHTS

NEW HAMPSHIRE AVE.

③

BF
L

Rock Creek

Rock Creek

MARYLAND

DISTRICT OF COLUMBIA

Rock Creek Park

GOLD
COAST

MT.
PLEASANT

EDGE-
WOOD

ECKIN
LE DRO
PARK

④

CHEVY CHASE

⑤

COLUMBIA
HEIGHTS

FLA. AVE. NW

U ST. NW

VERMONT AVE. NW

16th ST. NW

RHODE I. AVE. NW

RHOTE

CONNECTICUT

Zoological
Gardens

LANIER
HEIGHTS

CLEVELAND
PARK

WOODLEY
PARK

CALVERT AVE.

ADAMS
MORGAN

KALORAMA
HEIGHTS

NEW HAMPSHIRE AVE. NW

NW

MASSACHUSETTS   AVENUE   NW

U.S. Naval
Observatory

②

WISCONSIN AVE. NW

Glover Archbold Parkway

GLOVER
PARK

See inset
map

K. ST.

FOGGY
BOTTOM

Chesapeake & Ohio
Canal

WESLEY
HEIGHTS

BURLEITH

GEORGETOWN

CONSTITUTION

⑥

㉚

Potomac River

FOXHALL

㉟

D.C.
VA.

Arlington

V I R G I

LOGAN CIRCLE

⑧

NEW JERSEY
AVE. NW

㉗

㉘

⑨

NEW HAMPSHIRE

VERMONT   AVE. NW

MASS.

THOMAS
CIRCLE

NEW YORK AVE. NW

㉖

NEW JERSEY AVE. SE

CONNECTICUT

SCOTT

CIRCLE

AVE. NW

㉒

UNION
SQ.

DUPONT CIRCLE

AVE.

RHODE I.

16th ST. NW

㉔

AVE. NW

㉕

㉙

INDEPENDENCE AVE. SW

S. CAPITOL ST.

NW

⑲

PENNSYLVANIA

㉓

THE MALL

Rock Creek

⑫

⑱

K ST. NW

⑰

㉑

㉟

PENN. AVE. NW

AVENUE

㊱

㊴

Canal

⑯

⑳

㉞

⑪

㉜

㉝

Washington Channel

Fort
McNair

⑩

CONSTITUTION

⑭

⑮

㉛

㊳

㊵

0   ¼   ½ mile

Potomac R.

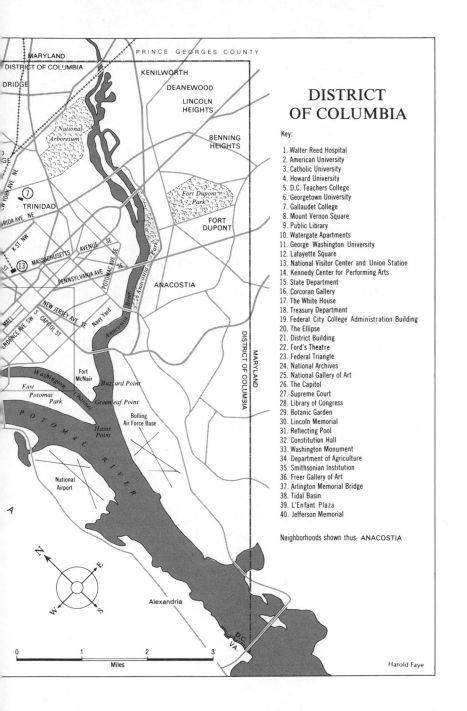

DISTRICT
OF COLUMBIA

Key:

1. Walter Reed Hospital
2. American University
3. Catholic University
4. Howard University
5. D.C. Teachers College
6. Georgetown University
7. Gallaudet College
8. Mount Vernon Square
9. Public Library
10. Watergate Apartments
11. George Washington University
12. Lafayette Square
13. National Visitor Center and Union Station
14. Kennedy Center for Performing Arts
15. State Department
16. Corcoran Gallery
17. The White House
18. Treasury Department
19. Federal City College Administration Building
20. The Ellipse
21. District Building
22. Ford's Theatre
23. Federal Triangle
24. National Archives
25. National Gallery of Art
26. The Capitol
27. Supreme Court
28. Library of Congress
29. Botanic Garden
30. Lincoln Memorial
31. Reflecting Pool
32. Constitution Hall
33. Washington Monument
34. Department of Agriculture
35. Smithsonian Institution
36. Freer Gallery of Art
37. Arlington Memorial Bridge
38. Tidal Basin
39. L'Enfant Plaza
40. Jefferson Memorial

Neighborhoods shown thus: ANACOSTIA

Harold Faye

Iowa Circle is known today as Logan Circle, Civil War Gen. John A. Logan belatedly receiving congressional recognition in 1930. On L'Enfant's original map, this intersection was a square until it was redrawn by Ellicott. It was developed about two decades before Dupont Circle, during the heyday of Boss Shepherd's building spree, and remains the most complete example of what prosperous Washington was like during the Gilded Age. Its high Victorian houses, though outsized by present standards, were modest by comparison with some of the marble behemoths on Dupont Circle. It was, in fact, the nurturing of Dupont Circle as the domain of the rich and the mighty which contributed to the decline of Iowa Circle after the 1880s, for, although there were rich residents around the circle, the real rich went to Dupont. Most of Logan's people belonged to the newly affluent middle class who desired, as the *Star-News* recalled, "to emulate the spectacular, gaudy mansions of the robber barons, but on a smaller scale." [6]

Logan Circle's architecture has been known to sober the tippling tourist nocturnally wandering through, such a marvel of the weird is it. Wolf Von Eckardt, the *Washington Post*'s architectural critic, has felicitously dubbed the style "Charles Addams Whim." There is a dollop of just about every architectural possibility; and yet the circle possesses the reasonableness of a Lewis Carroll limerick (internally coherent if a bit mad by normal standards). The owners of these houses ordered external embellishments from the same catalogue—loggias, pinnacles, turrets, widow's walks, bays, and so on—which they amalgamated with abandon. Side by side, the hybrid mansions rose, Italianate, second empire, Romanesque, Victorian.

Around the turn of the century Logan Circle began to change colors, to become black. Not all of the newcomers were less affluent than their striving predecessors, and almost all were as socially proper. For a time it was the professional and intellectual hub of black Washington, a diminutive Dupont Circle. The boxer, Jack Johnson, the religious leader, Bishop Charles M. ("Sweet Daddy") Grace, and Congressman Adam Clayton

6. *Washington Star-News*, January 19, 1975.

Powell, Jr., were just a few of the neighborhood's distinguished homeowners. Then, shortly after World War Two, the black bourgeoisie began leaving for the more modern, affluent enclaves of Brookland, upper Sixteenth Street, and North Portal Estates. Logan Circle's ten- and twenty-room dwellings were converted into boardinghouses and apartments. It was only a matter of time before the district commissioners, ever obedient to the House District Committee, approved the mutilation of the circle. "There has been no public hearing on the project," the *Daily News* neutrally commented in 1950, "and the Commissioners did not indicate they plan to hold any. It is considered merely a street improvement, a spokesman said." [7] The mere street improvement entailed slicing the circle's terrain with two wide roadways forming a parenthesis within the ring of the original artery. Today, General Logan's equestrian likeness prances in the heart of a circle whose ventricles are clotted by automobiles and busses. A few benches and exiguous trees are all that remain of a once green and shaded roundabout.

One of the penalties of what can only be described as colonial rule—congressional autocracy in District affairs—has been lumpish, official insouciance in matters of historic preservation. Logan Circle has survived the commercial and luxury high-rise fate of nearby Thomas Circle largely through neglect and luck. When Capt. H. C. Whitehurst, the District's chief engineer, proposed splitting Thomas and Logan circles by a highway, in 1931, Congress shelved his scheme for the duration of the depression. In 1964, when local real estate interests petitioned the zoning commission to authorize nine-story apartment buildings, the National Capital Planning Commission, supported by citizens' groups, just barely won a deferral. Eight years later, the preservationists were strong enough to nudge the Department of the Interior into designating Logan Circle a national historic district. In 1973, the Redevelopment Land Agency commissioned architect Nicholas Satterlee to study the area and prepare a comprehensive report, which Satterlee did in August of the same year. Although Satterlee's report appears to be lost in the

7. *Washington Daily News,* June 14, 1950.

vast files of the now defunct RLA, that special brand of private restorationist in which Washington excels has begun tentatively to renovate the neighborhood. Recently, the city has even toyed with plans to restore the circle's terrain to its original dimensions.

From Logan Circle, Rhode Island Avenue leads to the Le Droit Park neighborhood, one of the oldest developed outside the immediate limits of the original city. Le Droit stretches from Florida north between Seventh and Second streets, N.W., to Howard University. The neighborhood was assembled from four tracts of land known as the Miller, Gilman, Prather, and McClelland properties, which Howard's first president, Gen. O. O. Howard, purchased in anticipation of the university's expansion. When debts expanded more rapidly than the school's need for space, the general sold the four properties to a group of developers headed by Howard's white vice-president, the Reverend A. L. Barber. Four years later, in 1877, the Le Droit developers were able to issue an illustrated pamphlet announcing that ". . . eight large brick residences have been erected on the north side and ten on the south side of Maple Avenue [T Street]." On Elm (the only street still bearing its original name), Harewood (Third Street), and Spruce (U Street) avenues, more gabled homes rapidly followed. Purchase prices ranged from four to twelve thousand dollars. Vice-President Barber was careful not to mix Le Droit Park business with Howard University philanthropy. The few blacks who might have afforded his houses were signalled that their money was unwelcome. Not only were they unwelcome as residents, Le Droiters erected a wooden fence to force the blacks of Howard Town to circumnavigate their neighborhood when travelling to and from downtown Washington. Le Droiters won the 1889 law suit over their fence, but it was pulled down as rapidly as they repaired it. In 1890, the barbed wire replacement was permanently removed.

Le Droit Park remained exclusively white until the late 1890s. By then, Barber, having long since recouped his investment several times over, had transferred his energies to 120 acres northwest of Le Droit Park, the future Columbia Heights area. Gradually, prosperous blacks moved into the park until, by 1930, *The National Capital Magazine* reported, "now *only one* white family remains." The author added, "It is still an attractive, orderly suburb, only the tint of the complexions of the inhabitants has changed."

Christian Fleetwood, a sergeant-major and Medal of Honor winner in the Civil War, was the first acknowledged black to purchase in Le Droit Park. Invariably known as "the Major," Fleetwood taught drill and trained the spit-and-polish cadet corps at Dunbar High School. Paul Laurence Dunbar, the brilliant, tubercular poet, was among the earliest of the new residents. He and his attractive wife, Alice, lived there while the poet worked as an assistant to the librarian of Congress. The first black municipal judge, Robert H. Terrell, and his militant wife, Mary Church, moved to the park where they were soon joined by the Benjamin Davis, Sr., family. Davis would become the army's first black brigadier. Clarence Cameron White, composer and violinist, spent most of his professional life there. The blood plasma developer, Charles Drew, was another distinguished resident. With its encircling porches and spacious lawns bordered by aureoles of flowers ("the flower garden of Washington"), Le Droit Park was a diminutive Logan Circle where black cave-dweller families raised future wives of notables and West Point generals.

The ebb and flow of urban life has been unkind to Le Droit Park. Washington is divided into nine administrative or service areas. Le Droit Park is in Service Area Seven which, according to *A Demographic, Social, Economic, and Physical Profile of the District of Columbia,* is one of three containing more than half the 20,740 families living in poverty. Census tract 92, one of the city's most impoverished, abuts the neighborhood, dumping into it vandalism, burglary, drug-related crime, and gang warfare. A 1961 *Star* article reported that Le Droiters were being terrorized by the "Ramblers," marauding, pistol-packing juveniles from elsewhere. A decade later, conditions had continued to worsen: Le Droit's sixty-five hundred residents earned a median per capita income of $2,000 ($3,992 below the city median), and one-third of them were elderly. "Le Droit Park's

154 DISTRICT OF COLUMBIA

Two Faces," a 1971 *Washington Post* story, found that some of the more desperate Le Droiters had established a six-man "court" in the rear of a local barber shop to administer beatings to young hoodlums. Although the heart of the neighborhood is still well-kept, creeping decay seems irreversible, even though the mayor, Walter Washington, lives there. (A few doors from the mayor's home, Paul Laurence Dunbar's home was recently demolished.) Perhaps, nevertheless, the special if belated interest of Howard University's School of Architecture in the area and the location there of the university's new hospital will restore some of the bloom.

The poverty that began lapping at many of the older neighborhoods in the early 1950s and that turned into a floodtide by the early 1970s spreads to all sections of the city—even in sparsely populated Service Area Nine. Area Nine's eastern border slices the Capitol and contains the White House, Federal Triangle, luxurious Southwest, and much of commercial Washington, but census tracts 60.2 and 64 list 69 and 45 percent, respectively, of Area Nine residents below the poverty line. Service Area Four in Anacostia (including both Southeast and Southwest) is blighted by the horrible census tract 74.4, the triangular section bordered by Saint Elizabeth's Hospital, Suitland Parkway, and Alabama Avenue, where crammed public housing projects such as Frederick Douglass and Stanton account for a poverty ratio of 37 percent. By far, though, the majority of the city's 20,740 families earning less than $5,000 annually in 1970 lived in Service Areas Five, Six and Seven, the areas encompassing the center or inner city. These are the sections which have provided, in recent presidential elections, dubious credence to charges that Washington is the "crime capital" of the nation and that it has been ghetto-ized almost beyond redemption.

With a population of 114,400, Service Area Seven, comprised of Adams-Morgan, Edgewood, Eckington, Upper Cardozo, Columbia Heights, Lanier Heights, Le Droit Park, Mount Pleasant, and part of Dupont Circle, has the heaviest concentration of District poor—twenty-three thousand people, more than one in five. Service Area Seven's central region, stretching from Six-

teenth to North Capitol streets above Florida Avenue and below
Spring Road, has 55 percent of its population struggling below
the poverty line. It contains all the expected horrors of urban
destitution—fatherless families (about 40 percent headed by
women), disease, lawlessness, drug use, children attending
schools providing custodial care at best and on-the-job instruction in crime at worst, and a milieu characterized by total alien-
ation. Service Area Seven breeds much of the once supposedly
pandemic crime.

This part of the city, despite its blight, is one of the most
varied. If the Fourteenth Street corridor has lost much of its
demimonde glamor and many of its shops and clubs to the riots,
it is still the place where music, sex, drugs, fenced merchandise, pornographic literature, whatever, are available. A block
away, on Thirteenth Street's cross streets, there are row on row
of three-story brick houses that would be the envy of any Capitol Hill renovator but for their location. Some are mere shells,
teeming with matrifocal welfare families, rats, and roaches. In
others, however, the working—hard-working—poor maintain a
semblance of domestic grace and hygiene. Such families are, in
fact, in the majority. More than 55 percent of the total family
population in Area Seven has income from wages, although 20
percent of all income is supplemented by social security or
railroad retirement benefits.

On Clifton Street, the Clifton Terrace Apartments, early
twentieth-century luxury units designed by Harry Wardman, tes-
tify to what can be accomplished with community imagination,
minority business involvement, and public funding. Once one of
the worst high-rise complexes in the city, "a shorthand expres-
sion for exploitation, rent gouging, rats, roaches, deteriorating
services," according to *Washington Post* columnist William
Raspberry, Clifton Terrace was gutted and remodelled in the
early 1970s to provide moderate rental units with minimal displacement of the tenants. The Reverend Channing Phillips, a
black political activist in the Kennedy mold, helped organize the
Housing Development Corporation which purchased and renovated the complex. Aided by funds and technical assistance
from Boise Cascade Corporation and by loan guarantees from

the Department of Housing and Urban Development, Clifton Terrace Apartments, after heartbreaking delays and dumb mistakes, was ready for occupancy in mid-1972. But in less than a year the Housing Development Corporation directors had learned that by no means all the woes of the old Clifton Terrace had been the fault of its slumlord. What would have been just another costly miscarriage in the delivery of low-cost housing to low-income minority people currently has bright prospects for reaching maturity. Pride Incorporated, a local black mini-conglomerate created by city Councilman Marion Barry, now runs Clifton Terrace with a pitiless efficiency that would have made General Grant III flinch. As columnist Raspberry explains, "Pride has built for itself the sort of reputation that makes it possible to institute such no-nonsense policy without criticism." Pride seems to be proving that low-income housing can pay and that the poor can be encouraged to surmount the stereotyped behavior inherent in their poverty.

The real variety in this part of Washington comes with the Adams-Morgan area, a neighborhood shaped somewhat like the map of the United States, extending due north from Florida Avenue and U Street to Calvert and Lanier streets and Columbia Road, and bounded on the east by Sixteenth Street, on the west by Connecticut Avenue, Belmont Street, and West Side Drive. "In a city of sharp contrasts between rich and poor, renaissance and decay," said the *Washington Post,* "the neighborhood around Eighteenth Street and Columbia Road, N.W. seems perplexingly headed several ways at once." [8] This is the unique part of town reminiscent of sections in most large cities of the United States—ethnic areas where English has to compete, where customs are exotic, the food in the markets and restaurants superb, and the locals contagiously alive. In 1965, the population of Adams-Morgan was about seventeen thousand, more than half of which was nonwhite. More than a decade later, there are somewhat fewer whites and the population has slightly increased. Reluctantly, the shabby-regal apartment buildings were evacuated by most of their elderly white resi-

8. February 12, 1970.

dents and replaced by the poor, the marginal, and the upwardly mobile, almost all nonwhite and a near majority from Central or South America.

For middle-class families, the neighborhood became a purgatory. But the basic excellence of its housing stock still attracts adventurously liberal, middle-class white families. One such family, too pioneering and heroic, perhaps, to have been typical, dug in until the soil itself began to wash away. "From 1950, when I moved into the neighborhood, until 1958 . . . ," the anonymous family head confided,

> I watched the very rapid downhill progress of the area. The section in which I lived, considered the least deteriorated, was composed of fifty percent rooming and tenement houses at that time, and life was getting a bit strained. Between 1956 and 1958, my home was robbed four times (twice while I was in it), my car was stolen, then the wheels were stolen off it, my youngest daughter, aged four, was sexually accosted; purses were being snatched with uncomfortable regularity; roaming bands of disorderly teen-agers were afoot late at night; my home was worth about $20,000 less than I had in it. . . .[9]

Between 1950 and 1960, the median value of homes dropped from $19,196 to $16,400. Population dropped 17 percent in the decade after 1950. Still, there were young professionals like W. Deaver Kehne, a white physician, who explained his still being in Adams-Morgan in 1964 "because of a dream I had about life and people in America. . . . Practically the entire economic, social, racial, and cultural spectrum is represented here." [10]

Washington's local establishment realized that Adams-Morgan was too well endowed and too strategic to the city's core to lose. They feared that the buildings along Sixteenth Street, Mrs. Henderson's "Avenue of the Presidents," and mel-

9. Cited in Hope Marindin, "Adams-Morgan: Democratic Action Fails to Save a Neighborhood," George Washington University, 1967, p. 6.
10. "Urban Renewal Plan for Adams-Morgan Renewal Area," Redevelopment Land Agency Document, RLA Library, p. 9.

low Kalorama Triangle, a contiguous neighborhood, would decay beyond hope. The establishment moved with resolute circumspection. In mid-1958, the privately funded Bureau of Social Science Research undertook an impressionistic survey of Adams-Morgan's economic and social conditions. Its report was both a confirmation of fears and a corroboration of potential. At the end of the year, supported by a grant from the Housing and Home Finance Agency, Dean Richard M. Bray of American University mounted the Adams-Morgan Demonstration Project, a model example of university involvement in community affairs. During the two years of American University's pioneering activities in the neighborhood, some twenty-six community organizations coalesced and agreed upon a common program of renewal.

Approximately 114 acres were suggested for renewal with federal funds (about 28 percent of the total); the remainder was to be privately redeveloped. Light industry (printing, auto repair) in the Columbia Road area was to be evacuated and low-cost public housing and a complementary garage constructed. What became known as areas A and B exactly coincided with census tract 40—Adams-Morgan—and were separated by Columbia Road. Area B was poorer and blacker. Area A embraced Kalorama Triangle (bounded by Calvert to the north, Columbia to the east, Connecticut to the west; and with its southern point snipped by Kalorama Road), populated by senators and foreign dignitaries. The plan called for building row housing for moderate-income families in the triangle. In June 1960, Donald Gartenhaus of Furs by Gartenhaus became director of the Adams-Morgan Demonstration Project. In late July, despite some eleventh-hour opposition, the citizens of the neighborhood adopted the plan by a large majority. On August 14, the District commissioners gave their formal approval, authorizing the Redevelopment Land Agency (RLA) to apply to the Housing and Home Finance Agency for a grant to draft a final master plan.

What happened after 1960 is both unclear and complicated. The attitude of two powerful residents of Kalorama Triangle foretold trouble for the plan. In November 1959, Senators William Fulbright of Arkansas and Leverett Saltonstall of Massachusetts, among others, publicly protested the District zoning commission's decision to permit row housing in their community. At the July public hearing in 1960, John L. Barr, Jr., speaking for the Kalorama Triangle Restoration Association, wondered if area A should not be excluded from the plan in order not to "impede the restoration work already underway by creating an uncertainty in the public mind concerning the future of the neighborhood, thus disturbing the image so far created of a stable, high class urban residential area." [11] At the same hearing, congressional administrative assistant J. George Frain, owner of a co-op apartment house on Lanier Place, presented a petition signed by seventy-nine property owners opposed to publicly funded redevelopment. While the Redevelopment Land Agency and the National Capital Planning Commission (NCPC) perfected the plan, opposition hardened. "Unfortunately," the *Star* editorialized in 1962, "a few irresponsible citizens are attempting to create the view that disunity and factionalism have split this area, that residents' interests oppose business interests, that race opposes race, that class opposes class. This is untrue." [12] The Urban League was of the same opinion, charging that the light industry interests were sabotaging Adams-Morgan redevelopment.

Nineteen sixty-three was a bad year for Adams-Morgan. Congressman John Dowdy of Athens, Texas (population seven thousand), was the new chairman of the Housing Subcommittee of the Committee on Banking and Currency. Dowdy's name was also a fitting description of the congressman's politics. Federal funds for social engineering were anathema to the subcommittee chairman. Sixteen witnesses appeared before his subcommittee over a three-day period, only one of whom (Donald Gartenhaus) spoke favorably of the Adams-Morgan plan. Perhaps the unkindest cut was the withdrawal of the Henderson castle property from the plan. Mrs. Eugene Meyer, owner of the *Washington Post,* had donated this property to be used as a park for industry displaced by the plan. However, in April, she an-

11. Marindin, "Adams-Morgan," p. 20.
12. *Washington Star,* July 11, 1962.

nounced that it was being placed in trust for her children. One writer alleges, reasonably enough, that ''a number of the white residents of area A hoped to restore the area by the use of private funds in a manner similar to that used in Georgetown and Capitol Hill.'' On February 4, 1965, the directors of NCPC indefinitely tabled the Adams-Morgan plan by a vote of six to four.

The Georgetown–Capitol Hill dreams of J. George Frain's supporters will probably come to pass. Young professionals (almost all white) are painting and patching solid three-story houses with the frenzy of their Capitol Hill models. Along and off the Columbia Road there is a new aura of trendiness. Mercedes sedans and Volvo wagons double-park in front of Fields of Plenty on Eighteenth Street, a co-op offering soybeans, whole grains, and fresh fish at greatly reduced prices. The Omega, once the cheapest feed in the city, has burst through the walls of an adjacent building in order to accommodate the polyglot, scruffy-to-Foggy-Bottom-neat clientele washing down black beans and paella with Central American beers and domestic wines. Farther down Columbia Road, El Caribe, an authentic Hispanic restaurant, offers flawless service, devastating Pisco sours, good Flamenco guitarists (mercifully, no castanets), and sauces without compare. One of the major casualties of urban renewal retrenchment (federal) was the New Thing for Art and Architecture, a vibrant, free-form community center headed by the brilliant young black Yale graduate, Topper Carew.

Congressman Dowdy's highhanded hostility only accelerated the demise of the Adams-Morgan plan. The lesson of the failure seems to be that inevitably, private restoration means deportation of the poor and the aged. Adams-Morgan is still a decade away from massive middle-class displacement of the blacks and Hispanics, but, in the absence of a comprehensive plan and public funds for low-cost housing, only a depressed national economy will delay its certain *embourgeoisement*.

In early April 1967, Nicholas Von Hoffman explored an area which he called ''Lower Cardozo.'' Von Hoffman's description of its geography—from Mount Vernon Square to Florida Avenue—squarely fixed his terrain as being in what is usually known as the Shaw neighborhood and now officially designated the model cities area. Von Hoffman was smack in the middle of Service Area Six, the second-worst of Washington's nine area divisions. Twenty-nine percent of the Area Six population subsists below the poverty line, rising to 41 percent for families trapped in its central portion. Von Hoffman had found the real poor:

> They are the mute poor who sing no folk songs, who carry no placards but who pile in front of the Rent-A-Man office on Seventh Street, and stand, swaying and shivering, asking each other for money. They are the disgusting poor with bad teeth and sores on their skins who loiter in unsteady torpor in front of 'Chester's Express Shoe Shine Parlor' on P around the corner from the Ninth Street UPO office.[13]

Seventh Street, notorious in Jean Toomer's day for its ballooning, zooming Cadillacs, is Shaw's principal artery. The title for Langston Hughes's 1927 poem, "Fine Clothes to the Jew," was suggested by the street's profusion of pawn shops among the bars, pool halls, and flophouses. Since Toomer's and Hughes's day things have gone from bad to worse on Seventh Street—much of it, indeed, no longer exists because of the 1968 riot. One or two apartment buildings for moderate-income families have gone up; a complex of town houses (incredibly expensive to build) has been completed under the guidance of the Reverend Walter Fauntroy's community organization and in conjunction with RLA; Shaw Junior High School—"Shameful Shaw," a custodial Bastille at the intersection of Seventh and Rhode Island Avenue—will soon be replaced by a modern facility. The promise made by President Nixon, during a tour on foot of the area, of federal funds to rebuild has been indefinitely postponed.

Elliot Liebow has written a classic study of Washington ghetto life—*Tally's Corner*. Liebow's street corner is somewhere "within walking distance of the White House, the Smithsonian Institution, and other major public buildings of the na-

13. "Cardozo," *Washington Post,* April 9, 1967.

tion's capital.'' It might very well have been located in Area Six. The cast of twenty characters, semi- and unemployed black males who gather daily in front of the New Deal Carry-out, runs the gamut of personality types in the ghetto, from the strong-willed, brawny Tally and the lean, ''cool,'' ''Sea Cat'' to Richard the unconvincing braggart, and ''Bumdoodle'' the numbers runner. They have taken wives and fathered batches of children but the entangling responsibilities of family life have caused them to flee to the corner where they excuse their defections in a chorus of platitudes about real men being such ''natural born dogs'' that fidelity is unnatural. They may catechize themselves about better days to come, but Liebow deftly catches the prevailing sullen despair. Too many children to support on occasional wages, harried from their homes by welfare laws inimical to families with live-in fathers, these men know themselves for the social detritus they are.

But even in Area Six those who congregate on corners are in a minority. Two years after Liebow's book, Ulf Hannerz wrote *Soulside: Inquiries into the Ghetto Culture and Community* (1969), a less famous but no less instructive exploration of Washington's black poor. The locus of the study, the fictional Winston Street, ''a long, narrow residential street in the ghetto,'' may be almost anywhere in the city, but for present purposes, Area Six will claim it. Hannerz encountered three basic family models. There were the ''street families,'' the households deserted by Tally and his corner cohorts. Grandparents were absent. Drinking was heavy. Children ran wild and mothers sifted lovers like sand. Each day was an eternity; no concept of futurity existed. Then there were the ''swingers,'' some married but most not, people who could have been upwardly mobile but who preferred sybaritic dissipation of wages to frugality.

Hannerz described a third and final category in Winston Street—the ''mainstreamers''—families conforming closely to middle-class ideals. ''We want to get to a place where it isn't so noisy and where people aren't so rowdy,'' mainstreamers said. Often, these families were strengthened by the presence of grandparents who released husbands and wives into the labor market and enforced domestic discipline in the absence of the latter. Hannerz also spelled out the positive role of street-corner men which Liebow left to inference. "Again and again the men intervene when play brings the children too close to dangerous traffic," *Soulside* reports. "Sometimes they seek out the parents to tell them to take better care of their children." Von Hoffman's "disgusting poor" were not without redeeming qualities.

Area Six then, even with its riot damage and brownstone rot, is not a total disaster. Above Burnham's Union Station, now the National Visitors Center, North Capitol Street courses between Massachusetts and New York avenues, slicing laser-like through what were once some of the city's worst communities. In 1963, the halcyon days of city planning, RLA and NCHA set aside more than ninety acres on either side of North Capitol for urban renewal, the territory east of the street being reserved for light industrial and commercial development and that west for low-income housing (and renamed Northwest Urban Renewal). "It is a good thing," the *Star* editorialized, "for much of the City's future hopes for urban renewal are riding on the successful completion of this ambitious experiment." [14] To make sure that massive federal funding and shotgun condemnation proceedings would not result in the usual diaspora of the area's seven thousand poor, the Urban League organized a Neighborhood Development Center whose members raucously demanded consultation with and safeguards from city planners. With uncustomary enlightenment, the city government agreed to stagger the construction over a ten-year period and to guarantee the residents priority accommodations in the new garden and high-rise apartments. The city also exercised commendable supervision of building designs. Golden Rule, Sibley Plaza, and Tyler House, the huge apartment structures fronting North Capitol Street, are unusually well constructed, with balconies and entrances given a touch of the refinement of luxury housing. Sursum Corda garden apartments, with sharply sloping roofs and varied facades, and many with five and six bedrooms, have escaped the dormitory uniformity typical of the genre. Su-

14. September 23, 1966.

perficially, Northwest Urban Renewal was a neighborhood that worked according to plan. But there were increasingly bitter second thoughts in the air.

In October 1970, RLA's assistant director, Roy Priest, submitted his report to the agency, warning of disaster if middle-class families were excluded from Northwest Urban Renewal and if recreational, shopping, and expanded educational facilities were not included. The commitments to the original residents, Department of Housing and Urban Development regulations, and bureaucratic inertia combined to fix family income ceilings at a level too low to allow admission of middle-income residents. Resigning from RLA, Priest told the *Washington Post* in early 1971 that the area had become a "concrete jungle."

"Eight years of urban renewal . . . near the Capitol is creating a low income ghetto without adequate shopping, schools, or other community facilities," he charged.[15] One Safeway supermarket and the Martin Luther King, Jr., co-operative were serving eight thousand people. The Safeway soon abandoned its plant and the successful King co-op, a plucky black-owned business, eventually closed to make way for a railroad overpass. The shopping problem has been alleviated recently by the new Golden Rule supermarket, a Baptist enterprise comparable in commodity offerings and prices to the city's two large supermarket chains but hard pressed to meet the needs singlehandedly of a community now numbering more than ten thousand. Sursum Corda, the garden apartment complex owned by the Washington Roman Catholic archdiocese, has raised, in government, denominational, and foundation funds, most of the two million dollars needed for its recreation center. Northwest Urban Renewal's prognosis is uncertain. It may follow the pattern of Chicago's multimillion dollar high-rise ghettoes or become, like Saint Louis's Pruitt-Igoe, an aberrant solution even worse than the original problem. There is a good chance nevertheless, that community pride will stave off such an outcome. Moreover, as commercial and federal buildings advance along the North Capitol Street corridor, this will very likely encourage the city gov-

15. "Renewal Project Criticized," January 23, 1971.

ernment to expand playground and school facilities. And paren-
thetically, a note of commendation is owed Gonzaga College
High School, an excellent Roman Catholic school in the community which has elected to remain, to expand facilities, and
whose students are achievers with the *éclat* redolent of the old
Dunbar.

Outside the three central hardcore poverty areas—Service
Areas Five, Six, and Seven—there are dozens of neighborhoods
reproducing the depressed conditions so far described. But if
poverty exists everywhere in the city, it is not everywhere dominant. Across the Anacostia River, there is Service Area Three,
the fastest-growing section of Washington, with a population of
89,449, of which 96.4 percent is black. It contains the greatest
percentage of juveniles—slightly more than two-fifths of its
families are headed (officially) by females. Its slums are eye-
sores. But Area Three is by no means overrun by grim housing
or overpopulated by the poor. Its twenty-odd neighborhoods
range from well-cared-for Fort Dupont to valiantly middle-class
Kenilworth to ragged Deanewood and slum-ridden Benning
Ridge. Only 19 percent of the families in Northeast earn less
than $4,000. Twenty-one percent earn between $10,000 and
$14,999. Thirteen percent figure in the $15,000-plus category.
Obviously, mainstreamers live cheek-by-jowl with street families in Service Area Three. Similar extremes characterize Service Area Four, also across the Anacostia River.

Area Two in upper Northeast, the second smallest by population, has its pockets of poverty, but it is also one of the richest,
embracing Brookland, Brentwood Village, University Heights,
and Langdon, Michigan Park, Fort Lincoln, and Woodridge. A
small number of the city's whites, about nine thousand, live
here, mostly within walking distance of Catholic University, or
in Brentwood. Blacks who live here generally live well. In
Brookland, they live very well indeed. A 1965 report prepared
by the Bureau of Social Science Research identified Area Two
as the major outlet for black expansion—that is to say, black
displacement of whites. A decade later, the expansion into the
Northeast continues, although the thrust of blacks is now mainly
into the Maryland and Virginia suburbs. This part of Washing-

ton affords the student of urban history one of the most instructive laboratories in the nation. More than a half-century ago, whites and blacks settled Brentwood—whites in Brentwood proper and blacks in North Brentwood. Until the early seventies the twenty thousand or so black and white residents amiably ignored one another. Then a half-dozen black families moved into Brentwood's twenty- to thirty-thousand-dollar homes without a ripple. More came, encouraged by real estate agents. Suddenly, a burning cross ignited the neighborhood. Minuteman Jesse S. Stephens organized white teen-agers to preserve the "character of the neighborhood." Frank Kube, a recreation specialist, sponsored interracial sports in the local park. The crisis has passed. Brentwood has become blacker, but the thirty-thousand-dollar homes are as well kept as before, although family size has increased and more taxis are parked in driveways.

Brookland stands out as a model of assimilation. With its frame and brick late Victorian houses, its square stuccoes, its broad porches and deep lawns set back from shaded and secluded streets, it possesses the uncrowded charm of an earlier America. Brookland was established in 1887 with the breakup of the 137-acre Brooks Estate. It remained white until the late 1940s. Its black wedge was composed of well-heeled lawyers and physicians. Frugal civil servants and teachers followed and behind them came the striving postal clerks and taxi drivers. By 1970, Brookland's population of thirty thousand was 75 percent black. What the 1965 Bureau of Social Science report found to be true of upper Northwest—that nonwhite homes were generally better maintained than white, though slightly overcrowded—fully applied to Brookland in Northeast, for it was here that black families earning more than fifteen thousand dollars (at 17 percent, more than double the national 1959 black figure) were concentrating. Brookland was the new Le Droit Park. And because of the city government's assaulting folly, its successful attempt at self-defense made it much more. When it was announced, in the late sixties, that the North Central Freeway was to crash through the heart of Brookland, community militants organized the Emergency Committee on Transportation Crises (ECTC), and garnered support from other civic organizations throughout the city. After ECTC leaders Sammie Abbott and R. A. Booker were dramatically arrested for reopening sixty-nine condemned houses, the militants forced the city to abandon the freeway. It was the beginning of the beginning of official sanity in the District's highway planning, until then almost wholly governed by the highway lobby, the Army Corps of Engineers, and powerful residents of the suburbs.

Because all but a few areas north, east, and south of Rock Creek Park have become overwhelmingly black during the past decade, it has become routine to ponder Washington's future with aggravated alarm. The mere fact that the city has a black majority seems to compel doomsday syllogisms—viz., blacks are poor; most Washingtonians are black; ergo, Washington's future is bleak. In the next and final chapter the syllogisms of doom and the catastrophic statistics will be shown to be objectively unpersuasive.

West of the Park

"All Washingtonians," Georgetown author Burke Wilkinson wrote twenty years ago, "can be divided into two parts: those who would never live anywhere but in Georgetown and those who want no part of the place." [16] With a fine sense of seigneurial discrimination, Mr. Wilkinson excluded those Washingtonians who *must* live anywhere but in Georgetown because they can afford no part of the place. If Georgetown and the other enclaves west of the park—Burleith, Chevy Chase, Cleveland Park, and Foxhall, Glover Park, Tunlaw, Wesley Heights, and Woodley Park—were consolidated into counties, they would be the richest in the nation. Fifty-five and a half percent of the 21,000 families west of the park earn more than $30,000, an affluence resulting in one-eighth of the city's population paying one-third of the property and income taxes. This part of Washington is 95 percent white.

Since its incorporation in 1751, Georgetown has always been a good place for the rich and the distinguished—except for a period after the 1880s when it became 50 percent black and a

16. *The Georgetowner*, January 23, 1955.

haven for the poor of both races. The first settlers were Scots—Presbyterian, serious, and frugal—who built on the 795 acres granted by the colonial legislature, in 1699, to Col. Ninian Beall, commander-in-chief of the Maryland Provisional Forces. The place prospered through shipping and commerce; so much so that until the early nineteenth century, Georgetonians dreamed of surpassing New York as the principal seaport on the eastern seaboard. The new city of Washington was the undoing of these ambitions, for the bridgebuilding and digging of the canal between the Anacostia and the Potomac silted the Potomac and lowered the water table in Georgetown harbor. The larger ships could not be berthed. The Chesapeake & Ohio Canal, a costly gamble by the city fathers, failed of its purpose through lack of funds and competition from the railroad.

But whatever the limitations upon its prosperity, there was one aspect of its development which was incomparable—the erection between 1780 and 1830 of a raft of great federal period houses which today give Georgetown its unique flavor. On the acreage owned by Ninian's son, George Beall ("Rock of Dunbarton"), and on that of George Gordon's ("New Scotland Hundred"), the second largest landholder, rose the homesteads of the local aristocracy, the Coxes, Dunlops, Linthicums, and Mackalls, the Glovers, Peters, Tenneys, and Riggs, and a great number more. Houses such as Bellevue (now Dumbarton House, 1750), Decatur (1779), Laird-Dunlop (1799), and Sevier Place (1800), as well as Riggs-Riley (1805) and Linthicum (1826) adhere, in the main, to the simpler, nonmanorial designs characteristic of most of Georgetown's early homes—the New England type of frame house, the ell-shape, and the rectangular. Then there are the lovely manor creations such as Evermay (1792), inhabited by the Belins of du Pont wealth, Dumbarton Oaks (1801), successively owned by William Dorsey, Edward Linthicum, Robert Woods Bliss, and now Harvard University's Byzantine Studies Department, and the mansion Jefferson might have built for himself but for want of money, Tudor Place (1815), the William Thornton-designed homestead of Georgetown Mayor Thomas Peter and bride Martha Parke Custis, a granddaughter of Martha Washington. Illustrative of the longevity of Georgetown families is reclusive Armistead Peter III,

Tudor Place's current occupant and a direct descendant of the original owners.

By the last decade of the nineteenth century, Georgetown had fallen upon hard times. The panic of 1873 merely accelerated a decline that would, in the following decade, be sealed by the Shepherd-inspired growth of the city away from the old seaport settlement. Many old families moved away. More and more black families arrived. Congress esteemed the place so little that, in 1895, it obliterated the very name "Georgetown" from the map of Washington, abolished the boundaries and replaced the old street names with letters, numbers, and states. The town named after one of England's three Georges came to be regarded as a quaint outback by Washington society. Then came Mrs. Newton D. Baker, the wife of President Wilson's secretary of war, a practical woman with a large family. The large house at 3017 N Street met her needs perfectly. "That may have been the town's turning point," an old *National Geographic Magazine* speculates. But if so, it was a point which turned very slowly. Worse than the decay was the demolition of historic buildings. As late as 1935, a time when citizen preservationist concern was well underway, Union Tavern, a hospice whose guest register included Louis-Philippe, Jerome Bonaparte, Talleyrand, and John Adams, Washington Irving, Count Volney, Humboldt, and Robert Fulton, was razed to make way for a gas station. A quarter-century later, the buildings adjacent the Old Stone House, Georgetown's oldest structure (1765), were replaced by a parking lot—the same year (1939) in which Georgetonians raised $60,000 to restore the 1765 structure.

It would not be until the decade after World War Two that Georgetown would be recaptured by the affluent, and even then the victors were bitterly divided about the spoils. Surviving cave-dwellers and young restorers were adamant for restoration and residential zoning. The business community wanted more gas stations, parking lots, high-rise apartments, and commercial buildings. Battles were waged over street lighting, the Progressive Citizens Association violently protesting the 1959 introduction of the city's new vapor lights into Georgetown and the M Street merchants just as angrily demanding them: the District commissioners compromised, removing some of the harsh vapor lights but leaving a few. Feelings between the two groups became so raw that the pettiest misunderstandings between neighbors could explode in court as a *cause célèbre*. Real estate broker Lt. Col. Emil Audette explained to Judge Thomas Scalley that the fence he knocked down behind his property was rickety and useless. This was not the opinion of Pierre Gaunoux, his young restorer neighbor. The two men had fought; then Gaunoux brought charges. The *Washington Post* story of the trial describes a tense hearing, each man's partisans filling the courtroom. Colonel Audette testified that his opponent "had the most fierce look in his eyes I have ever seen, and I've seen Japanese on a banzai charge." Maj. Gen. Melvin Maas, a Marine Corps hero, submitted a deposition defending the honor and truthfulness of Audette. But the prominent real estate broker, Millicent Chattel, took the stand on Gaunoux's behalf and reported that Colonel Audette had a "pugilistic reputation." [17]

The price of restoration is vigilance. Despite setbacks, the preservationists have won most of the major battles. In 1950, Congress restored Georgetown's name and original boundaries and placed the area under the protection of the Department of the Interior. In the late sixties, citizen pressure finally closed the miasmic Hopfenmaier Rending plant. In the early seventies, Inland Steel's one-hundred-million-dollar plan for the face-lifting of the Georgetown waterfront area was scaled down by the commissioners after prolonged and bitter protest. Most recently, the Three Sisters Bridge, which would have been the aesthetic ruination of the Potomac and a disaster for Georgetown, has been abandoned. Today, Georgetown's character is assured. Month by month, it seems to become more "authentic," more chic, and more rich. Even the colorful sidewalk vendors have gone the way of yesterday's hippies and flower children— though the former were scattered by a mean-spirited city ordinance. A stroll along M Street and up Wisconsin Avenue past French, Greek, Indian, and Italian restaurants, English pubs and French creperies, Edwardian ice cream parlors and cozy pastry shops, past hardware and household stores ranging from early

17. October 30, 1959.

American to Champs-Elysées-elegant in style, on past the haberdasheries and specialty shops (some of whose items rival in price the wares in Harry Lunn's gallery) and past grungy and gay night spots—is like finding London's Chelsea and Soho slightly sanitized and placed end-to-end on the Potomac.

Whether or not the cave-dwellers are wholly contented with the new Georgetown is a tantalizing question, for they have had to share the place with the newcomers, many of whom are not only richer but possess what is, for all Washingtonians but those bearing the hoariest pedigrees, the talisman of the town—political power. Fifth- and sixth-generation Georgetonians are pleased to view the swirl of cocktail parties mounted by upper-level bureaucrats, garden variety ambassadors, and lobbyists, mere congressmen and even senators and cabinet members with mannered insouciance. For the old guard, this is an effluvial world of *plus ça change*. Admission to the inner circles of Georgetown's elite cannot, it is said, be bestowed by the electorate of Wyoming, the chairman of the board of ITT, mere occupancy of a Massachusetts Avenue embassy, or even by the occupant of 1600 Pennsylvania Avenue. The earliest notables, families such as those of Bowie and Clagett, Hagner and Sasscer, members, so to speak, of the *noblesse d'épee,* embraced the families of Carusi and Eustis, Noyes and Willard, members of the *noblesse de robe.* And both the old tobacco and the old business clans (the true cave-dwellers) came to blend in time with Auchincloss and Archbold, Belin and Folger, Roosevelt and Shouse. Thereafter, the boulder was rolled across the cave entrance. Old and wealthy Jewish families are not cave-dwellers, nor is there any evidence of grief at the fact on the part of those named Berliner, Cafritz, Hahn, Hechinger, Lansburgh, and Tobriner.

Still, the boulder has a large crack in it, one that admits, in the good old American way, those so rich as to make pedigree irrelevant or those so distinguished professionally that cavilling about eligibility would seem ludicrous. Moreover, it is significant that it tends to be the newcomers who infuse vitality and even set the tone of some of the cave-dweller clubs, particularly the Metropolitan and the Cosmos. And Sulgrave Club matrons now generally concede they were mistaken in believing Jacqueline Bouvier's marriage to John F. Kennedy was a fall from grace. If matronly verdicts about another controversial union, that of a blue blood debutante with the son of flamboyant Congressman Adam Clayton Powell, Jr., are still out, the event itself—albeit unique—suggests cave-dweller awareness of the perils of caste rigidity.

Georgetown is much more than an overcrowded, overpriced Williamsburg. Its homes costing $150,000 and up have more than architectural or historic significance. Georgetown, more than any other Washington community—Chevy Chase, Cleveland Park, or Capitol Hill—is where the federal government carries on after closing, the place where much of the real business of the nation is transacted, with or without attendant cave-dwellers. Here the press gathers much of its off-the-record information; senior officials and members of Congress poll one another on major issues; lobbyists and diplomats ladle their special concerns along with the caviar and terrapin. Politics—earnest, specific, voluble, and unending—fills a Georgetown evening.

A bit above Georgetown lies Cleveland Park, the community "Georgetown people go when their families grow too large for Georgetown houses." Cleveland Park began as a 998-acre plot known as Pretty Prospect owned by Gen. Uriah Forrest and Col. Benjamin Stoddert. In 1790, Forrest renamed the holding "Rosedale," and his descendants retained ownership until 1917. The present name emerged after 1886, the year the Rosedale owners sold land to President Grover Cleveland for "Red Top," his summer home. But the area really came alive during the 1930s, when Roosevelt braintrusters and their young aides moved in. Among those who settled the neighborhood at this time and somewhat later were Rexford Tugwell, William McChesney Martin, Tilford Dudley, James H. Rowe, and Max Kampelman. Cleveland Park was also home to the extraordinary lobbyist and cave-dweller Thomas G. ("Tommy the Cork") Corcoran, in 1976 still a natty, tireless presence in legislative antechambers on Capitol Hill. During the Johnson years, Cleveland Park received a second wave of luminaries: Nicholas Katzenbach, William Bundy, Walt Rostow, George Reedy, Birch Bayh, Walter Mondale, Lucius Battle, and a pride of other Democratic movers and shakers.

Cleveland Park is as ideologically liberal as nearby Wesley Heights (Vice-President Nixon's neighborhood) is resolutely conservative. When real estate brokers asked the New Deal elite to sign agreements not to sell its homes to blacks, it refused. In the sixties, its residents pushed for open housing and District home rule, opposed freeway construction, and fought runaway high-rise building. There are still very few blacks in the area—fewer than 5 percent—but those wealthy enough to buy (and the number is slowly growing) are about as rapidly assimilated into the community as they would be on the Gold Coast. The cost of Cleveland Park housing worries many residents. It was the old-fashioned, shabby-genteel character of the neighborhood that attracted the established settlers. Fifteen years ago, the rambling, stucco houses with their gabled roofs and wooden porches, and their deep backyards were superb buys for the middle classes. The area was fairly heterogeneous then—economically if not racially. In 1961, future Attorney General Nicholas Katzenbach paid $55,000 for his home. A few years later, a memorable party was given by Katzenbach in his home for Princess Margaret. In 1968, the house was resold for $185,000. "Right now, I think Cleveland Park still maintains its great heterogeneity," Sheldon Holen, a young dentist, told a *Washington Post* reporter in early 1974:

> But what's killing it is the high price of housing. Where the diversity may be going is when you begin to spot swimming pools in the back yards—and essentially you're left with fat-cat lawyers. That's not necessarily bad, but it means it will end up as homogeneous as Georgetown.[18]

Should the numerous heirs to the Joseph B. Davies estate, Tregaron, ever decide to sell the sprawling property to developers, the impact on prices and density in Cleveland Park will be enormous. Most residents hope that Tregaron will become the permanent home of the Washington International School, its present leaseholder.

18. March 7, 1974.

5

1976 and All That

$\mathcal{W}$HAT sort of place is Washington likely to become during the last quarter of the twentieth century? Increasingly black with even the $30,000-a-year white families west of the park decamping for the suburbs or (leapfrogging the parallel exodus of wealthy blacks) for Harper's Ferry and rural Pennsylvania? If blacker, does this inevitably mean poorer—so poor that housing stock, municipal services, and schools disintegrate? Or if whites survive at about one-fourth of the population, will it be at the cost of what one professional Washington-watcher calls the "urbanity of the District"—aging and rich whites desperately clinging to residential islets in a roiling black sea? Will the historian of Washington's tercentenary record that Congress intervened to "save" the capital from black ruination by annulling local government for the second time in the city's history? Or will the course of events surprise the urbanologists and make of Washington an exemplary achievement of racial comity and municipal imaginativeness?

In the twenty-two years since the end of legal segregation Washington has endured the best and the worst of times. Since 1968, when the city's civil cohesiveness seemed possible only at the price of constitutionally dubious crime prevention laws

174

and the addition of more than two thousand policemen, the signs of better times have been less than abundant. A fast reading of the recent past fails to inspire. Washington's population continues its decline from the 1950 high of 802,178. Its white population steadily diminishes. Ninety-seven percent of the public school population was black in 1974 as were 85 and 90 percent of the administrators and teachers. The 1966 *Report of the President's Commission on Crime in the District of Columbia* plots a curve of robbery and rape since the 1950s whose apogee is enough to make Wallaceites dance for joy. From 1964 to 1965 alone, the number of robberies shot from 1,312 to 3,945. Four years later Washington Board of Trade merchants were reporting to Sen. Joseph Tydings's committee that their shoplifting losses for a twelve-month period would range from eighty to one hundred fifty million dollars. With crime as the excuse but the suburban shopper as the quarry, large and small businesses either abandoned the city altogether or maintained a holding operation there while they expanded in Maryland and Virginia. Kann's and Lansburgh's, large and long-established department stores, simply gave up and liquidated.

Among the most alarming and dismaying statistics are those from the public school system. Skills in reading and math have dropped year after depressing year until they are now nearly three years behind the national norms, wringing from the head of the teachers union the concession that Washington's schools are "at rock bottom." [1] What good schools there are, with very few exceptions, are west of the park. Fifty-five percent of school-age whites attend private institutions; only 8 to 10 percent of the black youngsters do. In the eight years since Congress granted an elected board of education, five school superintendents (acting and permanent) have presided over the dissolution of local education, one of them, William Manning, being paid to leave, and another, Barbara Sizemore, having to be fired after weeks of mass demonstrations and legal fandango.

---

1. Joan C. Baratz, "A Quest for Equal Educational Opportunity in a Major Urban School District: The Case of Washington, D.C." (Syracuse, N.Y.: Syracuse University, 1974), p. 1.

Whatever is wrong with District schools, money is not the major cause. The beginning salary for teachers in 1976 was $9,940. The local average was $14,005, comparing favorably with Milwaukee's $14,250 and not unfavorably with Los Angeles's $14,985. Washington spent more per student—a hefty $1,399—than Boston, Cleveland, or Milwaukee, and if the additional federal payment of $229 was included the figure ranged near the national maximum.

Yet these efforts are perceived to have failed so abjectly that the Bureau of Social Science Research reports that a mere 18 percent of Washingtonians currently rate their schools favorably, a 10 percent decline in just one year. The 1975 school year was traumatic enough to have destroyed all faith in the city schools. Before Mrs. Sizemore departed, the community had been polarized almost as fiercely as in the days of Boss Shepherd.

To people who continued to believe in racial integration, Mrs. Sizemore's policies were an ignoble mockery of the efforts of academic trouble shooters like Julius Hobson and Kenneth Clark. Dr. Clark, a renowned New York psychologist, had presented his commissioned report to the Board of Education in mid-1970. His Academic Achievement Plan called for payment of teachers according to the performance of their students, a radical policy already rejected by New York City and nervously tabled by the District. The Clark plan may have been unworkable but its legacy of accountability was healthy. Hobson, formerly an economist with a federal agency, has been the city's magnificent windmill tilter for years. His 1967 court victory had abolished the District's "tracking" system (inflexible student placement in curriculum channels) and imposed equal allocation of funds among all city schools. Four years later and then a member of the board of education, Hobson returned to court to demand that Judge Skelly Wright's decree be enforced in order to end budgetary disparities between mainly white and mainly black schools. He won again. Clark and Hobson, championed by board members such as Anita Allen, Charles Cassell, Martha Swaim, and Bardyl Tirana, planned and sued for reforms inspired by certainties that Washington's black youngsters could be taught to read and calculate as well as white students—once the school system was overhauled. They were integrationists.

When Daniel Fader, the Michigan educator, wrote *The Naked Children* (1971), an account of his extraordinary experiences with students at Washington's Garnett-Patterson High School, he asked the anguishing question, "Who but a fool practices for a contest to which he will not be admitted, a struggle in which he will not be allowed to compete?" But Fader understood that blackspeak, dull classes, and miserable test scores could and must be overcome, thereby making the contest and the struggle worthwhile. Barbara Sizemore's answer to Fader's question was to defend bad grammar, bad math, bad classes, and bad test scores as the way black youngsters learned. Indeed, they were not bad at all, only perceived to be by whites (and some middle-class blacks), who are forever foisting their criteria on other races. When Sizemore's successor, Supt. Vincent Reed, announced his views, there was an audible sigh of relief from most citizens. "There are two things we have to do immediately," Reed told the *Washington Post*. "We've got to stop telling people the [school] system can't be managed. It can. And we've got to stop telling our children they can't learn because they're black, poor, or both. They can learn. We don't want them using racism as a crutch and an excuse." [2] Long overdue official straight talk in a city noted for evasion and obfuscation.

If the public school system now has nowhere to go but up, local housing problems are likely to become much worse over the next decade. From the Battle of Bull Run to Pearl Harbor, the decennial population increase averaged a steady fifty-five thousand. Because population density was unusually low (and still is, Georgetown excepted) and because tall buildings have been anathema since the Cairo Apartments (1894) alarmed Congress into imposing a heights limit to protect the majesty of the Capitol and the Washington Monument, Washington became a city of "attached" or row houses. Thirty-seven percent of its 262,000 housing units in 1976 were row houses, increas-

2. Lee A. Daniels, "Reed: 'Our Children Can Learn,' " November 17, 1975.

ing to levels between 66 and 71 percent in the center city. Detached houses comprise the second largest category. Nearly 75,000 of Washington's 102,000 one-unit structures were occupied by their owners in 1970, a statistic that continues to grow as more blacks become householders. In 1974, of the 89,500 owner-occupied units, about 56,000 were black-owned and, despite deteriorating municipal services and larger families, they are being well maintained.

Unfortunately, Washington is running out of housing for citizens with moderate incomes, and much of its housing stock is wearing out. The 262,000 housing units extant in 1975 are fewer than in 1970. The displacement of the fifties and sixties has about run its course. There are practically no more white neighborhoods into which most black Washingtonians can afford to move. This same limitation affects young white families. For the black who can meet the inflated price tags west of the park or on Capitol Hill, there is the crucial intangible of lifestyle. Newly middle-class, the black lawyer, physician, or GS-14 seldom has as an ideal a $50,000 turn-of-the-century brownstone without front yard and needing a minimum of $30,000 in remodelling. Something modern, with central air conditioning, deep yard, two-car garage, picture window, and, if possible, a swimming pool beyond the patio, confirms his affluence and banishes adolescent memories of inner-city row houses and density.

With the crime and the collapse of the schools, it is small wonder that 30,000 blacks have left Washington since 1970, more than twice the number of fleeing whites. Among both races, the city is losing its most productive and vibrant citizens. Between 1950 and 1970, almost 92,000 Washingtonians, or one-fourth of those Washingtonians aged twenty-one to forty-four, disappeared. Rapidly, the District is becoming a place for rich and older whites and for blacks just above the poverty line.

The causes of Washington's housing and demographic patterns are complex. Vagaries of time and place, taste and race are involved. One cause, however, is as patent as it is reprehensible. It is the mortgage lending policies of nearly all the seventeen savings and loan institutions in the District. According to a

Ralph Nader-supervised study of eleven savings and loans firms presented to the city council in early May 1975, "most of the money . . . went into neighborhoods that are either mostly white, including Georgetown, Cleveland Park, Embassy Row, and close-in Capitol Hill, or becoming white, including Adams-Morgan and the outer edges of Capitol Hill." [3] And while Councilperson Douglas Moore's subcommittee pondered this report, Sen. William Proxmire's Banking and Housing Committee released a more definitive and distressing Library of Congress analysis circumstantially establishing a pattern of neighborhood "redlining." Warning the savings and loan associations that they were violating federal civil rights laws, Proxmire spelled out the mechanics of redlining:

> A prospective home buyer will approach a lending institution for a mortgage loan. His credit rating can be excellent and the house can be in sound condition. But some lenders will reject the application because they don't like the neighborhood and steer the buyer to the suburbs. [4]

Only one Washington savings and loan institution gave 50 percent of its loans within the city—the tiny black-operated Independence Federal ($2.8 million). Interstate Building Association, the third largest, awarded $55.2 million in loans in 1973, of which, according to the *Washington Post,* "only $185,000—in three loans on property in white neighborhoods west of Rock Creek Park—was lent inside the District." Home Federal lent a fourth of its $40 million in the District, but most of it went for condominiums. Of the seventeen, only two, Perpetual and National Permanent, made racially equitable and sizeable District loans in 1973—$13.1 million of Perpetual's $85 million and $15.1 million of National Permanent's $69.2 million.

The savings and loan institutions have, of course, strenuously

3. Thomas W. Lippman, "D.C. Suburbs Got 90% of S&L Loans," *Washington Post,* May 4, 1975.

4. Thomas W. Lippman, "Savings-Loan Firms Lend Suburbs Most," *Washington Post,* April 27, 1975.

denied the imputation of racism, citing similar mortgage patterns in Milwaukee and Minneapolis. It seems only natural and reasonable that the District's chief financial officer select as favored depositors only those institutions whose lending practices promote the welfare of Washington. At a minimum, the council has been encouraged to enact legislation similar to Chicago's, compelling savings and loans firms to disclose the source and use of deposits.

The most significant event for Washington in the immediate future is, of course, the return of a semblance of local government. After the 1961 ratification of the Twenty-third Amendment permitting them to vote in presidential elections, the District's citizens clamored and politicked more strenuously than ever for the right enjoyed by all other Americans to elect their local rulers and to be represented in Congress. Congressman John McMillan of Florence, South Carolina, chairman of the House District Committee from 1948 until his defeat twenty-four years later, vowed never to let the national capital master its own affairs. McMillan had powerful congressional allies. William Natcher of Kentucky, campaign coffers biennially replenished by the highway lobby, and laboring mightily for a second bridge from Virginia to Georgetown (the "Three Sisters"), was apoplectic at the prospect of local officials having a say in highway construction. John Dowdy of Texas used his District subcommittee to probe and exaggerate error, waste, and supposed indulgence of the wastrel poor. Virginia's Joel Broyhill, the most enraging of the lot, possessed a fine talent for legislative foul play and an acidulous tongue, until his constituents removed him from office in 1974. The opposition of these congressmen to local government was, at bottom, racist.

But home rule somehow had been moving along. Although many Washingtonians, especially those belonging to the D.C. Statehood party, dismissed the Johnson adminstration's 1967 consolidation of the old three-man commission government into a single appointive mayor-commissioner and council rule as cosmetic, it was an important forward step. It removed the Army Corps of Engineers from its decisive role in local affairs and afforded at the least the possibility of reforming the Byzantine bureaucracies more or less responsible to the District Building. Then came the November 1968 elections for the new eleven-member board of education, the first time in ninety-two years that Washingtonians had voted for local officials. It was a rambunctiously disorganized affair with unknown candidates declaring at the eleventh hour and citizen interest remaining surprisingly dormant, even though perceptive citizens knew that the elections were a dry run for the day when local government became a reality.

In the rawest traditions of American politics everybody wanted a piece of the action. There were thirty-nine contenders for the six at-large and five ward positions. Mrs. Ilia Bullock, beautician, of Ward One, was a more colorful but not atypical candidate. Arriving just before the midnight deadline with her registration fee in brown paper grocery bags, she was informed that only checks or money orders were acceptable. Mrs. Bullock, a large, powerful woman, glared at the official and roared, "I'm poor! I don't handle checks. This is the way the money came to me." [5] A downpour of change and small bills covered the counter and the candidate huffed away officially inscribed.

Julius Hobson, Sr., was by far the best known and most respected (and feared) of the candidates. Washingtonians expected to hear Hobson's voice on important issues and, for the majority who understood him, his was a voice of integrity, intelligence, and guts. But there were many—some Gold Coast blacks, white businessmen, congressmen, and District officials—in whom Hobson aroused embarrassment, dread, and speechless anger. Ex-fighter pilot and Howard University graduate, Hobson had mobilized the local CORE chapter to picket discriminatory businesses in the early 1960s. By 1964, CORE reported that more than five thousand jobs had opened to minorities. It also expelled Julius Hobson, whose maverick radicalism had begun to distress its leaders. But Hobson was a civil rights organization of one. When officials were slow to respond to the inner-city rat plague, Hobson launched Saturday rat-catching rallies, placed cages atop a station wagon (the "Rat

5. "Last Minute Entries," *Washington Post,* September 22, 1968.

Wagon'') and announced that each Saturday's haul would be released in Georgetown. "The City immediately instituted a rat extermination program in Northeast and cleaned up a hell of a lot of rats," Hobson recalls.[6] Hoaxes were his specialty. While other civil rights leaders ineffectually deplored the brutality of Chief John Layton's police, Hobson designed and built a parabolic microphone and devoted Friday nights to tailing squad cars in his clearly labelled "Cop Watching Wagon." A directive was issued instructing patrolmen to mind their language and improve their manners.

Another candidate, the goateed and dashiki-clad Reverend Douglas Moore, quickly surfaced as a prominent contender. Later, he would become as controversial, though not as revered, as Julius Hobson. Moore was a founder of Stokely Carmichael's local Black United Front. If he was agreeable to genteel private discussions either in French or English, the candidate's capacity for public rage was outstanding even for that vintage year of racial passion, 1968. At the height of his campaign, Moore unveiled a plan to compel police to live in the District and to create an elected citizen review board empowered to select precinct captains and set professional standards for patrolmen. In the final days of campaigning, Moore's racial politics became increasingly jugular and sometimes hilarious. John Sessions, an incumbent board member seeking a new mandate, was attacked for his position as an AFL-CIO education specialist and a white man, "a union flunky . . . who doesn't see that your father gets into the union." During a high school speech, Moore championed another cause. "Every people has its own dog— Irish Setters, Scotch Terriers, and so forth," he railed. "But you'd never know that black people have a dog, too—the *basenji,* a dog native to the Congo. You never see a picture of the *basenji* in your school books." [7] The cheering students were assured that, if elected, the *basenji* would be recognized. The Reverend Moore lost.

6. "Hobson's Specialty," *Washington Post,* July 4, 1972.

7. "School Candidates Launch Personal & Racial Attacks," *Washington Post,* November 1, 1968.

When the votes were counted, only Hobson had won a seat. Runoffs were necessary for the others. Mrs. Anita Allen, former board member and employee in the Office of Education, was a conscientious, conservative public official. A successful runoff candidate, she returned determined to salvage Dr. Kenneth Clark's Academic Achievement Plan and to prevent Hobson's election as board president. The presidency went to a compromise member; Hobson was de facto head. Like many brilliant and unconventional public figures too much ahead of his times, Hobson was soon repaid with ingratitude. Running as an at-large candidate again the following year, he was defeated. His atheism, Marxism, litigiousness, and enraging public statements (Hobson blasted black and white opponents equally) strained the tolerance of his supporters. Then, when he was striken by spinal cancer two years later, Washingtonians more than forgave his iconoclasm, his radicalism, his pure cussedness, and even his new white wife. On the evening of November 14, 1972, at the Sheraton Park Hotel, they gathered, black and white, to pay extraordinary tribute to their dying rebel. Hobson not only survived the hypocrisy of his canonization, with the help of his wife, radical chemotherapy, and superhuman willpower, he even forced his cancer into remission.

The 1968 and the 1972 presidential elections were mixed blessings for the capital. D.C. became known as the "crime capital of the world," thanks to the president's inflammatory campaign rhetoric. It became the most heavily policed city in America, with a 5000-man municipal constabulary, 450 park police, 1000 Capitol police, an 800-odd-member Executive Protection Service (for embassies and federal buildings), and thousands of other federal and military law enforcement personnel. Perhaps police saturation did slow the rate of crime acceleration. But there were also the truly frightening signals emanating from the Nixon White House and the Justice Department of a police-state mentality. Few Washingtonians doubted that the administration intended to make the city a laboratory for law and order, a reassuring prospect for commuting conservatives and panic-stricken inner-city residents, but an alarming portent for civil libertarians.

Nixon's reappointment of Walter Washington as mayor-commissioner was only barely reassuring. John B. Duncan had been the first black commissioner, serving competently from 1961 to 1967. After the abolition of the three-man commissioner arrangement in 1967, President Lyndon Johnson appointed Walter Washington to the new single commissioner post. Walter Washington possessed a wealth of experience in public housing management, knew first-hand the capital's labyrinthine channels of power, and would evince a fine *sangfroid* during the 1968 riots. Through his wife, a Le Droit Park Bullock, his roots in Washington's black bourgeois community ran deep, and his long professional career had won him respect on Capitol Hill and in the white business community. He meant well and, despite imperious Nixonian constraints, he continued to inspire confidence even as his public relations role was being crimped. "What is the clout of the Mayor?" Thomas Fletcher, his deputy, rhetorically bemoaned in a seminar at the Washington Center for Metropolitan Studies.

> The clout of the Mayor is almost zero, other than his own personality. . . . "Why doesn't he speak out? Why doesn't he come out and stand on his own two feet and shout and yell and attack?" How *can* he attack? What is his base of attack? Is it the citizenry of the District? No. Is it Congress? No. Because once he stands up they can just turn around and flatten him. Now, if he were elected he would get flattened, if he didn't do the job right, when he came up for reelection. That is the process we ought to have.[8]

The best and the worst came wrapped together. In late September 1970, without a public statement and with no ceremony, Nixon signed the bill creating a nonvoting delegate for the District of Columbia. But the president had already signed the District of Columbia Crime Control Bill, a piece of legislation that the White House spiritedly advertised as the prototype for the nation. Three courts—general sessions, juvenile, and tax—gave

8. *Managing the Nation's Capital: An Interview with Thomas W. Fletcher, Deputy Mayor-Commissioner* (Washington, D.C.: Washington Center for Metropolitan Studies, 1971), p. 4.

way to one, the new superior court, for which fifteen new justices were needed. A public defender service was created. Then came the bad parts. The law authorized invasion of domiciles without warning (the ''no-knock provision''), greatly expanded electronic surveillance, and allowed pretrial detention of certain categories of criminal offenders. Old Sen. Sam Ervin, not yet immortalized by Watergate, denounced the legislation as unconstitutional. Washington's new police chief, downhome, accessible, and smart Jerry Wilson, was a topflight professional, but his independence from the District Building, coziness with the White House, and willing endorsement of the Crime Control Bill made liberals and home rulers uneasy. Uneasiness turned to outrage in early May 1971 when Wilson's men behaved like Spanish riot police, indiscriminately arresting some thirteen thousand people during three days of antiwar demonstrations, a Justice Department-directed tactic for which Washington's police department eventually received a stinging rebuke from the Supreme Court.

Still, there was progress during the Nixon years. The Reverend Walter Fauntroy, a young, Yale-trained lieutenant of Martin Luther King, Jr., and city council appointee, was elected nonvoting delegate to Congress in November of 1971. There was something of the choirboy about Walter Fauntroy then, a mannered loquacity quite belieing the hardhitting, no-holds-barred summer primary campaign he mounted against the urbane Reverend Channing Phillips (first black to be a nominee for president in a national party [Democratic] convention) and council member Joseph Yeldell, beloved of the Board of Trade. In vain, Julius Hobson (D.C. Statehood party candidate) protested that Martin Luther King, Jr., was not running for delegate. With Coretta King at his side, Fauntroy's motorcade, blaring soul music, swept through inner-city streets and on to smashing victory in the general elections over Hobson, Douglas Moore, and Republican John Nevius. Congressman John McMillan and several of his allies were defeated in the 1972 elections. Michigan Congressman Charles Diggs, a gruff and wily black veteran of Capitol Hill, assumed the chairmanship of the House District Committee. On Christmas Eve 1973 the president signed the

Home Rule Bill. Finally, in January 1975, a mayor and thirteen-member city council, popularly elected, were installed.

But the shaft of light cast by self-government is still much too dim. "Despite Home Rule, Distrust Remains," the *Washington Post* reported on September 7, 1975. "About 59 percent of the District's residents now feel their officials 'cannot be trusted to do what's best for all citizens'," the newspaper claimed, citing a Bureau of Social Science Research poll. In extenuation, though, the survey "also shows distrust towards officials increasing in all suburban jurisdictions except Arlington. . . ." There is ample reason for lack of citizen confidence. Authentic home rule is still to be won and, when they voted in the May 7, 1974, referendum on the Nixon-signed charter, Washingtonians were mindful of Missouri Sen. Thomas Eagleton's admonition that what Congress gave it could also take away. The Home Rule Charter reserved the power of presidential veto of all municipal legislation. Congress retained final control over budgetary matters. The federal government carved out an enclave, extending from Capitol Hill along the Mall and Federal Triangle and beyond, over which it exercised exclusive domain. The city's closely supervised taxation powers explicitly precluded the enactment of a commuter tax. Finally, the language of Section 601 of the Home Rule Act excludes all doubt about where ultimate sovereignty lies:

> Notwithstanding any other provision of this Act, the Congress of the
> United States reserves the right, anytime, to exercise its
> constitutional authority as legislature for the District by enacting
> legislation for the District on any subject. . . .

Real self-government will not be possible until the Constitution's Article I, Section 8 is amended, or until the territory over which it stipulates that Congress "shall exercise exclusive legislation" is congressionally redefined to exclude the area beyond the new federal enclave.

To home rule purists like Julius Hobson and his supporters in the D.C. Statehood party, the appearance of local government was worse than the old reality of congressional bondage. Sam

Smith's *D.C. Gazette* expressed their special bitterness toward Delegate Fauntroy for his role in the charter outcome. Fauntroy had prevailed upon the 1972 Democratic standard bearer, Sen. George McGovern, to renege on his promise to include statehood in the party's platform. Statehooders said that the delegate sabotaged them to preserve his power. Fauntroy argued that statehood would have cost the District its hefty federal subsidy. After months of one of the most energetic and resourceful lobbying campaigns ever sustained by a member of the House, Walter Fauntroy won congressional consideration of a District representation formula which even inveterate statehooders can accept. On February 18, 1976, the House Rules Committee agreed, for the first time in more than a century, to release a constitutional amendment proposing voting District representation in the Senate and House. Delegate Fauntroy's bill ignored the issue of statehood, although opponents smelled a dangerous hybrid. "They will have all the benefits of statehood with none of the responsibilities," said Michigan's Republican congressman, Edward Hutchinson. The Fauntroy bill was voted down by the House (March 23, 1976), but it marks a significant step forward for complete home rule.

The reasonable supposition is that the more local autonomy, the better it is for the locals. But Washingtonians have been disappointed by the costly unresponsiveness of many city departments. What has really changed since Royce Hanson's American University dissertation or Martha Derthick's oft-cited monograph, "City Politics in Washington, D.C.," exposed the yeasty amorphousness of the commission government? "There is neither top nor bottom to the structure of government," Derthick explained.

> Authority does not come to a peak, in a single individual or agency, nor does it rest on the broad foundation of a voting public. It is distributed not vertically, but horizontally—among an elite that circulates in the Capitol and its offices, the White House, the District Building, and the many federal and quasi-federal agencies that have a share of authority over the district.

After a century of topless and bottomless government, home rule has seemed to do little more than fatten Washington's middle.

Gone are the days, one hopes, when District Highway Director James Carberry would be summoned to discuss trees in front of a senator's house. "The spectacle of a $17,000-a-year City department head being summoned to the Hill to account for the presence of three trees may appear ludicrous," the *Washington Post* admitted.[9] "But to a greater or lesser extent, this sort of thing takes place daily." Audits and budgetary deficits have now replaced trees as matters of Capitol Hill concern. In recent months the state of the city's finances has been described by Senate District Committee Chairman Eagleton as so dire that home rule would have been delayed "a decade or maybe even a century" and Mayor Washington would have been "destroyed politically" if Congress had known the full facts.[10] How Senator Eagleton and Congress could be ignorant of such matters is a puzzlement the supposedly astonished senator left unsolved. In demanding a total audit at the moment the District government was about to float $50 million in commercial bonds, Eagleton warned that Washington would soon find itself in New York's quasi-bankrupt predicament. While the citizenry staggered under these unexpected revelations, U.S. Comptroller General Elmer Staats astounded everyone by declaring that the District's finances were not possible to audit because of chaotic bookkeeping! Congress pondered a veto of the city's duly authorized bond sale and the local press reported budgetary anomalies and obligations of stupendous dimensions throughout the final weeks of 1975—for example, $1.5 billion in generous future pension obligations (firemen, police, teachers) for which no sinking fund existed.

The worst fears of Board of Trade pessimists appeared to be coming true. Home rule was not only destructive of traditional political arrangements, it was becoming a downright ripoff of the taxpayer. Or so it seemed. In ten years, the local debt rose

9. July 30, 1961.

10. "Eagleton Plans Total Audit," *Washington Post,* November 26, 1975.

tenfold, from $101 million in 1965 to $1 billion in fiscal 1975. Washington now ranks after New York City with the highest per capita indebtedness. Since 1968, the size of its government increased more than 30 percent, saddling the city with about five times more employees per thousand population than twenty comparable cities. The ratio of personnel workers to employees (1 to 50) is exceedingly high. The example of federal agencies had been followed with relish. Although roughly a third of those hired after 1968 are black, the 1972 report of Rep. Ancher Nelson's Commission on the Organization of the Government of the District determined that more than two-thirds of the executive slots were held by whites, and that 91.6 percent of these executives were males.

The Nelson commission also reported that Washington's work force, whether black or white, was much less efficient than that of comparable municipalities. Nor has home rule improved conditions one whit. The District's version of the federal Department of Health, Education, and Welfare, the new Department of Human Resources (DHR), a hydra accountable neither to Congress nor to the electorate, feeds on the detritus of its own enveloping chaos. Even the disaccreditation of D.C. General Hospital barely ruffles the composure and silence of Joseph Yeldell's DHR leviathan. Meanwhile, where once the city's sales, gas, entertainment, hotel, and individual income taxes were the lowest in the metropolitan area, they are now the highest. The District taxes families earning between $15,000 and $40,000 more heavily than do two-thirds of the thirty largest cities in the nation. Significantly, the tax burden on family incomes in the $5,000–$10,000 range is about average. But high tax receipts on the upper middle classes and the hefty annual federal subsidy of $280 million are being outrun by galloping expenditures.

Desperate for new revenue to finance expenditures rising 12 percent annually while income increases only by 4, Mayor Washington (formerly trusted by business interests) has presented a $1.5 billion budget for fiscal 1977 which raises $119 million in new taxes by a business gross receipts tax, hiked income and commercial property taxes—and (if possible) a commuter tax. Whatever slashes the council makes in the mayor's proposals, the billion-dollar-plus budgets of the immediate future will not only force taxes upward, they may rise geometrically and very rapidly. For bicentenary Washington residents home rule seems to mean no relief from taxation even with quasi-representation.

Escalating taxes and bureaucratic elephantiasis are not peculiar to the District of Columbia, even if they seem to thrive better here than most places. But the passivity of leadership in the District Building has been one of Washington's severest civic debits. During the first week of July 1972, the *Washington Post* serialized one of its most memorable interviews. For four days the reading public feasted (though some suffered chronic indigestion) on the infernal wit and superior wisdom of infirm Julius Hobson. What Hobson said then about government ills still applies. "I think that the District of Columbia government itself is not run on an honest basis," he charged. Not that Mayor Washington "puts his hand in the cash box every morning." Hobson had in mind the dishonesty of not "facing up to an issue and admitting as a City official that, 'Yeah, there's something wrong in my department. There is waste in my department.' " The evasion, delay, and incompetence of some Washington public servants have greatly refined the Peter Principle. In recent years, citizens have complained about, courts have enjoined against, and Congress has investigated conditions at D.C. General Hospital, Lorton Reformatory, the center for the retarded at Forest Haven, Saint Elizabeth's Hospital (a federal-municipal hybrid for the mentally disturbed), the Redevelopment Land Agency, and the public school system and the department of sanitation with zero to minimal results.

According to anonymous staff sources and some hard evidence, conditions at D.C. General Hospital resemble the disordered, insanitary Civil War cloacae described in Walt Whitman's letters to his mother. Florence Nightingale herself might well have despaired of a hospital where patients' crutches are routinely purloined by emergency room attendants to prop up makeshift stretchers, and nurses "liberate" critically scarce drugs and other supplies to replenish their wards. To compound the disaster, the head of the department of human resources has issued a directive interdicting hospital officials from responding to enquiries by citizens and newspaper reporters. The laxity of surveillance at Lorton Reformatory recently resulted in custodial and inmate murders and a stream of escapes causing Virginia legislators to demand either the removal of the facility to the District proper or a takeover by the federal government. Charges of corruption in the sanitation department and gross mismanagement at RLA trail on unanswered and uncorrected. Finally, there is the benighted school system.

It was this general sense of elementary duties being badly discharged, if at all, that resulted in a serious 1974 summer primary battle for Walter Washington on his elected way to the District Building. With a little less Harvard (B.A.) and Yale (LL.B.) and a little more Fourteenth and U in his campaign style, Clifford Alexander might not have lost the Democratic primary by 4 percentage points. In a "Today Show" appearance on January 20, 1976, Walter Washington talked about the "terrific pressures" of running his city, citing the constricting surveillance of Capitol Hill and the White House. Awesome pressures, indeed. Yet, as Alan Grip, chief assistant to the city council chairperson explains,

> Home rule didn't change the executive branch way of doing business much. Over here, it's like a whole new government. There's no comparison between the appointed Council and this Council, in every respect—not the least of which is the amount of work done.

The amount of work *not* done by the executive branch has occasioned a crescendo of complaints not only from citizens and newspapers but also from council members. "It's the style of the administration," Council Chairperson Sterling Tucker says of the mayor's dilatoriness. "Things are held very closely to the chest. . . . I'm not sure how well-connected his network is." [11] It is not just a question of bureaucratic creakiness, a malady common enough in city halls nationwide. His critics

11. A. Grip and S. Tucker, taped interviews, January 21, 1976.

charge that the mayor and his closest advisor, City Administrator Julian Dugas, regard the new thirteen-member council as an adversary. If it is an adversary, it is a formidable one because it combines youth and experience.

The council's recent demand to be empowered to confirm the appointment of the mayor's director of the new consumer affairs office evidences its encroaching aggressiveness. Its enactment of a complicated and probably unworkable rent-control law (initially vetoed by the mayor), imposition of a stinging nonresident tax on unincorporated professional incomes (doctors, dentists, lawyers from Maryland and Virginia practicing in the District), and its determination to pare his 1977 budget so severely that municipal employees might be fired ("social dynamite, my friends") have aroused Mayor Washington from his usual phlegmatism. His public utterances (rarer and rarer after 1968) have increased and his language (customarily an amalgam of bureaucratic blather and blackspeak) has become sharper and richer as the initiative passes to the astute Sterling Tucker and to Marion Barry, one of the council's most aggressive members.

However, the growing feeling among many Washingtonians is that executive unresponsiveness is more a matter of dumbness than of pressure or conservatism. "Just how numb is everyone in the city government?" a 1976 *Washington Post* editorial wondered of the plight of a wheelchair-bound Library of Congress employee whose parked, specially equipped automobile had been badly damaged by an out-of-control squad car. His complaint having been duly filed, and after having taxied to work and lost job hours for months, Emmett Anderson's $2,300 claim was approved. But the money, Anderson was told, must come from the "regular deficiency appropriation" which Congress may not replenish before the summer.[12] If this were just one of those occasional horror stories inevitably extruded by the clattering gears of big government and small people, it would merit sympathetic publicity but not a verdict of incompetence. Unfortunately, inanition in matters large and small seems to

---

12. "Red Tape and Personal Ruin," *Washington Post,* February 6, 1976.

have become the rule rather than the exception with the executive. "Is Mr. Anderson's problem too complex for Mayor Washington to resolve immediately? Can't the City Council find him a ride? Must Congress enact a special bill for the relief of Emmett Anderson?" asked the *Washington Post*. "It boggles the mind." [13]

The Best of All Possible Cities

Because of what it is, Washington draws attention completely out of proportion to its size and its problems. Almost anything written about the city is good copy, but far too much has been printed that is insidious or inflammatory. Not all the carefully researched, readable publications of the Bureau of Social Science Research, the Potomac Institute, or the Washington Center for Metropolitan Studies (WCMS) have a teacup's solvent power on the dross of misconception, prejudice, and just plain cheap politics covering the real Washington. Indeed, the real city is usually written off as "The Washington Tourists Don't Visit," as was the case in a recent *Fortune* article describing it as "a city of marble built on sand." A little earlier, a *Harper's* article, "The Worst American City," listed Washington as the worst place on the East Coast, a ranking all the more puzzling because of the perfect score given by the author to Tulsa! The catalogue of local ills is lengthy and chronic but, all in all, Washington is comparatively healthy and getting better, a conclusion reached by the small Midwest Research Institute of Kansas City under a grant from the Environmental Protection Agency. In its survey, Washington ranked twentieth among sixty-five large metropolitan areas, well ahead of Baltimore and one of only four East Coast cities receiving a "B" rating. Still, as *The Washingtonian* magazine said in February 1976, "two major factors overshadow all considerations about the District: It is black and the streets are unsafe." That citizens are safer at night on Washington's streets than on San Francisco's somehow carries little weight. San Francisco is not the nation's capital.

13. *Washington Post*, February 6, 1976.

A recitation of positive Washington attributes could be as interminable as an undelivered speech in the *Congressional Record*. The average level of education is the highest among large American cities. Nor is this one of those tricky statistics so inflated by legions of economists and lawyers and GS-14's west of the park or diploma-bearing aids and technicians in Southwest and on Capitol Hill as to have dubious value. Washington's blacks are also exceptionally well educated. A 1973 survey found that between 1960 and 1970, the decade of maximal black increase and white decrease, the number of persons with graduate level education rose 25 percent. "By 1970," according to the study, "almost one D.C. resident out of six who had passed his or her 25th birthday had completed college." [14] By 1974, persons with some college education had risen from 29 to 32 percent. Washington even looks fairly good in terms of population stability, too much of which tends to stultify but too little of which promotes community indifference and anomie. Turnover figures for the metropolitan area are, as WCMS director Atlee Shidler gasped, "staggering." But in Washington, four out of five heads of households dated back at least to 1970.

There are still too many fatherless households in Washington, about 40 percent of all families in Service Areas Three through Seven (a figure distorted by massive concealment of resident fathers because of public assistance regulations). There are also too many unemployed young persons from low-income homes; the bulk of city crime being committed by males under twenty-five. In the twenty years after 1950, the fifteen- to twenty-four-year-old population rose from 11 to 24 percent. Once again, though, statistics reassure. Since 1970 the population has begun to age and the size of households to shrink. In 1970, the median age was 28.4; now it is about 30. Average household size decreased during the same period from 2.72 to about 2.5 persons. If unemployment remains slightly higher than the official national figure for early 1976, local incomes

14. Eunice S. Grier, *People and Government: Changing Needs in the District of Columbia, 1950–1970* (Washington, D.C.: Washington Center for Metropolitan Studies, 1973), p. 24.

continue to rise. A July 1975 Bureau of Social Science Research poll reported that 71 percent of the residents in the metropolitan area were "satisfied" with their salaries, with satisfied blacks in the District expressing somewhat greater contentment than whites. Of course, rising taxes have accompanied rising incomes, and Washington's tax base will crack if too much more weight is placed upon it. But a commuter tax, in one form or another, is inevitable, unless Congress secretly wishes to see the capital slide into bankruptcy.

In an era of municipal hard times when the prospects of New York, Detroit, and even Los Angeles are debatable, Washington holds a trump card: it is as immortal as the Republic it symbolizes. Whatever Washington's maladies—however debilitating— they will never be allowed to become terminal. Not even the most inveterate neo-Jeffersonians, those voters and politicians who inveigh against creeping federalism and urban sin, are really prepared to deny the city the wherewithal not merely to survive but to thrive. A ghetto-ized, moribund Washington is unthinkable. But there is a joker in the pack, forebodingly expressed by Austin Kiplinger:

> The future of Washington as a black center depends as much on the rest of the nation as it does upon itself. The willingness of Congress to let District citizens govern themselves (real home rule, not the strings-attached variety practiced now) will hang on how each Congressman thinks his constituents like him to vote, and how liberal he thinks they are in matters of race relations.[15]

Translated into the blunt language of earlier times, Kiplinger's statement is a warning that, if Washington's blacks are perceived as being too uppity, Congress may strike down their rights once again. That would be a calamity both locally and nationally. Race has been the District's nemesis of local autonomy for decades. Otherwise, why not grant statehood or a variation of it to an entity with a population larger than that of Alaska, Delaware, Idaho, Nevada, Vermont and four other states, and comparable to Hawaii and New Hampshire?

15. Austin Kiplinger, *Washington Now* (New York: Harper & Row, 1975), p. 318.

Today's Washington, feeling its way to independence, and wobbly in its unconventional governance, is like the America of yesteryear. If it can be run well, if its black and white citizens retain faith in the efficacy of collective effort and the ballot, and if luck prevails, Washington will become a metropolis more splendid for the quality of its life than for the grand architectural legacies of L'Enfant, Shepherd, and McMillan.

Although sporadic and unformed, the mood of confident commitment is definitely abroad in the city: the friendliness of people riding the few miles of completed Metro; the increased feeling of safety on the streets; the tentative return to the public schools of middle-class children; the cautious but certain drift of whites back to the city; the enthusiastic reception by public school teen-agers of the People United to Save Humanity campaign for the simple virtues of good manners and good grades. These are unmistakably benign ripples moved by deep currents of urban change. That terrifying expectancy of the worst, which gripped the city for so long, is finally being washed away. July Fourth may have had an even more profound significance for the District of Columbia than elsewhere. One million people celebrated the nation's two-hundredth birthday without political violence and virtually free of petty crimes while thousands of hidden police and troops stood ready to save the city, if necessary, from chaos. From now on, Washingtonians can take care of themselves. Black or white, rich or poor (though most will be richer than poorer), heavily taxed, denied political equality, they will continue to grow into the comity of their new roles of cultural pace-setters and urban innovators.

Suggestions for Further Reading

The following selective list of books and other materials will enable readers to pursue particular subjects in more detail. Many of the sources listed here can be found in public and university libraries, although a few may be available only in Washington, D.C., repositories.

GENERAL SOURCES

Bryan, Wilhelmus Bogart. *A History of the National Capital from Its Foundation through the Period of the Adoption of the Organic Act.* 2 vols. New York: Macmillan Co., 1914.

Cable, Mary. *The Avenue of the Presidents.* Boston: Houghton Mifflin, 1969.

Furer, Howard B. *Washington, A Chronological & Documentary History, 1790–1970.* New York: Oceana Publications, 1975.

Green, Constance McLaughlin. *Washington: Village & Capital, 1800–1878.* Princeton, N.J.: Princeton University Press, 1963.

―――. *Washington: Capital City, 1879–1950.* Princeton, N.J.: Princeton University Press, 1963.

Kiplinger, Austin. *Washington Now.* New York: Harper & Row, 1975.

Kite, Elizabeth. *L'Enfant's Washington, 1791–1792, Published & Unpublished Documents Now Brought Together for the First Time.* Baltimore, Md.: Johns Hopkins University Press, 1929.

Leech, Margaret. *Reveille in Washington, 1860–1865.* New York: Grosset & Dunlap, 1941.

Proctor, John Clagett, ed. *Washington Past and Present, A History.* 5 vols. New York: Lewis Historical Publishing Co., 1930.

Smith, Sam. *Captive Capital, Colonial Life in Modern Washington.* Bloomington, Ind.: Indiana University Press, 1947.

Tindall, William. *Standard History of the City of Washington from a*

Study of the Original Sources. Knoxville, Tenn.: H. W. Crew, 1914.

Truett, Randall Bond, ed. *Washington, D.C. A Guide to the Nation's Capital.* New rev. ed. New York: Hastings House, 1968. Originally published 1942 and compiled for the Federal Writer's Program of the Works Progress Administration.

ARCHITECTURE AND ENGINEERING

Duryee, Sackett L. *A Historical Summary of the Works of the Corps of Engineers in Washington, D.C. & Vicinity, 1852–1952.* Washington, D.C.: n.p., 1952.

Goode, James M. *The Outdoor Sculpture of Washington, D.C., A Comprehensive Historical Guide.* Washington, D.C.: Smithsonian Institution Press, 1975.

Maddex, Diane. *Historic Buildings of Washington, D.C.* Pittsburgh: Ober Park Assoc., Inc., 1973.

U.S. Government. *The Improvement of the Park System of the District of Columbia.* 3rd ed. Washington, D.C.: Government Printing Office, 1906.

AUTOBIOGRAPHY AND BIOGRAPHY

Adams, Marietta M. *My Studio Window, Sketches of the Pageant of Washington Life.* New York: E. P. Dutton, 1928.

Bedini, Silvio. *The Life of Benjamin Banneker.* New York: Charles Scribner's Sons, 1972.

Carpenter, Frances, ed. *Carp's Washington.* New York: McGraw-Hill, 1960.

Colman, Edna M. *Seventy Five Years of White House Gossip.* New York: Doubleday and Co., 1926.

Dickens, Charles. *American Notes.* New York: George Munro, 1885.

Douglass, Frederick. *Life & Times.* New York: Macmillan Co., 1926. Originally published 1893.

Drayton, Daniel. *Personal Memoir of Daniel Drayton.* Boston: Bela Marsh, 1855.

James, Bessie Rowland. *Anne Royall's USA.* New Brunswick, N.J.: Rutgers University Press, 1972.

Hines, Christian. *Early Recollections of Washington City*. Washington, D.C.: 1866.

Moore, Charles. *Daniel Burnham, Architect & Planner of Cities*. 2 vols. Boston: Houghton Mifflin, 1921.

Nicolay, Helen. *Our Capital on the Potomac*. New York: Century, 1924.

Poore, Benjamin Perley. *Perley's Reminiscences of Sixty Years in the National Metropolis*. 2 vols. Philadelphia: Hubbard Bros., 1886.

Royall, Anne. *Sketches of History, Life & Manners in the United States*. New Haven, Conn.: 1826.

————. *The Black Book or a Continuation of Travels in the United States*. 3 vols. No publisher or date [ca. 1828].

Samuels, Ernest. *Henry Adams, The Middle Years*. Cambridge, Mass.: Belknap Press, 1958.

————. *Henry Adams, The Major Phase*. Cambridge, Mass.: Belknap Press, 1964.

Terrell, Mary Church. *A Colored Woman in a White World*. Washington, D.C.: Ransdell, Inc., 1940.

Trollope, Frances. *Domestic Manners of the Americans*. New York: Alfred A. Knopf, 1949. Originally published 1832.

EDUCATIONAL AND INTELLECTUAL

Baratz, Joan C. "A Quest for Equal Educational Opportunity in a Major Urban School District: The Case of Washington, D.C." Syracuse, N.Y.: Educational, Finance and Governance Center, Syracuse University Research Corp., December 1974.

Daley, John M. *Georgetown University: Origins & Early Years*. Washington, D.C.: Georgetown University Press, 1957.

Durkin, Joseph T. *Georgetown University: The Middle Years (1840–1900)*. Washington, D.C.: Georgetown University Press, 1963.

Fader, Daniel. *The Naked Children*. New York: Macmillan Co., 1971.

Flack, James Kirkpatrick, Jr., "The Formation of the Washington Intellectual Community." Ph.D. dissertation, Wayne State University, 1968.

Hundley, Mary. *The Dunbar Story (1870–1955)*. New York: Vantage Press, 1965.

Kayser, Elmer Louis. *Bricks Without Straw, The Evolution of George Washington University.* New York: Appleton-Century-Crofts, 1970.

Logan, Rayford W. *Howard University, The First Hundred Years, 1867–1967.* New York: New York University Press, 1969.

POLITICS

Commission on Organization of the District of Columbia. *Report of the Commission.* Washington, D.C., Government Printing Office, 1972.

Derthick, Martha. *City Politics in Washington, D.C.* Washington, D.C.: Joint Center for Urban Studies of Massachusetts Institute of Technology and Harvard University and the Washington Center for Metropolitan Studies, 1972.

Grier, Eunice S. *People & Government: Changing Needs in the District of Columbia, 1950–1970.* Washington Center for Metropolitan Studies, 1973.

O'Keefe, John Dennis. "Decision-Making in the House Committee on the District of Columbia." Ph.D. dissertation. University of Maryland, 1969.

Young, James Sterling. *The Washington Community, 1800–1828.* New York: Columbia University Press, 1966.

DEMOGRAPHY, RACE, AND SOCIETY

Bigman, Stanley K. *The Jewish Population of Greater Washington in 1956.* Washington, D.C.: Jewish Community Council of Greater Washington, 1957.

Brown, Letitia W., and Lewis, Elsie M. *Washington From Banneker to Douglass, 1791–1870.* Washington, D.C.: Education Department, National Portrait Gallery, Smithsonian Institution, 1971.

———. *Washington in the New Era, 1870–1970.* Washington, D.C.: Smithsonian Institution, 1971.

District of Columbia. *The People of the District of Columbia, A Demographic, Social, Economic and Physical Profile of the District of Columbia by Service Areas.* Washington, D.C.: Office of Planning and Management, District of Columbia Government, 1973.

Edwards, G. Franklin. *The Negro Professional Class.* Glencoe, Ill.: The Free Press, 1959.

Gilbert, Ben W. *Ten Blocks from the White House, Anatomy of the Washington Riots of 1968.* New York: Praeger, 1968.

Green, Constance McLaughlin. *The Secret City, A History of Race Relations in the Nation's Capital.* Princeton, N.J.: Princeton University Press, 1967.

Hannerz, Ulf. *Soulside, Inquiries into Ghetto Culture and Community.* New York: Columbia University Press, 1969.

Herron, Paul. *The Story of Capitol Hill.* New York: Coward, McCann, and Geoghegan, 1963.

Johnson, Haynes. *Dusk at the Mountain, The Negro, the Nation and the Capital.* New York: Doubleday and Co., 1963.

Liebow, Elliott. *Talley's Corner, A Study of Negro Streetcorner Men.* Boston: Little Brown & Co., 1962.

Marindin, Hope. "Adams-Morgan: Democratic Action Fails to Save a Neighborhood." George Washington University typescript, 1969.

Noyes, Theodore. *Our National Capital and Its Un-Americanized Americans.* Washington, D.C.: Judd & Detweiler, Inc., n.d.

Thurz, Daniel. *Where Are They Now: A Study of the Impact of Relocation of Former Residents of Southwest Who Were in an HWC Demonstration Project.* Washington, D.C.: Health and Welfare Council of the National Capital Area, 1966.

U.S., Congress, Senate, Committee on the District of Columbia, *Hearings on Crime in the National Capital.* 91st Congress. Part I. March 11, 12. Government Printing Office, 1969.

Weller, Charles Frederick. *Washington, Neglected Neighborhoods, Stories of Life in the Alleys, Tenements & Shanties of the National Capital.* Philadelphia: John C. Winston, 1909.

Index